The Diaries of Mr Lucas

'Extraordinary... *The Diaries of Mr Lucas* is a thrilling page-turner intersecting a criminalised queer scene with the liberations of the Swinging Sixties and the drama of London's criminal underworld.' Arifa Akbar, author of *Consumed*

'At turns funny, poignant and thrilling, this book is so much more than a secret diary of 20th century gay life. Hugo Greenhalgh provides avuncular commentary and crucial context, shining a light on overlooked aspects of British social history.' Paul Baker, author of *Fabulosa!*

'A provocative and mordant humour... Greenhalgh has published only choice extracts, which are enlivened by his own sparky commentary. The result is a human document of real interest.' Richard Davenport-Hines, *Literary Review*

'I absolutely love this book. I couldn't get enough of the outrageousness, the unbridled indiscretion, the danger, the blackmail and the lust for love. *The Diaries of Mr Lucas* is a real page turner, told with panache and affection.' Lord Michael Cashman, author of *One of Them*

'At once heartfelt and hilarious, Hugo Greenhalgh's selection from Mr Lucas's diaries offers a sympathetic and occasionally steamed-up window onto a previously hidden world.' Robert Douglas-Fairhurst, author of *The Story of Alice*

'By turns tender-hearted, romantic, obsessive and plain scared, through his diaries Mr Lucas offers an important commentary on a period of sexual repression now largely forgotten. Both his ongoing internal battles with temptation and the insight he offers into the backstage lives and doings of the prominent figures around him draw irresistible and justifiable parallels with Samuel Pepys.' Sarah Burton, author of *The Strange Adventures of H*

Hugo Greenhalgh has been a journalist for more than thirty years. Now a full-time writer, he is the former LGBTQ+ editor of the Thomson Reuters Foundation. Before that he worked at the *Financial Times*. In 2024, he was named an LGBTQ+ trailblazer on the *Attitude* 101 list. Previously he has been nominated for the European Press Prize, Amnesty International's Media Awards and the GLAAD Media Awards. He is also a former activist. Aged nineteen, he took the British government to the European Court of Human Rights over the gay male age of consent in the UK.

The Diaries of Mr Lucas

Life in 1960s Gay London

Hugo Greenhalgh

Atlantic Books
London

First published in hardback in Great Britain in 2024 by Atlantic Books,
an imprint of Atlantic Books Ltd.

This paperback edition published in 2025 by Atlantic Books.

Copyright © Hugo Greenhalgh, 2024

The moral right of Hugo Greenhalgh to be identified as the author of this work has been asserted by him in accordance with the Copyright, Designs and Patents Act of 1988.

All rights reserved. No part of this publication may be reproduced, stored in a retrieval system, or transmitted in any form or by any means, electronic, mechanical, photocopying, recording, or otherwise, without the prior permission of both the copyright owner and the above publisher of this book.

No part of this book may be used in any manner in the learning, training or development of generative artificial intelligence technologies (including but not limited to machine learning models and large language models (LLMs)), whether by data scraping, data mining or use in any way to create or form a part of data sets or in any other way.

Every effort has been made to trace or contact all copyright holders. The publishers will be pleased to make good any omissions or rectify any mistakes brought to their attention at the earliest opportunity.

All images © Hugo Greenhalgh, with the following exception:
Page 180: © Trinity Mirror / Mirrorpix / Alamy Stock Photo

10 9 8 7 6 5 4 3 2 1

A CIP catalogue record for this book is available from the British Library.

Paperback ISBN: 978 1 83895 814 5
E-book ISBN: 978 1 83895 813 8

Printed and bound in Great Britain by Clays Ltd, Elcograf S.p.A.

Atlantic Books
An imprint of Atlantic Books Ltd
Ormond House
26–27 Boswell Street
London
WC1N 3JZ

www.atlantic-books.co.uk

Product safety EU representative: Authorised Rep Compliance Ltd., Ground Floor,
71 Lower Baggot Street, Dublin, D02 P593, Ireland. www.arccompliance.com

To Liam and Will. Just because.

Contents

Preface 1

1 George Leo John Lucas 12
2 The Early Years 29
3 A Fateful Night in Germany 46
4 The Tragic Tale of Flannan O'Hehir 70
5 Irish Peter 98
6 England on Trial 136
7 A Brush with the Krays 162
8 Out on the Scene 192
9 The Slow Train to Ireland 219
10 Sex, Money and Death 239
11 The Death of Mr Lucas 258

Postscript 278

Notes 293
Acknowledgements 301
Index 305

Preface

WHAT DO YOU think of when you look back to the UK in the sixties? Miniskirts, The Beatles and the Kray twins? Maybe thoughts of hippies, demonstrations against the Vietnam War or England winning the World Cup? Or the Profumo Affair and the birth of women's liberation? Maybe some or all of these, but what you will most definitely not think of is George Leo John Lucas. A rather timid civil servant, Mr Lucas – never George to me – would turn thirty-four as 1960 ushered in some semblance of multicoloured change to a nation shambling out of the grey shadows of the fifties and the remnants of a collective hangover from the Second World War.

Rationing, for example, continued right up until 1954. The women who had served alongside their male counterparts were expected to return to the kitchens. Gay and bisexual men, who had experienced a brief flicker of equality during the war, despite frequent crackdowns, went from heroes to hunted once more. And then the sixties started; a chance for change as the youth movements of the fifties – the Teds, or Teddy Boys

– solidified into the first true generation of youthful rebellion. Suddenly, as Mr Lucas struggled to find a place at his usual lunchtime restaurant, he writes, 'it was difficult to enter or leave for the hippies, male and female, cluttering outside'.

Society was in flux and Mr Lucas was there to record every detail in his diaries, some sad, some funny and some, indeed, drenched in sex – and, remarkable for then and perhaps even today, gay sex. As a gay man, not 'out' by modern standards, but active on the scene of the times, his diaries stand as an unequalled record of same-sex love and desire of the mid-twentieth century. Mr Lucas was our very own 'gay Pepys', as writer, actor and director Mark Gatiss once described him. Employed by the Board of Trade by day, at night he would slip out silently along the darkened streets, avoiding both the lights and the police before scurrying home to write up everything – and everyone – he had seen and done. The sheer fact of his sexuality, as he writes in March 1948, at almost the start of his diaries, 'can turn one who by day is a respected and useful official into a furtive night prowler driven by dark lusts till the fit has passed'.

A mild-mannered man, not quick to anger or seek confrontation, he was the very personification of the buttoned-up civil servant. Not for him, the raffish flamboyant air of a Quentin Crisp, whose 1968 memoir, *The Naked Civil Servant*, became a popular film seven years later. No, Mr Lucas hogged the shadows, kept his feelings and views to himself, but, fortunately for us, not from his diary.

That is not to say that Mr Lucas was ashamed of or embarrassed about being gay. As he writes in April 1968, '[It was] my molecular structure, my genetic inheritance, the environment that shaped me.' A religious man, a devout Catholic, his sexuality and beliefs do clash and overlap, but ultimately are reconciled by Mr Lucas's determination that what he gets up to in various bushes, public lavatories and occasionally at home, isn't morally wrong.

As Mr Lucas muses on his father's temperament and character, it's clear that, by dint of his sexuality, he's had a lucky escape from the horrors of heterosexuality.

23 February 1968 (Friday):

It's fortunate that whatever sexual tensions lay deep buried in [my father's] *mind have, in me, become frank and fluid homosexuality, preserving me from the disasters of marriage and procreation.*

The diaries trace these tensions, devoting space – among the millions upon millions of words – to his bowel movements as much as to his nocturnal activities. They are an incredible record of a lost queer London, of a man battling to retain his identity in a world that hated homosexuals.

What, can we say, is the significance of his diaries? For me, they represent the gold standard of diary-keeping: waspish and witty, sleazy and circumspect.

The first question to address, though, is whether we have the 'real' Mr Lucas. Is he pouring out his thoughts and feelings in a purely undiluted manner or carefully crafting a persona, the 'Mr Lucas' he feels himself to be, unrecognized and unadmired by others? I'd argue the latter. Reading through his diaries, year after year, one thing quickly becomes clear: you are reading the idealized Mr Lucas. The person we know as Mr Lucas is a creation of his own: wittier, cleverer and, crucially for any diary writer, misunderstood by those around him. Which might explain his enthusiasm when I initially broached the idea, when we first met back in 1994, of publishing his diaries at some stage.

To be fair, though, he was always clear this would only happen after his death – and he left them to me with that express instruction on his death in 2014. He never sought fame, but surely such dedication to diary-keeping indicates some desire to be remembered in some form? Or perhaps, more accurately, to be liked.

19 February 1948 (Thursday):

Unquestionably, my greatest desideration has always been sympathy and affection. Not friendship, not even passion, so much as affection. Friendship is a good plodding drudge that will not be over driven, passion is a fine high metal or a thoroughbred, but affection will carry on to the world and back, or beyond if need be, for those that I have loved.

He and I were friends for almost twenty years, but it is only since I took possession of the diaries that I have truly come to know him. An arch conservative, but social liberal, his views are very much not my own, but I recognize how he has been moulded by the times and the environment in which he grew up. Is he dislikeable? Most certainly, particularly when it comes to class, where his views can tend to an almost cartoonish dismissal of those he sees as 'below' him in terms of social standing.

13 July 1965 (Tuesday):

One thing I must take care of for the future, not to make friends with one's social inferiors. Be friendly with them, yes, be helpful, listen to their troubles, advise them, have sex with them – what else are the lower classes for? – but not to be confined to them or to rely on them. People of one's own sort have the same standards, attitudes, codes of ethics.

No diary is a perfect record of the time in which it was written, and Mr Lucas's diaries are no exception. Some dates and names may not be exactly right, though they are always as they appear in the diaries. Idiosyncratic, repetitious and in places incomplete, the entries that follow are his reminiscences, his thoughts and feelings. The entries are verbatim, as much as is possible in terms of making them make sense in their truncated form, and I've retained Mr Lucas's punctuation and grammar throughout. History, in Mr Lucas's hands, isn't malleable, but it is personal.

Conservative politician Alan Clark said it best, in the preface to his own published diaries:

These are not memoirs. They are not written to throw light on events in the past, or retrospectively justify the actions of the author. They are exactly as they were recorded on the day; sometimes even the hour, or the minute, of a particular episode or sensation... And as for taste, it, too, is subjective. There are passages that will offend some, just as there are excerpts that I myself found embarrassing to read when I returned to them... Sometimes lacking in charity; often trivial; occasionally lewd; cloyingly sentimental, repetitious, whingeing and imperfectly formed. For some readers, the entries may seem to be all of these things. But they are real diaries.[1]

I've chosen to focus on the sixties for many of the reasons above – the pace and speed with which Britain experienced change, culturally, socially and sexually. As a gay man born in 1926, and who eventually died at the age of eighty-eight in 2014, Mr Lucas's life marked the milestones of queer liberation: seeing the first fruits of freedom during the Second World War (he was nineteen at its end), to the partial decriminalization of gay sex in England and Wales as he turned forty-one. He even lived to see the first same-sex marriages in the year he died. His life was one of the last lived under threat of arrest; he was one of the few remaining guides to a world of blackmail, violence and police harassment. But it was a life also filled with a sense of community, laughter, parties and the need to protect one another from a society that hated us then and still holds its nose at times today. And it was a life full of sex. Lots and lots and lots of sex.

PREFACE

19 November 1958 (Wednesday):

Tonight, I took home an Irish lad introduced to me by stout Charles the [General Post Office] *security officer some time ago – spent in all £1* [£28.69 – all currency conversions are in today's money] *on him – willing lad, if not able, and quite pleasant. Then, as I was relaxing over cocoa before going to bed, I was surprised to receive a visit (at 11.30 at night) from Charlie, a pleasant lad who is active heterosexually and passive homosexually. I obliged him as he wanted, and finally went to bed feeling pleased at my ability to have sex twice in an hour and a half and extremely flattered that an attractive young man more than ten years my junior should find such sexual satisfaction in me as to call on me at 11.30 at night.*

I first met Mr Lucas when I was working on a documentary about male prostitution and, while he eventually declined to appear on screen, asking instead for his words to be read by an actor, he and I remained friends until he died. He left me the diaries in his will, but in the chaotic aftermath of his death and the clearance of his house, I had to literally fish some out of the attendant skip. But ultimately, the entirety of the fifty-six diaries I managed to rescue – with only a few missing – each marking a year from 1948 to 2009 when his health started to falter, represents one man's attempt to find love, to assemble meaning in a society that would, at times, wish him dead. As the diaries open in 1948 when Mr Lucas is a twenty-one-year-old army conscript serving out the final moments of his National Service duties, his desire, his need for love, is evident.

13 February 1948 (Friday):

I fell to reflecting on my melancholy situation, forever cursed to love those that can never love me, tormented by love in a hell of loneliness, reduced to loving, silently, lance-corporals and drivers met by chance on inspections.

I have also chosen to focus on the sixties to show that Mr Lucas is more than a product of his passions. Hero or antihero, victim or villain, is something we will not shy away from answering, but for me – and I hope for you as the reader as well – our diarist acts as the most perfect psychosexual guide to Britain as the country unfolds from the privations of the forties and the strictures of the fifties. Never an ardent activist, just as his place was never at the barricades of any of the demonstrations of the sixties, his role was watcher, an observer noting everything down in his tiny handwriting, scratched out every night without fail in the diaries I have before me today.

Yet beyond the pathos, there is also humour from Mr Lucas, armed with a dry waspish wit and ever a scabrous pen; the takedowns he writes of his 'frenemies' are endless and delicious. The side characters, who appear throughout the sixties and then, like many diary accounts, disappear again into the margins of history, into the detritus of someone else's life, are simply magnificent. From the melancholy of the journalist Tokyo Rose, forever mourning a lost love or nursing a black eye from the current one, to H. D. Williams, an early victim of conversion therapy (the discredited practice of trying to change someone's sexuality or gender identity), Mr Lucas's friends act as ciphers to the decade and its changes. And that's to say nothing of the fabulous old Mr Niece and his 'phallomania'...

15 April 1963 (Easter Monday):

Old fat Charles Niece is an intolerable nuisance at times with his phallomania. When I am told (as tonight) that 'such-a-one has got a nice piece of meat' or 'a big packet' or a 'huge chopper', my interest in the young man is at once quenched, however attractive in features or conversation. My imagination pictures some disproportionate penis, unduly elongated, hideously pendant between his legs. Why Niece and so many other homosexuals should have this intense interest in the size of the penis, I don't know...

I also chose the sixties for one other crucial reason: the decade details the ten-year, slow-moving car crash of a friendship that almost leads to Mr Lucas's ruination and, at one point, we see him contemplating murder. The potential victim? Irish Peter, a scheming rent boy as the decade opens; a hardened member of the Firm, the notorious gang headed up by the

Kray twins, at the close of it. Obsession becomes love and then turns to hate over those ten years, as Mr Lucas comes close to the real underworld of sixties London, the gangsters of the East End head west and the overlap between the gay and criminal worlds is complete. 'The world [Peter] moves in is a cannibal one and its denizens prey on each other,' Mr Lucas writes presciently in 1961.

When I think of the sixties, I think of Mr Lucas ambling through life, always in the background, at times unnoticed, at others his head bobbing above the parapet, but always writing, writing, writing – his diary his only true friend, the one constant to his life for more than seventy years and our guide now to a lost queer world of sixties London.

5 September 1965 (Sunday):

On my way home I reflected that my diary-keeping – it's twenty-three years since I first felt the need to set down something of what I thought and what I saw – would be understood by few or none of those I knew. Most homosexuals, in any case, dread the written word, and would entirely concur with Boswell's observation that 'a plan of this kind is dangerous, as a man might, in the openness of his heart, say many things and discover many facts that might do him great harm if the journal should fall into the hands of his enemies'. There are the great diarists and recorders, Pepys, Walpole, Boswell himself; the host of lesser writers – Croker, Greevey, Greville, Fitzroy, Kilvert,

PREFACE

all the scribbling generals, politicians, litterateurs; and the little people like me, with the same compulsive itch to record and repeat, but neither style nor interesting matter, who benefit only the ink and paper makers, or at best turn out a phrase or two that would be worth remembering.

1

George Leo John Lucas

IT WAS THE plates that struck me first. Row upon row of grubby porcelain plates; some cracked, others held together with greying Sellotape, each sporting its own parabola of dirt and dust.

On each one, as I climbed the stairs of the grotty maisonette flat in Clapham, listening to the wheezy sounds of Mr Lucas quadruple-locking the door behind me, a face stared back – photographs of young men in their twenties or thirties; some clothed, others with dicks in hand or waggling their penises eagerly at an out-of-sight cameraman.

'What on earth are these?' I asked, gripping the handrail and turning back to Mr Lucas.

'My boys,' he rasped. 'My boys.'

Mr Lucas had been buying boys for almost forty years. I should make it clear from the outset that by 'boys' both he and I mean men in their early twenties – Mr Lucas makes it clear many, many times, that his tastes are for the 'sturdier' young men – but he probably spent many thousands of pounds paying for sex over the decades.

It was 1994 and I was down from the University of Edinburgh where I had just finished my third and penultimate year of an English Literature degree. In need of cash over the summer, I had taken on a job as a researcher on a documentary about male prostitution in the twentieth century. Quite a smart job for an undergrad, but helped somewhat by the fact that my boyfriend at the time, Will Parry, was down as the lead researcher and hired me to help.

The documentary, sadly, faltered at the pre-production stage and never got made in the end, but my job was to find both the punters and the 'boys', the rent boys who were active in the fifties and sixties – and then probably solidly into retirement age – or those still on the scene. My first port of call had been to place an advert in the gay papers of the day – *Capital Gay* and the *Pink Paper* being the main two.

And Mr Lucas, George Leo John Lucas, then aged sixty-eight, got in touch.

6 September 1994 (Tuesday):

In Capital Gay *on Saturday, I noticed a brief reference to a research study on male prostitution whose researchers ask 'sex workers and their clients' to get in touch with them. I wrote saying I'd be glad to assist, and this morning a Mr Parry replies very civilly, requesting an interview and remarking on 'the invaluable historical knowledge I must possess of how prostitution has changed over recent decades', which is true and perceptive.*

Yes, he'd been active on the rent-boy scene for decades, and yes, he'd be more than happy to talk to a researcher, with an eye to possibly appearing on screen at some point.

So round I went, nervous and inexperienced, but keen to find out more about this mysterious man.

The flat on Mandalay Road in Clapham was in a terrible state. I've described it since as a Miss Havisham flat, not having been cleaned for what looked like decades, but frankly it was much, much worse than that. It stood as a firm rebuttal of Quentin Crisp's comment about there not being any need to do housework because 'after the first four years the dirt doesn't get any worse'.[1]

As I climbed those stairs, wondering whether I'd ever make it back alive or end up being dragged down, stair by jagged stair, wrapped in a moulding carpet, these are the things I noticed: the plates; the peeling wallpaper; the almost neat tramlines up the worn carpet where Mr Lucas and his friends had gone willingly to their fate; the splintered handrail, paint having been worn off years ago; and the smell.

My god, the flat reeked. Not that musty, old-person flat smell, but as if something – someone? – had died many, many years ago and been left to rot happily in a corner. As I turned into the living room, on the right at the top of the stairs, it all sort of made sense.

The living room was a cocoon. Lined by books of all shapes, sizes and ages, more pictures of 'boys' hung on every wall. There were at least three, maybe four, rugs on the floor. An old armchair – 'worn' is not a good enough word to describe just how knackered it was – in one corner, crowded in by free-standing bookcases and piles and piles of old newspapers and magazines.

A door on one side opened to the kitchen, unmodernized since Mr Lucas had moved in in 1969 and the source of at least some of the smell (and that's before we get to the ever-present dildo neatly parked on one of the lower shelves).

And then there was Mr Lucas himself. He was never George to me, always Mr Lucas. Partly because calling him George Lucas – hello *Star Wars* – just sounded silly, and partly because, well, to play the game, I consciously made him into a character; a character both in his own life and, over a period of more than twenty years, in mine.

He wore an old black three-piece suit; almost certainly the same old black three-piece suit he was wearing every time I saw him subsequently. Back in 1994, it was already worn, with a rip down the left arm that had been sewn back together of sorts with an arrangement of safety pins. All of varying sizes, of course. His voice was slightly cracked and veering towards the croaky: he sounded – and looked – like a relic from a bygone era. Pallid, his white skin pocked by liver spots, face discoloured by age, his fingers, slightly bloated, poking out from beneath the wrecked sleeves of his suit.

And, like the flat, he also stank. He smelled, sorry to say this, very distinctly of shit (which, when I dared to enter his bathroom a few visits later, also made sense). And, like the flat, he was also covered in dust. The collar of his white shirt was grubby; his tie neatly tied but stained; and the shoulders and waistcoat of his suit lightly coated in what could have been dandruff, but was almost certainly something much worse.

He looked as if he'd risen from the grave.

Needless to say, I was gripped. Fascinated and gripped – and then, my eyes scanning the room as if casing the joint, I noticed the diaries. Taking up most of one wall, all filed neatly in order of year. On each fraying spine, I could just about make out a year – 1952, 1968, 1983. The earlier years were slim, almost neat. But by the time they reached the eighties, as I would soon discover, each volume was overspilling with photographs that fell into your hands as you turned the pages.

'Before we start, could I ask you what those are?' I squeaked.

And down they came. The diaries, each one a year in the life of Mr Lucas. Each one stuffed full of photographs – of rent boys (clothed and unclothed), of his house, of the lost queer world of decades ago. Each one a tale of a London long since passed.

Interlaced into each were newspaper clippings, mainly of middle-aged men being robbed by those in their twenties, receipts, cinema tickets – all manner of collected crap from a life that spanned almost nine decades.

'Would you like a drink?' he asked in his curiously gravelly voice, sort of like the light graveyard rumble you might hear when a tomb is opened for the first time since the fifteenth century. And someone emerges…

16 September 1994 (Friday):

The interview lasted two hours almost, 'till 1.25. Hugh [sic] Greenhalgh is a good-looking dark-haired young man in his early twenties, well-spoken, who asked few questions and let my recollections and reminiscences flow out, unstructured, digressive, omitting much, as I realized after he'd gone.

Born on 16 June 1926, Mr Lucas grew up in Chadwell Heath, a small suburb of Romford now on the eastern edge of London's urban sprawl, then a forty-five-minute train ride to the centre of 'Town', as he always called it. His was a typically lower middle-class upbringing. Not poor exactly, but one in which the pressures of little money exacerbated the tensions between his constantly warring parents, Edmund and Johanna, a clerk at Customs and Excise and a housemaker. An only child, he attended West Ham Grammar School (now known as St Bonaventure's) in Forest Gate between the ages of twelve and eighteen, years informed by genteel poverty and the outbreak of the Second World War in 1939, when Mr Lucas was thirteen. He was bullied badly during his school years, writing many years later when he returned to the area in July 1979 of the 'streets of pain and fear' and trying to avoid his classmates who 'would torment me'.

Mr Lucas grew up to be a shy, somewhat introspective young man, very conscious of his receding hairline (parted in the middle, much to the amusement of his mother) and often the target of scorn from both parents. And when he ducks their brickbats, they take glee in screaming at each other. 'I have learned better since 1952,' he writes, looking back in 1969. 'Seventeen years ago – living at home, amid the jangling and bickering of mother and father reproaching and reviling one another and joining to reproach and revile me.'

His mother, a staunch Irish Roman Catholic, and his father, a rabid atheist, are quite spectacularly ill-matched and religious war flares regularly at number 14 Bath Road.

22 March 1951 (Thursday):

Father railed against the church, Pope and priests. He said he'd leave his money to the Protestant Alliance and the Communist Party, and said he'd die happy could he see the Pope burned alive in the Red Square at Moscow.

Mr Lucas is often caught in the crossfire, not least as both his parents are very aware of his sexuality. Entry after entry details the almost daily abuse he endured – until his parents moved to Holland-on-Sea in 1955, leaving him living at Bath Road for another couple of years.

26 January 1953 (Monday):

This evening at home a horrible outburst of rage by my mother – her worst since her unforgiveable tirade of last August 19th. I arrived home to find my mother and father shouting and grimacing at each other because the coal was not in. She suddenly snarled at me, 'If you were a man, you'd punch him in the face.' I resented this and said so; and a flood of the most filthily malignant abuse was poured out on me. 'You humpy backed old homo, go and join Field [an M.P. convicted in 1953 of 'importuning for immoral purposes']... *go and hang round conveniences and wait for them. You filthy toad, you old homo... you came home from Germany with a filthy disgraceful past and I went and humiliated myself to Mr Atkins* [at the civil service] *to get you reinstated... you ought to be down on your knees to me... you've got no gut in you' (this several times). Then, to the cat, 'That old homo made me forget to give you your milk.' She continued to croon endearments to the cat and make filthy allegations of sexual immorality against me, while her husband snarled and gibbered to himself in another room. This is terribly distressing, especially when the peace and serenity of love in my heart are so defiled, so stained, by filthy insinuations.*

His father is no better.

2 May 1948 (Sunday):

I was awakened by my father shouting below, 'I want him to lose his job, I want him dragged down as low as he can be, the homosexual!'

His sexuality became evident to his parents in 1940, when Mr Lucas was just fourteen. The exact details are unclear, but his father, in particular, constantly returns to the young Mr Lucas's 'attempted seduction of a housepainter', although Mr Lucas does reflect in 1979 how he first had sex in a public lavatory aged fourteen. We'll come back to the fractious relationship with his parents a little later, as this explains much about Mr Lucas and his many insecurities.

Let's return for now to that book-stuffed, newspaper-strewn room when I first met him in 1994, Mr Lucas stretching to pick a random diary from the bookcase. And so we started – with his account of being robbed in 1968 when he was aged forty-one. A tale that I had no idea would come to define both my relationship with him and that of his with a certain Irish Peter.

3 January 1968 (Wednesday):

What I have so long dreaded, the terror whose shadow has lain cold across the last two years, fell on me tonight.

I had just gone to bed this early Wednesday morning, about 1.45, when the door buzzer sounded again and again. John Joyce[*]*, coming round at 2 o'clock, I thought, huddled in my dressing gown, and hesitated at the head of the stairs.*

The buzzer sounded again, I thought of banging on the front door and of the Hemsworths[†]* roused, and went down. There were two shadows silhouetted in the glass, and a thought of Peter came into mind.*

'Who's there?' I called out, rather low.

'Police. We're police officers.'

Someone else, used to the idea of the police calling on my account, on Lavin's or Williams[‡]*, would have drawn back and phoned the police station; but I, credulous, had the door open in the next moment, and before the idea the police might be come over for little Maher*[§]* had faded, I*

---

[*] An occasional friend of Mr Lucas's and one-time pash.
[†] The downstairs neighbours.
[‡] Two friends of Mr Lucas's.
[§] An occasional rent-boy friend.

found myself seized by a tall young man and a shorter stockier one that rushed in, turned round and forced me up the stairs into my sitting room.

A third man came in behind them... but he went off into the bedroom before I could see his face or anything much of his figure.

Pushed down into my armchair, the tall young man holding the opened blades of the scissors close before my face, I spoke as fair as I could for terror and shock, asked that personal papers and matters of no value to them be left, and watched as the sideboard drawers were pulled open, my £14 [£300] spending money counted, my watches examined – the tall youth a glum and spruce cold-eyed eighteen-year-old with the flat lower-class secondary school accent of the type, enquired 'are you a shoplifter?' on seeing four watches.

The shorter youth – Dublin, by his voice, and also spruce in a grey overcoat, picked over the old pennies I had accumulated in an envelope. Another pouncing on the gold locket with my mother's picture enquired 'is this your grandmother?'

Being told it was my mother's picture he observed 'We'll leave you that' and put it out of sight. Then, looking at the faces in the Victorian lockets on the wall, he exclaimed 'I know that one – that's Eddie Johnstone.'*

After this I was hustled out into the front room to be left under guard of this Dubliner. I glanced into my

---

* Another rent boy.

bedroom as we passed but could see only a dark figure leaning over suits and coats thrown on the bed – bending to avoid recognition – before I was hurried on.

The Dubliner was less intimidating by himself, and even apologetic, seemed concerned over my uncontrollable trembling, and, enquiring what the 1914–18 war medal was he'd found in the envelope of coins, restored it to me when I told him it was a souvenir of my deceased uncle.

Presently the tall youth returned and made some cryptic remarks about 'we get paid for this, we're doing it for a firm, you aren't the only one'.

Some discussion ensued about tying me up, and in fact my hands were tied behind me with a short length of my own string.

The Dublin youth proposed locking the door, but when I objected to the inconvenience and disturbance changed his mind. With warnings not to move they departed on to the landing, I heard a muttered 'stall him' as the third man, no doubt, having plundered the sitting room, went off.

I heard the telephone moved (and to my pleas it should be left undamaged got only 'we can't take risks' from the tall youth, and a contemptuous dismissive 'can it' when the Dubliner began to say, 'Will you give me your word as a gentleman…?') … and then they were gone.

I crept to the window but could see nothing and hear nothing but heavy driving rain.

My sitting room had been well rummaged, when I stood, at 2.30 in the morning, gazing on the wreck of what would never more be a secure home. All the glass-fronted Victorian lockets I have collected over eight years were gone, save for that of my mother the Dubliner spared, another they had missed, and two large brass ones still on the wall.

The silver tea caddy, too, was gone (and its contents neatly poured on a plate in the kitchen – a house-trained burglar, probably the Dubliner), the silver apostle sugar tongs and the silver Indian bowl I bought my aunt in 1956, with the silver napkin ring that came from my childhood home, dented where I'd flung it, nearly thirty years ago, at my father.

Gone too, was the silver artillery medal I bought last year; and only my old metal pocket watch was left of the four watches I had before. It was no surprise to see my umbrella gone – I had seen the tall youth with it on his arm; and I didn't grudge the Dubliner the badly worn pair of nylon socks he had said he fancied.

It was distressing to see the telephone flex torn out; but by now I felt I would do no good contemplating my losses, and I retired to my bedroom, where suits and overcoats were piled higgledy-piggledy on the bed, the drawers pulled open, and my black gloves gone.

But to my great satisfaction I found the old artillery ring, the heirloom of my great-grandfather Captain Lucas, was still in its case.

In bed, it was past 4.30 a.m. before I fell asleep. For nearly two hours my thoughts were busy with the third man – obviously someone known to me, who had recruited these two novice bandits to plunder by proxy and keep his identity hid; obviously someone who knows my flat sufficiently well to press the night bell.

Peter, very likely, but though the episode bore traces of a crafty sinuous mind like his, I would not have expected him to be so moderate. My records were untouched, and my porcelain figures.

Who else knows my address and could find his way here?

Maguire, for one, and Tony Brown, for another. Either could have planned the details.

Others who know where I live are rather less probable – Sleman, Riordan, Clarke, Tilford, in descending order of likelihood.

Joyce it almost certainly wasn't, for he'd never have left my diaries untouched. There are others, more casual visitors, might have conceivably found their way back – Lyons, Ross, Dignam – but they don't seem very probable.

It must be, I think, Peter or Maguire or Brown, and Eddie Johnstone himself as an outside possibility.

Why not inform the police? It's true the police might catch this trio and recover my missing property; but I don't fancy being named in the South London Press *with the chance of very disagreeable allegations made against me at the trial, and the rogues in the end given a very light sentence.*

Bald middle-aged homosexuals do not excite much judicial (or police) sympathy when they have the misfortune to be robbed by young men. Though not exactly hors la loi [outside the law] *any longer, I would prefer to endure my loss in silence.*

The loss of the money is an inconvenience, though I hope the money left over from the sale of the Redbridge house will cover it. (If I had moved to Redbridge how far and for how long would I have averted a similar episode?)

The loss of those glass-fronted photograph lockets is irreparable. I wonder if I'll ever see one, still with a colour photograph of Leo Sutton or Johnston or Peter looking out, in some shady jewelled display.

The caddy and sugar tongs and bowl I regret, but not half as much as I regret that silver napkin ring my childish fingers handled in those long-past years. The loss of my own wristwatch is an irritation – though when I put it on in the spring of the year before last I wondered, now I remember, how long it would be before I was robbed of it.

The worst is the loss of any illusion of security, I shall always be frightened, now, of a ring at the door, I shall always taste the fears shared by Jews in Nazi Germany, by the politically obnoxious in all the tyrannies of the world, the ever-present lurking dread of the ring at the door in the small hours, the sudden invasion of one's private home, the pitiless faces uttering cold questions... throughout all the remaining years now, into old age, I shall go fearful, and with cause, anxiety born of experience chilling and shadowing every encounter with a young man, near certainty of loss souring the possession of any piece of gold or silver ware.

It is eighteen years that I wrote of someone going forward 'down a stony and sorrowful road to a future of aching years'.

The road I have walked to 1968 has been stony and sorrowful enough, and the years will ache worse as I go on from this ambush.

The sight of my sitting room, forlorn in the cold morning, was dispiriting; it was a good thing that the constant pressure of business at the office should keep me on the strict, unable to think of what I'd lost or how. Work is an opiate.

To the bank to withdraw £10 [£216], and straight away to spend £4-15s-6d [£103.21] on a calendar watch with clear luminous figures on a black dial I'd noticed in the jeweller's window in Charing Cross Road and half-decided I'd buy.

It's a mercy I'd put off buying it on Monday.

It's an elegant enough watch, a German make, a little like that I'd had of Gale in Hanover Street seventeen years ago and lost to the thievish young men in 1955. I think it's three watches that have been stolen from me now.

To Piccadilly Circus tonight, very wretched, and was a little inebriated by the ready sympathy and understanding that Smith expressed. I have suspected him a little in the past, but I know he's had nothing to do with robbing me; and his expressions of contempt and anger for the robbers rang true.

Fred, the Scots lad, too, was as mannerly and sympathetic as I could have wanted, though I've spoken to him but once before. I can rule out Lyons, at any rate, for I'm told he's in Wandsworth gaol. Whatever he's done, he's done nothing to me.

I ran into Ross, with his older ex-guardsman companion, in the 'Dilly underground, and mentioned my having had an unfortunate experience and unpleasant callers last night.

'Did you have your telephone flex cut?' said he, which has set me thinking. I don't see how he could be concerned, but I'm sure he must have heard someone describing how 'they'd turned a chump over and cut the geezer's telephone cord'.

No duplicate season ticket at Leicester Square station – but John Leround in the ticket queue, who insisted on buying mine, introduced me to a girl he was taking to his new lodgings, and pressed on me a prize he'd just won at bingo, a carving knife and fork, cheap but useful. This was heart-warming. I must not rule everyone out, nor suspect everyone overmuch. Better to think of those who have not robbed me, those whose acquaintanceship I am glad of. I remember it's a year since 'Tokyo Rose'* had a similar experience.

---

* Journalist friend of Mr Lucas's. The origins of his nickname – sometimes shortened to Rosie Toke – are unknown.

2

The Early Years

WHO WAS THE man who found himself being burgled by three young men that night in January 1968? The earlier diaries give a fascinating insight into the young Mr Lucas. We join Mr Lucas, an earnest, deeply religious and very dreamy bespectacled twenty-one-year-old on Thursday, 1 January 1948. In the UK, King George VI, father of Queen Elizabeth II, has just bestowed the annual New Year Honours; the General Agreement on Tariffs and Trade, a precursor to the World Trade Organization, has come into effect; and Mr Lucas is searching for his socks.

Britain as a country is weary. Battered and bruised economically after almost exactly six years of war, the capital is pockmarked by bomb sites, its inhabitants still mourning those lost. Clement Attlee is in power for the Labour Party and, in July that year, would oversee the creation of the National Health Service, still creaking on all these years later.

And so the backdrop to the earliest diaries is set. Counting down the days to the end of his National Service, we come to the first entry of Mr Lucas's surviving diaries. It opens in a typical nitpicking way with a reminder note to himself: 'Investigate socks prior to kit check.' This is a man for whom every detail must be recorded. Not just his moods or those of others. Not just the sexual encounters, coy in the forties and fifties; more explicit as we drift into the sixties and seventies. But everything around him, whether it is the political climate or the actual temperature.

For the time being, the most important matter on his mind is not the baronetcy awarded to William Sholto Douglas, former commander-in-chief and military governor of post-war Germany, nor, oddly enough, the vagaries of global trade. National Service has been a long stretch – three years and four months in total. And it can't finish quickly enough.

4 January 1948 (Sunday):

So the dreary expanse of years that I surveyed ahead of me in September 1944 has insensibly narrowed down to these last nine days. The years and months and days have passed, some rapidly, some with an infinite tedium: what seemed intolerable has been tolerated; what seemed unendurable has been endured; and so at last it is all hurrying to an end.

At the outbreak of war on 1 September 1939, Mr Lucas was evacuated, first to Trimley St. Martin, a small village in Suffolk close to Felixstowe, and then to Clacton-on-Sea in Essex. As he writes in 1948, looking back at his twelve-year-old self: 'Nine years ago, I was in Felixstowe, alarmed and alone, waiting for war to be declared and wishing I were home.'

The ragged aftermath of the war, however, offered other opportunities; the bombed-out parks of London's East End provided the perfect location for illicit late-night sex. 'Victoria Park [in Tower Hamlets] is a great haunt of inverts. I must explore its possibilities,' he writes in April 1949, ever keen to find new cruising grounds despite the evident dangers, not just of arrest but also assault from a deeply homophobic general public.

Mr Lucas had his first sexual experience at just fourteen in 1942 with a man called Ronald Terry (whose own age we don't know) in a public lavatory in St Chad's Park in Chadwell Heath. It is a moment he comes back to time and time again. In August 1948, he looks back: '(To) the happenings of that idyllic twenty minutes six years ago... that white lily of love whose beauty I then feasted on. At the beginning of 1941, my sexual inclinations were becoming definite [and] my interest in homosexual activities was beginning.'

But, as a committed Catholic, Mr Lucas spends his adult life torn between his sexual needs and the desire to live a life according to the church's teachings. 'A believing Catholic, who is also a practising homosexual, is forever fighting a war on two fronts – good for the intelligence, and pretty hellish for the emotions,' he muses in 1961. Gay sex would not be legalized – and then only partially – until 1967 when the Sexual Offences Act permitted consensual same-sex relations

in England and Wales in private for those over the age of twenty-one.

Society remained riven by homophobia. As Mr Lucas was growing up in the late twenties and thirties, the conviction of Irish playwright Oscar Wilde in 1895 was still fresh in many people's memories. The trial of Irish revolutionary Roger Casement – author of the notorious *The Black Diaries*, which explicitly detailed his same-sex sexual exploits, and some now believe were faked by the British Secret Service – had ended with Casement's execution just ten years before Mr Lucas's birth.

Gay culture might have bloomed in London during the Roaring Twenties, with weekly drag balls and a thriving queer scene played out in the personal ads of national newspapers, but very much only for the privileged few.

In 1932, thirty officers from F Division of London's Metropolitan Police stormed a ballroom in a private house on Holland Park Avenue, several worlds away from Mr Lucas's childhood home in suburbia, where they found sixty men dancing, many in 'female attire'. The subsequent court case of 'Lady Austin's camp boys' cast a long shadow over social attitudes, with hundreds of men prosecuted each year for offences connected to homosexuality (such as gross indecency, soliciting for immoral purposes, indecent assault and buggery) in the thirties.

Gay-friendly bars and clubs did exist, with many gay men and lesbians – and bisexual men and women – frequenting the Kit-Cat Club in the basement of the Capitol Theatre, right in the heart of London's West End. Gay members' clubs would appear and disappear with ruthless regularity. The Caravan in Covent Garden, which at one point had 445 members, lasted for a month before being raided by the police and shut down in August 1934. But otherwise, it was a life of cottaging and cruising, centred around public lavatories and late-night visits to parks.

In the sixties, we'll see how Mr Lucas becomes a fixture on the London gay bar scene, flitting between the Welsh Harp, White Bear and Golden Lion in search of fresh guardsmen. But in his early twenties, his sex life and social life are kept strictly separate: the gins and limes with his best friend Pat Connolly, a very serious, bookish young man the same age as our diarist, in the Charing Cross Hotel or the White Swan in Covent Garden, do not cross over into his night-time activities in Raphael Park, three miles from his home in Chadwell Heath, or around Marble Arch, one of the main cruising grounds at the time.

And, like every other twenty-one-year-old, he is desperate to find love. For Mr Lucas, stuck with his homophobic hateful parents and a black cat – very prosaically called Geoffrey – in a 1920s terraced house, however, the idea of escape, the idea of finding love, remained at that point just a dream, not least because of the internalized feelings of disgust he felt about his burgeoning sexuality. 'How vain, unsatisfactory, gross, is this perverse carnality,' he writes in July 1948.

But what is love for Mr Lucas? His feelings for Pat, with his love for literature and the arts, is building into something more serious. And yet, while Mr Lucas is becoming closer to Pat, he has also found a hint of the 'noble and exalted love' he so keenly desires.

10 January 1948 (Saturday):

What balm, what medicament, can give ease to an aching heart? Not cocaine nor morphia, nor any drug known to physicians, can soothe the gnawing cancer of desire for what is lost. For a year and a half, I have been consumed by a pure flame of love for F. It burns clear as ever now, though I've not seen him for six months – and oh! The pain of longing for him and knowing there's no hope. As a thirst-parched wanderer in the stormy wastes of Arabian Deserts seeks for the pool of water that may cool his mouth; as Dives in Hell cried for Lazarus to comfort him, I cry with all my heart for my most dearly loved one: and there is no answer given to me.

F is the 'casual, cynical and fairly arrogant' Fred, who does not reciprocate, leaving Mr Lucas to seek solace in the arms of others in London's bombed-out parks and dark-lit alleyways. Fred disappears quickly as the 1948 diary unfolds, leaving us to presume the 'grand passion' was played out in the 1946 and '47 diaries now lost to us, though the initial passion is strong and deeply felt. But we can see a deeper, perhaps more obvious, motive at work here: as the unhappy child of two unloving parents, Mr Lucas simply wants someone to like him. For now, though, Mr Lucas is moody, introspective and oh-so-pretentious, keen to record every bon mot or witticism made. But then what are diaries other than an extended wail of the unappreciated? This one, from nearly five years later, sums up his need for people to appreciate the real George: the witty, erudite Mr Lucas.

4 December 1952 (Thursday):

I made a good witticism this afternoon. Seeing House [colleague at the Board of Trade] *munching sandwiches when I returned at 3 p.m., I remarked, 'I see you're still masticating... I once made that remark to a man who was hard of hearing.' H. turned purple and choked with laughter for five minutes.*

Pat Connolly was one of the few who perhaps came closest to knowing the younger Mr Lucas. We know little about him, other than they met sometime during the war. We never quite find out whether Pat, 'so calm, gentle and courteous', is gay or not. 'I dare not hope he is like me,' Mr Lucas writes early in 1948. Frankly, from the vantage point of two decades into the twenty-first century, Pat sounds deeply tedious: tortured, another dry pseudo-intellectual and as soaked in religion as our protagonist. But for Mr Lucas, he is the best friend: someone he can call on for an early dinner at the Adelphi in Villiers Street followed by 'two films at the Warner ("mutilated shorts") and a gin and lime at the Fitzroy'. A weekend holiday with Pat in Clacton-on-Sea – 'the first I have spent with a sympathetic friend' – leads Mr Lucas to come close to coming out, in the typically pretentious way of a highly literate, if rather gauche, twenty-two-year-old.

23 August 1948 (Monday):

I wrote a long letter to Pat, touching at some length on the topic of homosexuality and quoting Proust.

Pat, perhaps unsurprisingly, does not reply, leaving Mr Lucas even more tortured the next time they meet. 'Home, with Pat to London Bridge,' he writes, 'possessed by a violent desire to embrace him, so that when I left him, I was quite weak.'

Their friendship, very close in the late forties, meeting at least two or three times a week, drifts on awkwardly until a sudden stop in 1952. 'Pat Connolly has taken offence at something I have said or written and won't meet me again,'

Mr Lucas writes in April that year. It was a hump that would last for six years.

3 February 1958 (Monday):

Today, I saw my erstwhile friend Pat Connolly, now long estranged from me, and was astonished to observe how old he seemed, with dry skin, faded eyes and worn features, drawn pinched face, tight lips and a complexion that has lost all freshness. Yet he is a year younger than I. At first, I could not believe 'twas he, so dry and faded he looked, but some man ten years older that looked like him. I went on my way a good deal cheered by this – his prim puritanism evidently agrees with his health very ill.

The glee at the physical decline of his former friend is evident, but the break in the friendship is, unfortunately, very typical of Mr Lucas. His earnestness quickly tips over into stubbornness and a youthful conviction that he is right, often at the expense of retaining even very old friends and acquaintances.

Was Pat actually gay? I'd say probably yes. Applying a contemporary eye to attitudes, styles and feelings of seventy years ago is both dangerous and probably futile, but he certainly sounds the archetypal tortured young gay man, sublimating his sexuality into his religion. Either way, better to give the last word to Mr Lucas: 'We have been long estranged,' he continues in February 1958. 'My liberalism in political and sexual fields grated on him. He is, I am convinced, a true homosexual who has, consciously or unconsciously, suppressed his affections and stifled all his natural desires.' It is precisely this refusal by Mr Lucas to stifle his own 'natural desires' that leads him into such trouble – as is the sheer fact that, several years later, he comes to see his sexuality as natural and not against God.

This need to be loved leads him to Raphael Park one fateful night, where, deep along the dark paths, he feels the heavy hand of a policeman upon his shoulder, his first encounter – but very much not his last – with the law.

2 May 1948 (Sunday):

Horror and ruin mark this calamitous day... unless God once more intervenes miraculously, I'm ruined, and my career blasted. My hopes gone: name, reputation and future destroyed at one stroke. After dinner to Raphael Park, where I met judgement in the form of a police constable, who took my name and address and demanded my identity card. When I could not produce it, he advised me to take it to Chadwell Heath police station, which I did as soon as I was arrived home.

He had spent the night, as he often did at the time – sometimes twice in one night – cruising for sex in Raphael Park, a good hour's walk from Chadwell Heath.

Today, the park is rather spruce. Neatly laid out, it is bracketed by a tennis court at one end and an ornamental lake at the other. But in 1948 it was a mess. The neighbouring town of Romford was bombed badly, with extensive damage to many houses in the borough and 143 residents reported killed.[1]

Sports pitches were dug up and emergency air raid shelters were built, and the park lost its railings as the war effort drove a desperate search for available iron. Trees overhung paths unswept for years; a deep trench at the north end was left unfilled. And one particularly perilous path led deep into the undergrowth, where men crept silently and softly into the dark, unseen by the cars on the main road heading into the slowly recovering capital. Perfect, indeed, for cruising. Or so Mr Lucas thought before one last stroll around the ageing bandstand would prove disastrous.

Mr Lucas is not the first to feel the tap of the law on his shoulder late at night. Friendship is the idealized form of love for him, but only because he knows its sharper, more intense version comes with the constant risk of arrest – and the consequences are harsh.

2 May 1948 (Sunday):

I imagine [the police officer] *means to charge me with either loitering with felonious intent or indecent exposure; either charge might stand. I do not know whether he would charge me. If he does, I am ruined for conviction means instant dismissal from the War Office for an offence that entails disgrace and obloquy.*

Secular laws policing same-sex behaviour stretch back to the Buggery Act of 1533, introduced under Henry VIII. With a penalty of death by hanging, sentences were carried out up until 1835 when James Pratt and John Smith were executed for sodomy. The death penalty was repealed in 1861 under the Offences Against the Person Act. But same-sex love remained very much against strict Victorian sexual mores (despite a heterosexual age of consent of twelve up until 1875). In 1885, Liberal M.P. Henry Labouchere introduced a last-minute change to the Criminal Law Amendment Act, designed to raise the straight age of consent to sixteen, bringing in a new charge of 'gross indecency' that would stalk queer society for decades to come.

What constituted gross indecency was left deliberately broad, covering everything except buggery, and carried a potential sentence of up to two years' jail. It was under a charge of twenty-five counts of gross indecency that Oscar Wilde was prosecuted in 1895, eventually receiving the harshest possible sentence of two years' hard labour.

The charge would certainly cover Mr Lucas's activities in Raphael Park. Yet while he is fully aware that his sexual desires are criminalized by society, he knows the risks he takes every night he sets foot in the park or simply strolls round Marble Arch. But what choice does he have? His diaries at this stage are full of conflict and turmoil; they show a man trying to suppress his desires and failing – and then attempting to deal with his conscience and set his mind at rest once more. It is not an easy process and one that Mr Lucas comes back to time and time again like, I'm sure, many other gay or bisexual men of the period who were desperately trying to be straight.

21 December 1948 (Tuesday):

I met a young fellow, tall and very well-looking, ex-RAF who took me to a field and used me indecently. He prefers women but likes lying with men. I was in such torment when I went to bed, I could not write in this diary but sought oblivion anxiously.

'An attempt to procure the commission by a man of an act of gross indecency with another man' was undoubtedly the charge Mr Lucas feared the most, a trap set for gay and bisexual men with a possible sentence of up to two years in jail. A parliamentary question in December 1953 by British Conservative M.P. William Shepherd to Sir David Maxwell Fyfe, then Secretary of State for the Home Department, revealed that in 1938 there were 822 attempts to commit 'unnatural offences', but it should be noted that figure covers both indecent assaults and importuning.[2] The same year, the police recorded 320 offences of gross indecency.

By 1952, the number of reported cases had risen considerably to 3,087 and 1,686 respectively. Of the overall 5,443 offences, including those for sodomy and bestiality – both of which still carried a maximum life sentence – Fyfe records that 'about 600 offenders were sent to prison'.

Attitudes remained fixed – and harsh. Replying to a further question of how many had received the maximum sentence for any of the charges, Fyfe was blunt: 'There is no reason to think that these penalties are inadequate.' And in a simple answer in the House of Commons, ruined lives were reduced to statistics for M.P.s to score political points. But real life was not very far away. A newspaper clipping Mr Lucas kept from May 1948 details how the law reached into the heart of the British Establishment, indeed into the House of Commons itself.

COMMONS OFFICER ACCUSED IN COURT
REMANDED ON £25 BAIL: NO EVIDENCE GIVEN

Fitzroy Hubert Fyers, aged 49, of independent means, of Ovington-court, Ovington-Road, Chelsea, appeared at West London to-day accused of persistently importuning at South Kensington District Line Station. No evidence was given and Fyers was in the dock for less than a minute. Sergeant Harding immediately asked for a remand until June 12. When Fyers was asked if he had any objection he bowed to the magistrate Mr J. L. Pratt and said: 'None at all, sir.' He was thereupon remanded on bail in his own recognisances of £25. Major Fitzroy Hubert Fyers is Assistant Serjeant-at-Arms at the Houses of Parliament. He was formerly Equerry to the late Duke of Connaught.

This is the fate Mr Lucas might face: a career ruined, public shame and the possibility of a six-month jail sentence. He rushes straight home from Raphael Park to detail the evening in his diary. Yet while he knows his father 'will exult over my downfall', suicide is 'out of the question', he writes on the evening he was stopped by the police. ''Twould be folly to lose all chance of happiness in the future life, because I've lost all chance of it in this.'

His prospects, though, are stark. At this stage, with his heart pounding, his handwriting becomes noticeably more scrawled, the fs and ps leaning even further from left to right as his nerves frazzle and fray. All he can imagine is the worst: '[I must] close all correspondence, contact, etc., with my friends. 'Twould be too painfully embarrassing for, say, Pat or Joan to continue to know one convicted of such an offence.'

The days stretch painfully and endlessly. 'As yet, no summons to judgement and condemnation has come,' he writes the day after he is caught in Raphael Park. 'No policeman with notebook or pencil. But what tomorrow, or the next day, or next week, may produce, I cannot dare to hope.'

Around him, life continues as normal. His 'miserable old father' is as irascible as ever, 'displaying all his usual evil temper and malignancy'. Missing the Royal Fusilier he has taken a fancy to on his morning train to Sidcup, he ogles instead the 'young private in the Royal Signals' with 'dark rather curled hair [who] rarely wears a hat'. But once home, the terror increases.

4 May 1948 (Tuesday):

This evening, as I sat by the fire, came a knock at the door. With beating heart and fluttering breath, I hurried to open it. Outside, stood a man, his car parked in the road. 'This is it,' thought I. But no – not yet. He merely wanted to know where Mr Leyton lived.

A month passes and Mr Lucas assumes he is safe – and returns once more to stalk the paths and bushes of the rundown park. It might be seen as a compulsion for sex, but I feel it's more of a simple need for love, for human affection and intimacy. But he is not off scot-free yet.

6 June 1948 (Sunday):

I received today a very terrible shock, being informed by my mother that Mrs Strutt, the fat woman next door that is a clerk in the police station, had seen my name on a charge sheet in the police station, the charge being indecent exposure on May 2nd. 'Tis true, 'tis pity and pity 'tis 'tis true. This is dreadful. I cannot imagine whether the police mean to proceed with a charge or no. 'Tis more than a month since it occurred. But I go in fear and dread. Whether the police mean to pounce, or whether my continued liberty is dependent on my good behaviour, I do not know, but I pray G-d to give me a good deliverance.

His diaries do not tell us what happened next, nor can I find any record of a charge being processed, so it is likely that the case was simply never pursued – or a caution issued, and no record kept. But this is what I love about the diaries: having to tug on the ragged ends of history to guess what happens next, find out where these characters end up and how their lives pan out. As a diarist, Mr Lucas is interested in the here and now, and specifically, of course, in how it relates to him personally. As such, reading his daily entries provides a necessarily choppy narrative: characters appear and disappear, events are truncated. We gain individual snapshots of his life and the times and events around him, but it is for us to fill in the details, to bridge those gaps, which I shall endeavour to do as we leave the underground queer world of London in the forties and travel with Mr Lucas, newly commissioned into the army, to Germany in the early fifties. And once more he is in trouble...

3

A Fateful Night in Germany

HAVING REJOINED THE army in December 1949 as a twenty-three-year-old lieutenant after lolling about at home with his parents for almost two years after the end of his National Service, Mr Lucas is about to face his worst nightmare: arrested while cruising the parks and public lavatories of Düsseldorf. The details of how exactly Mr Lucas made his way to Germany are a little patchy, partly determined by the fact that much of the 1950 and '51 diaries are missing; pages hastily ripped out following his arrest; photos presumably burned in an attempt to destroy incriminating evidence. This is, in fact, the only period over the almost seventy-year period of diary-taking that Mr Lucas attempted to self-censor. And who can blame him? The stakes are high, and his very liberty is at threat. But how did he get into this mess in the first place?

At the tender age of twenty-three, Mr Lucas is a dreamy young army officer, enamoured as much by the position as a servant of King George VI as the allure and effect of the uniform.

8 January 1950 (Sunday):

Now that I am once more in the army, as a commissioned officer, I have acquired an identity separate from my own personal one – I'm not merely myself but exist also as one of the King's officers, with a title and uniform to sustain me. As an officer, I must try to keep and cheer my soldiers; my duty and my romantic passion for troops directing the same. Caution and discretion, of course, I need; but I may hope for some measure of success in achieving an amorous comradeship with some attractive soldier.

Indeed, he wastes little time, kissing guardsman Ray Gardler just days later, 'a piquant tableau, had there been any to see – an officer in uniform kissing a guardsman's lips and hand'.

The Second World War had ended a little over four years earlier and the relative ease with which gay and bisexual men were accepted during wartime fighting alongside their heterosexual peers had come to a crashing end.

Historian Stephen Bourne writes eloquently about how war provided a moratorium on ostracizing gay men. 'What surprised me was the number of gay men in the Second World War who were not only known to be gay but were accepted by their heterosexual comrades,' he wrote in a blog for the London School of Economics and Political Science. 'Some gay men who joined up did face hostility to begin with, but found that if they used humour they could overcome homophobic attitudes and make friends.'[1]

But peacetime in September 1945 brought with it a return to the Edwardian attitudes and mores – and laws – of the thirties. In his 1996 book, *Heterosexual Dictatorship: Male Homosexuality in Postwar Britain*, Patrick Higgins estimates that 1,069 gay men were in jail in England and Wales for 'crimes' that would not be illegal today.[2] Their average age was just thirty-seven. The Sexual Offences Act 1956 repealed the nineteenth-century Labouchere Amendment – and then promptly re-enacted it.

INDECENCY BETWEEN MEN

It is an offence for a man to commit an act of gross indecency with another man, whether in public or private, or to be a party to the commission by a man of an act of gross indecency with another man, or to procure the commission by a man of an act of gross indecency with another man.[3]

Mr Lucas's concerns are less about the inequities of the law than wanting to get laid. And, having been sent to Germany a few weeks into 1950 in his newly elevated position as a commissioned officer, that's proving distinctly difficult. 'Even to be on terms of ordinary social friendship with soldiers is fraught with difficulty,' he writes in March 1950 stationed in Bad Oeynhausen, an hour's drive west from Hanover. 'The military officer, 'tis evident, must regard soldiers as a kind of animal, to be cared for, fed and rigidly controlled.'

The British Army of the Rhine, which had been formed to oversee the British zone of Allied-occupied Germany, was headquartered in Bad Oeynhausen in North Rhine-Westphalia. The military would remain in the town until 1954, overseeing the housing and administration of the approximately 800,000 British and Commonwealth soldiers stationed in Germany after the war. 'Finding barracks and camps for them all in a ruined country was a major headache,' notes the National Army Museum detailing the occupation of Germany.[4]

However, the headache for Mr Lucas was more visceral: the lack of available young men.

21 April 1950 (Friday):

I am like Major Rohm in Bolivia [when the gay Nazi politician was a military adviser in the country], *surrounded by exquisitely beautiful young men and unable to form a liaison with any of them – Casanova in a convent! There are no opportunities here, no convenient meeting places, for the beastly German mind has not thought to provide any public lavatories...*

And so Mr Lucas seeks respite in Düsseldorf, finding sexual success – if not ever satisfaction – with a young Scots guardsman a few months later.

16 July 1950 (Sunday):

My second visit to Düsseldorf – a charming city, urbane and civilized and a blessed relief from Bad Oeynhausen – has provided me with a pleasant evening entertaining a young Scots guardsman, who was touchingly grateful, and, yesterday, with the first complaisant soldier I have met since leaving England seven months ago. He is a short stocky Welsh lad of nineteen from Swansea (where he was a carpenter's apprentice and a gunner in the 19th Field Regt), fond of women but enjoys homosexual intercourse, which he has had before and liking both the active and passive roles. So this week has been productive – a pleasant innocent friendship and a pleasant guilty one.

Fraternizing with the lower ranks was frowned upon at the time by the military high command, with a keen eye on retaining discipline as well as class distinctions. The top brass is also well aware of other reasons for officers mingling with soldiers – and soon clamps down on Mr Lucas's extracurricular activities.

13 September 1950 (Wednesday):

The restriction of life in Germany has had a result I have long expected: a note of mine to Gunner Green, my military clerk and friend, has resulted in a sharp reprimand and warning of an adverse report, unless I mend my ways and cease to be familiar with troops... It is attributable to the restrictions imposed here on one of my temperament. Still, if this is the worst trouble my homosexuality ever leads me to face, I'll be thankful: le troisième sexe is a magnet for troubles and I fully expect I shall sooner or later find myself ruined by my peculiar tastes.

How right he was. But why do we – gay and bisexual men – take these risks in the first place? Of course, in 1950, there was little choice, but in the early nineties when gay sex was legal, if still not widely accepted, I gleefully went cruising and cottaging, and, yes, the thrill of the illicit was part of its appeal. Was sexual excitement heightened by the danger of being caught, beaten up or worse? Of course it was – and that's certainly what drew me time and time again to a freezing-cold Calton Hill on many dark nights in Edinburgh, where I was studying, or the glory hole drilled rather ineptly in the downstairs loos of the university library. That same thrill drew Mr Lucas to his fate one early-autumn evening in Düsseldorf.

18 October 1950 (Wednesday):

At 6 p.m. I was a useful and respected staff officer taking a walk; at 7 p.m. I was under arrest for an alleged indecent assault offence with a young German who reported me. After interrogation by Finnerson [of the Special Investigations Branch of the military police] *until after midnight, I was removed to the 1st Norfolk barracks to spend the remainder of the night in a dismal guardroom under escort of a 2nd lieutenant Sanderson – an agreeable, bespectacled subaltern who no doubt found the situation as disagreeable as I did. So my career as an officer comes to an end, sordidly.*

Our hapless lieutenant was released the following morning from 'close arrest at 11 a.m., to my relief and, I should fancy, that of poor second lieutenant Sanderson. Lunch at the Rhine Centre was followed by the journey to Bad Oeynhausen, during which I sat with my thoughts, except for a few words with an elderly civilian in my carriage. How I envied him.'

In *Which People's War?: National Identity and Citizenship in Wartime Britain 1939–1945*, Sonya O. Rose provides compelling evidence of a wartime perception that real men served their country and unmanly men 'pretend[ed] to believe in "peace". The tabloids were not far behind,' she writes. 'On the 2nd June 1940, the *Sunday Pictorial* offered a damning indictment of the "elegant sissies who fester in the restaurants of London, gossiping like girls... they've got more scent than sense." A week after Dunkirk, the *Sunday Pictorial* pushed its anti-pacifist stance even further with an article called "Pacifists and Pansies".'[5] The link between service, masculinity and heterosexuality was clear.

A ban on openly serving gay and lesbian personnel in the British military would last for the next fifty years, finally being scrapped under Tony Blair's government in 2000. Even after homosexuality was partially decriminalized in England and Wales in 1967, between 100 and 300 men and women were thrown out of the armed forces for the sake of their sexuality during the eighties, according to human rights campaigner Peter Tatchell.[6] 'It was unacceptable then and it is unacceptable now,' Minister for Veterans' Affairs Johnny Mercer, himself a former British Army officer said in a much-delayed apology twenty years after the ban was lifted.[7]

The 1950 Army Act sets out the armed force's stance very clearly, if starkly:

Any person subject to this Act who commits any of the following offences, that is to say,- (a) is guilty of any disgraceful conduct of a cruel, indecent or unnatural kind; or (b) malingers, or feigns, or produces disease or infirmity in himself, or intentionally delays his cure or aggravates his disease or infirmity; or (c) with intent to render himself or any other person unfit for service, voluntarily causes hurt to himself or that person; shall, on conviction by court-martial, be liable to suffer imprisonment for a term which may extend to seven years or such less punishment as is in this Act mentioned.[8]

Being thrown out of the army is the least of Mr Lucas's worries at this point – and he knows it.

His thoughts turn immediately to incriminating evidence, and to his diary in particular. 'I destroyed all the earlier pages of my 1950 diary for fear of possible scrutiny that might incriminate any of the lads I have been friendly with.' Yet he also reports that despite the severity of the 'crime' for which he stands accused, he is dealt with courteously and calmly by his superiors, who are perhaps used to this annoying occasional incident.

20 October 1950 (Friday):

I must say, Major Miller has been wonderfully kind. As I waited for Lt. Col. Alexander this morning, he [arrived and] *remarked that 'no man knows what another man has to bear', spoke a few consoling words about the comforts of our religion, and shook my hand. The colonel, too, though he said little, was most kind in his manner. Until my re-arrest and court martial, I am carrying on with my normal duties. My colleagues believe I have been recalled for a Court of Inquiry on the traffic accident in which I have recently been involved. What they will say when they learn the truth, I prefer not to think. Meanwhile, work goes on…*

The incident itself sounds like a set-up: Düsseldorf's finest pretty Polizei following in the footsteps of their West End counterparts. Either way, Mr Lucas is screwed – and not in the way he was hoping for that evening.

21 October 1950 (Saturday):

On Wednesday evening last, at seven, I was in the hands of the Düsseldorf police, accused of an indecent assault on a young German in a lavatory on the Kleverplatz. In point of fact, the young fellow was one that, coming back and forth to this lavatory several times, had persuaded me he was comme ça. When I perceived him masturbating, I was sure of it, and approached him, whereon he departed and presently two Kriminal polizei men in plain clothes arrive, arrest me and, after much talk at the police station, hand me over to the military police.

The worst is expected, despite Mr Lucas claiming to be 'in fact, innocent of this alleged assault'.

21 October 1950 (Saturday):

Yet in the face of the German's positive testimony and the absence of any reason why he should lie, no court martial can but find me guilty. I expect three years' gaol at most, nine months at least; thereafter, God knows. I must be dismissed from the civil service as well as discharged with ignominy from the military.

His sense of injustice is tempered, perhaps amusingly for us today, by the sheer fact that not only did he not actually do anything – but that, well, he didn't get to do anything. The irony – and the rueful admission of a lost opportunity – is killing: 'Many times have I run the risk of arrest for homosexual intercourse in the past and have not been arrested: this time, when in fact I have not had such intercourse, I am. 'Tis curious. Still God is the end of all things, and He will at last make all things well.' Not quite this time, Mr Lucas, I'm afraid.

A few days later and things start to move quickly. On 26 October, Mr Lucas spends the morning tidying his effects, 'having an idea that this was my last morning of liberty – and so it was'. His kit bag is packed and stored away, and he is taken to Hanover Transit Centre 'under the escort of Capt. Reeves and there handed over to Maj. Scott, U. C. Court Martial wing'.

He is deposited in the holding centre with two others, one bound over for 'drunkenness, gambling and assaulting

a [woman officer]' and the other for 'drunkenness'. Yet it is a somewhat bizarre form of detention, as, that evening, Mr Lucas spends the night at the cinema with the two other detainees, watching *Abbott and Costello Meet the Killer, Boris Karloff*, a horror comedy of the time that was subject to a wonderfully sniffy September 1949 review in the *New York Times*: 'Most of the humor—if that's what you'd call it—is derived from the slapstick display of the two comedians juggling a couple of very stiff corpses in a hotel,' writes reviewer Bosley Crowther.[9] Mr Lucas was equally unimpressed by the movie. 'A weak film, during which I nearly fell asleep,' he writes with quite impressive insouciance considering his impending fate.

His diaries do almost tip towards the glib, perhaps parsing the terror he must feel. But more, to my mind, they reveal just how young he still is. Although twenty-four, he is a very young twenty-four: naïve, completely the opposite of worldly wise and still torn between seeking out his heart's desire and wanting to be part of decent society; wanting to be liked, not least by whomever he imagines might be reading his diary, more than seventy years on.

27 October 1950 (Friday):

Today, we had the first snow of the autumn, which promises a long and hard winter. Where and how will I spend it, I wonder. The day passed tolerably in reading of magazines and conversation with [fellow detainee] *Lt. Col. Moore a* [former] *subaltern and Winfield (a* [lieutenant-corporal] *in the Queen's* [Guards]*). This evening, I was rather pleased at solving a* Times *crossword puzzle clue – 'Horace Walpole's word had a dip in it', to which the correct answer is 'serenity' – Mr W. having coined the word 'serendipity'.*

Sonya Rose writes of how '1,813 servicemen of all ranks were tried by courts-martial for indecency in the Army, the RAF and the Navy between 1939 and 1945 and there were 1,428 convictions'.[10] This is compared with the huge number of

British men who served in the armed forces during the war: more than 5 million.

For Mr Lucas, given what else is happening around him, his almost childlike delight in solving a difficult crossword clue is telling: even at times of extreme distress or terror, he is conscious of trying to impress, trying to fit in. Mr Lucas is also keen to bond with his fellow inmates, although his moral compass is distinctly off in terms of where his sympathies lie. 'Upstairs in this block, I learn, are confined fourteen soldiers, one group for rape, one for sodomy... I saw the rape and buggery boys being led out to exercise today – lads with seven years and three years respectively to serve in gaol.'

The first hearing of his case is in a few days' time. 'The summary of evidence on Monday is to be taken, I learn, by Major Symonds – a man I have often lunched with and chatted with. I am not looking forward to it.' Growing close to Lieutenant Colonel Moore – a product of Cheltenham and Sandhurst, so very much the type of person the acutely socially aware Mr Lucas would like to have become acquainted with under different circumstances (but on remand here for sexual assault) – our diarist starts to adjust to his new reality.

28 October 1950 (Saturday):

Both Lt. Col. Moore and myself are in the same position – wondering how to earn a living once we are thrown out of the service. Meanwhile we must enjoy our confinement as best we can – 'tis quite tolerably comfortable, and one is much better off than in comparable circumstances in civil life.

Indeed, quite bizarrely so. The initial trip to the cinema turns out to not have been a one-off, with the inmates' 'confinement' regularly interrupted by trips to the movies. 'To the cinema after tea, with Col. Moore and Winfield, to see *The Interrupted Journey* – a film with good points, but in general weak and badly planned. Then to a late dinner, accompanied by a bottle of beer, light conversation and to bed at 11 p.m.'

Monday comes quickly – as does a face-to-face meeting with the young German man who has filed the accusations.

30 October 1950 (Monday):

The summary of evidence against me this morning taken by Major William, a stumpy elderly man, who, to my satisfaction, spoke pretty sharply to my accuser, Wilhelm Hermann, once or twice. H., a shifty unreliable fellow, impressed me very badly; I can but fear that he must have had some secret or sinister motive – positively psychological – in reporting me to the police. He and Metzinneck, the police serjeant, are the only two prosecution witnesses.

Shaken by his ordeal – and confined in perhaps the most civilized jail of all time – 'after this was over, I had a glass of sherry to restore my disturbed spirits'.

Life continues in a similar vein for the next few weeks: confinement of sorts punctuated by visits to the cinema and even to regimental football matches. And the occasional bit of gossip about his fellow inmates: 'I was amused to hear that two quartermasters in succession of the B. M. H. Hamburg [a British military hospital] were cashiered for driving out into the countryside wearing only a greatcoat and there exposing themselves to small girls...' Mr Lucas's 'crime' somewhat pales by comparison.

The gossip he picks up from his fellow confined officers shows how time can wipe sexuality from the history books.

6 November 1950 (Monday):

I was interested to hear Winfield's reminiscences of a Major Loftus-Tottenham of the RE Bridging Camp, Chatham, who about 1934, was cashiered with his friend

Captain Case and served a term in Maidstone Gaol for sodomy. The major, a wealthy man from a good family, son to a major-general, had, with his friend the captain, kept a flat in Chatham to which they had taken band boys etcetera – and there seduced them. But, says Winfield, though Major Loftus-Tottenham was cashiered in 1934, in 1939 he returned to the army as a major, for he, RQMS Winfield, met him then on a bridging course.

The 'good family' included Major-General Frederick Joseph Loftus-Tottenham, renowned for his bravery in the First and Second World Wars. The National Portrait Gallery has a wonderful photograph of him from June 1947 looking straight out of Central Casting: bog-brush moustache, grumpy expression, hand on walking stick and all. We don't know much about the three sons other than two died during the war and the third is lost to history. These snippets give us a feel for the value of Mr Lucas's diaries. The tale of the unfortunate Major Loftus-Tottenham is only a footnote in this book, let alone in history – but it's our history and our lost queer history that Mr Lucas captures so elegantly. And, as ever, it's all in the detail, particularly the description of Colonel Moore's 'last supper':

13 November 1950 (Monday):

This evening Col. Moore gave a small dinner party on the eve of his trial – hors d'oeuvres, trout, duck, compote of fruit, cheese, with sherry and crème de menthe – very agreeable.

The next day, 'Col. Moore returned much shaken after a grim day in court, hearing Lt. Col. Campbell, that vindictive mountain, speak for eighty minutes and then listening to the array of prosecution witnesses'. Judgement arrives a day later: 'A severe reprimand and loss of two years' seniority – light enough for conviction on both charges, one of which was of assault with intent to commit grievous bodily harm.' A relatively lucky escape for Moore, but Mr Lucas is now left with just Winfield, who is 'sure to leave on Tuesday or Wednesday next. The prospect is beginning to alarm me.' As the trial date nears, Mr Lucas's fears are mounting. He is well aware that a guilty verdict will haunt him for years to come. For civilians, the penalty for gross indecency at the time was two years' jail. Military personnel would have been dismissed for 'disgraceful conduct' with a possible jail term of up to two years, depending on the severity of the charge.

18 November 1950 (Saturday):

On Monday, after thirty-three days of waiting, is my trial by General Court Martial for gross indecency. I have no doubt of the outcome – I shall be convicted and dismissed from the service, and my career ruined, all because of a moment's imprudence. The young German who for some sinister motive of his own reported me to the police after acting in the most suggestive manner, and masturbating in front of me, has done more than he expected – though I appreciate my dangerous situation and realize that in no long time I shall, for the first time in my life, have no occupation and no source of income, I cannot yet feel more than a general apprehension. Terror and dismay will no doubt come later – at present regret that this catastrophe should come so soon and that the occasion of my fall should be so mean and sordid, are my chief emotions, mixed with anger and contempt for my denouncer and gratitude to my soldier friends for their sympathetic letters. Had I been arrested for sodomy with, say, Gunner McAdam, I'd have been better pleased – the affair would have been on a nobler and more romantic plane. I recall a conversation last year in a bar in the Edgware Road, at which I predicted to Gdsn Johnnie Fisher and Gdsn Limb that I'd be court-martialled. A homosexual subaltern could scarcely expect otherwise.

Then the trial begins – and it's not looking good.

20 November 1950 (Monday):

Today I was tried before a Brigadier and four other officers (one major and three captains) – a very shattering ordeal, in the latter part of which I felt sick and ill. The prosecution was fair: the judge advocate was fair, and his summing up favourable; my defending officer, though he bungled his job, was at least immoderately convincing: yet the court (swayed, I believe, by the brigadier) found me guilty (what I had expected) and sentenced me to be cashiered and to serve six months' imprisonment – which I had not expected. Lieutenant 'Porky' Gale, RWK [Royal West Kent regiment], *tried before me, has the same sentence for nine charges of selling* [War Department] *stores: and he, I, and our two escorts, will occupy the mess until our sentences are confirmed and we removed to gaol. God be compassionate to all poor souls in prison or awaiting imprisonment!*

Shattered by the judgement, Mr Lucas returns to his holding centre, passing a miserable few days in the same pattern: movies, to bed by 11 p.m. and watching as, one by one, his fellow inmates are taken off to jail.

24 November 1950 (Friday):

The last of the Welsh Fusiliers convicted of 'gross indecency' was taken away this morning – a smart lad I have noticed before, with a plumpish perky face and laughing eyes, who, for the next two years, will be inside a gaol. I felt most distressed to see him so – another victim of that conspiracy of respectable society to maintain its conventions. I wish I could help him.

The fiftieth anniversary of the death of Oscar Wilde a few days later does not pass unnoticed – nor the comparisons to

Mr Lucas's own predicament. 'Oscar Wilde died today, fifty years ago – another victim (though in a different way) to the general dislike of homosexuality.' And, as the year turns, and Mr Lucas remains for now at the detention centre, his worries grow about what 1951 will bring.

31 December 1950 (Sunday):

I saw 1951 in in unusual circumstances – Gale and Frankish playing patience, Col. Palmer on the sofa in pyjamas and dressing gown, Jock Moncur and I drinking beer – I with a bad cold.

1 January 1951 (Monday):

Today, the first of the New Year, began with a heavy shower of snow: and I spent it in the court martial wing, where Gale and Lt. Knight played cards, and Martin Merry slept. To an increasing degree I am becoming afraid of going to prison. At the cinema tonight, the thought crossed my mind that soon, perhaps, I shall be in a place where I shall have neither wireless nor cinema.

The days pass; the films mount up. *Under the Sun*: 'a mediocre gangster film'; *East of Java*: 'with Shelley Winters, a good actress with an attractive, rather vulgar, face'; and *A Run for Your Money*: 'a richly comic film, at which I had a pleasant chat with an RASC [Royal Army Service Corps] lad from Yorkshire whom I think I have met before somewhere.'

I'm trying to gauge Mr Lucas's frame of mind here: despite the unconscionable terror of what lies in front of him, he remains dedicated – almost quite comically – to trying to retain some sense of normality. Even if it involves endless dreadful films. And then mercy strikes; he finally receives some good news.

9 January 1951 (Tuesday):

The [Deputy Adjutant-General – a military chief administrative officer] *visited today and, from him, Major Scott learned that my sentence has been reduced to one of simple dismissal. God be thanked! But I wish my fellow prisoners were so lucky!*

Three days later, Mr Lucas is released from 'close arrest', but – rather amusingly – 'to my annoyance, since I wish to see the [regimental] football match tomorrow'. He had spent a total of eighty-one days at the detention centre, 'fifty-three of them under close arrest' before he is shipped home aboard the *S.S. Vienna*, which, before it was scrapped in Ghent in 1960, served as a permanent leave ship for the British Army of the Rhine. But while he might be free – and heading home in some style – he still has to face the consequences of having lost his position and his career.

And, quite understandably, he lies through his teeth once he's back home. Meeting his friend Pat Connolly as he arrives in London, 'I told the story of being on leave and went to the War Office in plain clothes for a distressing interview with Frankie Atkin, the assistant secretary of C.4 [one of the departments] who, though very kind, made it clear that I was likely to be dismissed.'

But he is not alone in both his distress and his circumstances. Along with many, many thousands of others, his friend – and one-time lover – Johnnie Fisher tells him over a pint at the Victory Club in London later that evening of his brother Jim's 'posting to Tripoli: after a homosexual scandal involving a Captain Alexander'.

Life continues as ever in London, as Mr Lucas settles back into the round of bars and cruising grounds and once more living with his hateful parents.

28 February 1951 (Wednesday):

My mother in a savage humour and asking me, as I shaved, why I didn't draw the razor across my throat and end it. She cooled later.

Reading the diaries at this point, the trauma of the arrest and jail in Germany has very much been, if not forgotten, then certainly parked to deal with another day.

1 March 1951 (Thursday):

At the Arches [in Piccadilly Circus] *tonight, met my young Jock Reid – George Mackay Reid – and had an interesting chat with him, as he described various encounters with 'queers' – Richard, for instance, who will only pay £2 [£81.56], or the potman at 'The New Inn', described as a 'dollar touch'.*

4 March 1951 (Sunday):

I've lately made the acquaintance of sundry of the riff-raff that lurk about Marble Arch and eke out a pernicious living by some male prostitution – Christy O'Connell from Cork, short, impish, an ex-corporal in the Airborne; George Reid, seventeen, and fragile-looking, from Dundee; Frankie Harrill, a tough-looking ex-sailor, etc. They are an interesting social phenomenon. The homosexual habitués of the area, who provide their chief clientele, are interesting, too, though mostly elderly and repulsive to my own fastidious taste.

But, as we jump ahead a decade, scandal haunts Mr Lucas – as indeed it did many gay men of the time. Yet this particular scandal to come was one that had its roots in love, a fervent passionate love that Mr Lucas would come to regret as it brought him nearer to his downfall than even a close encounter with a wanking Wilhem in downtown Düsseldorf.

4

The Tragic Tale of Flannan O'Hehir

TUCKED AWAY IN the diaries, among the more than 10 million words that Mr Lucas poured out on paper over the course of seventy years, is a short, blink-and-you'll-miss-it, four-month period straddling 1958 and 1959 that explains much of what is to come in the sixties and the relationship with Peter. Mr Lucas falls in love, a love so pure – and so platonic – that it is heart-wrenching to read and poignant in the extreme.

The tale of Flannan O'Hehir, one-time barman and native of Ennis, a small town of just under 8,300 in 1956 in western Ireland, is one of tragedy. It starts with Mr Lucas, as ever an observer, becoming, by modern eyes, a stalker.

8 December 1958 (Monday):

At Marlborough Street [Magistrates' Court in London] *this morning, young Patrick Murphy was duly sent off to Dublin – I don't doubt he'll be back here before very long 'earning his living', as the policeman put it, 'by associating with men of a certain type'. But there was another and sadder case today. A well-dressed, pleasant-spoken, very Irish young man named Flannan O'Hehir, of medium height and build, was sent for trial on a charge of buggery. On Sunday the 30th of November, a prowling policeman in Hyde Park had found young O'Hehir with his trousers down and his coat up being buggered by a man. A struggle ensued, the other man got away and poor O'Hehir, hampered no doubt by his trousers around his ankles, was arrested. The policeman, I feel, need not have charged the full offence, at any rate.*

Mr Lucas was attending court in his newish role at the Board of Trade, as part of the Solicitor's Department. He had rejoined the civil service in April 1951, having first worked there in 1948–49, but was fortunate indeed to find an employer willing to hire him after his military service debacle.

9 April 1951 (Monday):

My first day at work, after five months of inactivity, was spent in my new office – the Import Licensing Branch of the Board of Trade, in Romney House, a large office block near the Abbey. Here I am set to learning the technique of licensing of imports into the country from an [executive officer] *soon likely to be promoted. 'Tis no very attractive task and inferior to those I have hitherto performed not unsuccessfully – but 'tis an officer post with a salary which I need.*

As such, in his new official capacity he is there to monitor ongoing cases for the Board of Trade, usually no more than trademark infringement and contract disputes. But unofficially, he uses the time to scour the noticeboards for cases of gay men arrested simply for their sexuality – those caught for having sex in public parks and lavatories late at night.

Marlborough Street refers to the magistrates' court that used to be at 19–21 Great Marlborough Street in Soho, central London – and now, perhaps typically, is a swanky hotel. Readers of queer history might remember it most poignantly as the scene of the start of Oscar Wilde's doomed libel action against the Marquess of Queensbury in 1895, before the case moved to the Old Bailey – and Wilde's eventual downfall a few months later. The court also played host to a number of other notable trials, including that of Christine Keeler on charges of prostitution that would eventually lead to the Profumo Affair of 1963. But for now, Mr Lucas is busy checking the notices for charges relating to gay sex – and those are many and easy to find.

9 December 1958 (Tuesday):

Three more people this morning at Marlborough Street charged with masturbating together in the park. A

Dutchman named Van Dyck, a Mauritian law student and a twenty-year-old electrical engineer named David Edwards, in London on a technical course. They were fined £5, £3 and £3 [£143 and £86] *respectively. At lunchtime, I was glad to see young Edwards in Falconberg Mews* [home to a public toilet known for gay sex at the time]. *Perhaps I should manage to get to know him there.*

Among the everyday were the remarkable – and the public figures. Ian Harvey was a promising Conservative career politician. Everything in his life had so far fallen in his favour: after attending Fettes College, he went on to Christ Church, Oxford, where he had been president of both the Oxford University Conservative Association and the Oxford Union. After the war, he joined the advertising industry in 1949, becoming the Conservative M.P. for Harrow East (a suburb in Greater London) the following year. But eight years later, his name was on the board of upcoming cases at Bow Street accused of gross indecency following a liaison in a bush in St James's Park with a nineteen-year-old Coldstream Guard.

10 December 1958 (Wednesday):

I was, of course, at Bow Street this morning for the hearing of the charges against Ian Harvey, and the unfortunate Guardsman Plant [the nineteen-year-old co-accused]. *The court had been full from its opening, so I could not get in and learned what had happened from the midday papers. The gross indecency charges against them were not proceeded with, it appears, so that the matter could be settled before the magistrate. Both Mr Harvey and the guardsmen – to whom my heart goes out in deepest pity – pleaded guilty to a charge under the Parks regulations of indecent behaviour and were fined £5 each. This is the usual procedure for Hyde Park cases (Cecil Edwards* [a friend of Mr Lucas's] *was so dealt with in May 1949) and it is regrettable that it was not adopted by the police at the outset, so that the affair could have been settled at Bow Street* [magistrate's court] *the next morning.*

While Harvey's career in politics might have ended 'sordidly', his post-parliamentary life was both honourable and deeply admirable. Having resigned his Harrow East seat, he went on to become the vice-president of the Campaign for Homosexual Equality in 1972 and then, eight years later, was elected chairman of the Conservative Group for Homosexual Equality, a brave public position during a particularly poisonous time for gay and bisexual men. Unfortunately, however, his last years perhaps typify the public view of the single gay man. One 'friend', quoted in David Kynaston's book, *Modernity Britain: 1957–1962*, recalled: 'I remember him, a sad old man living alone and forgotten in a small flat.'[1]

The trial closes badly for all concerned, but not before this rather wonderful analysis from Mr Lucas.

13 December 1958 (Saturday):

I did not get up till 1 p.m. almost. In Forte's tonight an exceedingly pushy young grenadier most insistent on my taking him home, till I was obliged to leave. 'Persistent soliciting' well describes his behaviour. From a queen who was able to hear the Harvey-Plant case, I learned that the actual 'misbehaviour' consisted of the guardsman's masturbating Mr Harvey – a pleasant act of courtesy on the young man's part, as I see it.

But along with the bold-type names of the fifties are the lesser-known characters, and it is Flannan O'Hehir who catches Mr Lucas's eye. Mr Lucas is now thirty-two and going through a very religious period, attending mass every second he can and trying to, as he sees it, save his soul by saving the souls of others.

6 November 1953 (Friday):

Meanwhile, I fall in and out of sin, not willingly, but through weakness and I aim to stand firm. My mother's acid tongue sneers and gibes at 'homos' and the 'filthy soldiers you pick up'. The public press, stimulated by my Lord Montague's and Sir John Gielgud's scandals, are hysterically denouncing homosexuals and sharper laws are likely to be made to punish those of us who slip into physical intercourse and are caught. Well, we must trust

*that our God will temper the wind to His shorn lambs –
and to His black sheep as well.*

Flann's case is one in need of simple Christian charity. And, while his mother is a crashing snob – warning him a few months later that 'most Irishmen [are] thieves and criminals' – Mr Lucas, while very class-conscious himself, is aware of the ease with which gay men, both then and now, can mix and mingle with those from different stations of life.

18 December 1958 (Thursday):

For most people, counter assistants, barman and such like, are people with whom one can be on the most amicable terms, yet never meet elsewhere than in the particular ambience to which they belong. They remain, so to speak, on the wrong side of the counter – people with whom one passes the time of day and discusses the weather, but who cease to exist for all practical purposes, as soon as they are out of sight. With me, it is rather different – my inquisitive interest in people impels me to try to bridge the gap to get to know the bus conductors, fellow passengers, coffee bar attendants, I encounter. Even the people I see in the dock on homosexual charges, I would like to know – Flannan O'Hehir, in particular, at the moment (while I am sat in the theatre with [friend] John Cullen and enjoying the show, my mind thinking of Flannan O'Hehir and wondering how I could comfort him).

Admirable on the part of Mr Lucas, and true to his role as a kind of 'street philanthropist' – a type of Victorian moralist who helped rent boys not just financially but morally, attending their court cases, paying their fines and lecturing them on the rights and wrongs of theft and violence. Still, his pursuit of Flann is no less than stalking. Piqued by O'Hehir's plight, Mr Lucas decides to try to find him to see how he can help, believing that Flann had already been released on bail. I know this is stretching credibility – and Christian kindness – but I think our diarist's intentions are honourable. His almost daily attendance at mass suggests a need to feed something more than his sex drive, which, it should be said, is already pretty healthy. His diary entry from 31 December 1958, tallying up his expenses in more ways than one, notes with a certain satisfaction: 'I've had sex forty-five times [this year]. I hope to the pleasure of those having it with me.'

History does not tell us whether that's true or not, but in terms of O'Hehir, Mr Lucas does have a track record of helping others less fortunate than himself, even to the extent of opening his home – at that point in Como Street, Romford – for his friends and acquaintances to use for sex. 'I left my back door open for G. Coe and Young Jeff, this evening,' he writes on 21 December 1958. 'They enjoyed themselves, I see from a note left on the table.'

To track down Flann, Mr Lucas first turns to his friends.

20 December 1958 (Saturday):

I visited Peter Austin this evening at his café and asked him to try to trace Flannan O'Hehir through his address in Wincott Street from the electoral register at Kennington.

Christmas that year passes uneventfully, with Mr Lucas sequestered in Clacton with his mother – his father having died at the age of sixty-nine earlier that year – in an uneasy truce from their usual quarrels. It was, as he writes, 'a dull, depressing day'. He had spent part of Christmas Eve at mass at the Catholic church in Warwick Street, Soho, asking the priest, Dr Fuller, to 'remember Flannan O'Hehir in his mass'. Mr Lucas is also moved to go to confession, something he does very rarely (perhaps as he has rather too much to confess to). 'I confessed "homosexual intercourse", but with a mental reservation that I did not believe it to be sinful.'

Boxing Day was no better in the Lucas household.

26 December 1958 (Friday):

Very much depressed – perhaps because of the uncheerful atmosphere of Clacton on Christmas Day with my mother in her chill, uncheerful bungalow. Perhaps because of my feeling and distress for Flannan O'Hehir. If my own lowness of spirits can help him at all, can thus bear some of the poor lad's distress, by way of substitution, I am glad of it.

So Inspector Lucas again picks up the trail, before realizing he needs to find another way to track down the elusive O'Hehir.

29 December 1958 (Monday):

I went to the Lambeth Public Library this morning in hopes of finding Flannan O'Hehir's address from the electoral register, overlooking the fact that, as the poor lad is only twenty, he will not be on the register and is too young to vote.

Born in 1938 in Kildysart, County Clare, a village of no more than 400 even today, Flann left school when he was fourteen. He was taught how to serve mass by Father O'Dea, the curate at Kildysart for whom he used to do odd jobs in the garden. In May 1954, aged just sixteen, Flann started work as a barman in County Galway before moving on to the Red Island holiday camp in Skerries, a seaside town in County Dublin. He moved to London the following year with his sister Mary, who had just married Jerry McKay, to work at Mooney's Irish House in Fleet Street, where he was a barman while living with his sister and brother-in-law at their flat in Victoria. And in January 1959, we find him in the dock of the Old Bailey.

8 January 1959 (Thursday):

At the Old Bailey all today – two days of waiting for Flannan O'Hehir's trial to come on, in deepening embarrassment [as Mr Lucas was terrified of being spotted as a member of the Board of Trade solicitor's team] *and nervousness. Today, the poor lad was put in the dock, the jury sworn in – before it was found that his counsel had not appeared. So the trial is put off till tomorrow.*

9 January 1959 (Friday):

This morning, Flannan O'Hehir's trial at last came on. While I sat tense, feverishly praying in the public gallery, his counsel today was one Davidson; and the lad, on his advice, pleaded guilty to the charge of gross indecency. The prosecution accepted his plea of not guilty to the charge of buggery. Prosecuting counsel briefly related the facts and the medical evidence that buggery had occurred. A detective sergeant said that he had been in custody since his arrest... and had worked since his arrival in England in 1955 as a barman in Irish public houses. Counsel for the defence made a brief but good plea, stressing the lad's youth and good character and his long spell in hospital. Then Mr Justice Hinchcliffe, who could hardly be unmoved by the lad, so slim and neat and young, said that justice would not be served by sending him to prison. He then imposed a fine of £25 [£720] *with three months to pay and six months' gaol in default. I left the court enormously relieved and thankful to Hinchcliffe J.* [Justice] *who seems a judge of humanity and sense. God be thanks, blessings on Mr Justice Hinchcliffe too, for his clemency. Now, I must try to find the poor boy, who will presumably return to one or other of the Irish bars in London. There are not so many of these, so I may reasonably hope to find him. My feelings for this lad are of the tenderest pity and affection, not physical attraction. Heaven knows, I have felt enough grief and distress of mind over him since I first saw him in the dock at Marlborough Street. What a silly romantic queen am I. How most people, homosexual or not, would smile at all this!*

Smile indeed. 'My feelings for this lad are of the tenderest pity and affection, not physical attraction.' Do we believe Mr Lucas, silly romantic queen that he is? Is this not someone struck by the first pangs of love – for a young man with whom he has yet to exchange a single word? The night of Flann's appearance in the dock – and several nights thereafter – see Mr Lucas pounding the streets and hopping from bar to bar with a view to meeting his hoped-for paramour. At this point, it's not love – but obsession. And the pursuit goes on.

9 January 1959 (Friday):

Bitter cold tonight, though no snow in London yet. I went up to Marble Arch in hopes of seeing Flannan O'Hehir; I must now try to locate him in the various Irish bars and other places of London. God grant I succeed!

10 January 1959 (Saturday):

Thinking much of Flannan O'Hehir and, in considerable dejection of spirits, lest I fail to find him in town. The cold kept most people away from Marble Arch.

11 January 1959 (Sunday):

To Wincott Street [the last known address for Flann], *to Marble Arch, to 'Mooney's', to the 'Quebec' hoping vainly to see Flannan O'Hehir. No one who has not experienced the same emotions could form any conception of how I am tortured by a passion of pity and love for him and an intense desire to meet with him, and, so far as possible, console and cheer him for the trouble of the past six weeks.*

It is a lonely trudge. Mr Lucas visits pub after pub: 'Irish bars in Oxford Street, Charing Cross Road, Piccadilly Circus, the Strand and London Bridge', pained by the idea that his trek might be in vain. 'And so at last home, with the tears heavy behind the eyelids, and the mind wrecked and twisted at every fresh thought of him.'

The bigger question remains unanswered: why? Why is he going to such trouble for a man he has caught only a couple of glimpses of in the dock, whom he does not know and may never know? Perhaps it's a reflection of Mr Lucas's deeply Catholic soul:

Isaiah 58:10: *If you pour yourself out for the hungry and satisfy the desire of the afflicted, then shall your light rise in the darkness and your gloom be as the noonday.*

I'm not suggesting Mr Lucas sees himself in a Christ-like light, but there are distinct echoes here of him dreaming of finding salvation through helping others. The notion of being the Good Samaritan is most definitely at play – whether consciously for Mr Lucas or otherwise.

John 15:13: *Greater love has no one than this: to lay down one's life for one's friends.*

His pursuit of Flann is devouring not just his time, it's also eating into his work life. 'Very little work at the office,' Mr Lucas writes on 13 January 1959. 'I pass my days vainly not in "delight". It certainly is not delight; with every thought of Flannan O'Hehir, a sharp anguish, and prayer for him, and, for me, that I may meet him, my only comfort.' But soon a plan – if a completely ludicrous one – forms.

15 January 1959 (Thursday):

It came to me that the quickest and surest way to find him is simply to call at every house in Wincott Street until I find that in which he lives or used to live. This will be a horribly embarrassing task, but I mean to undertake it on Saturday.

Completely nuts. And entirely obsessive. Yet in keeping with the religious fervour that affected Mr Lucas in the fifties. Disillusioned with the gay scene – and the lack of love – he turned to the church. But this is also the passion of a man in his late twenties and early thirties – he starts the decade aged twenty-three, turning thirty-four as it ends. The ten years trace a man torn between desire for sex and the need to subscribe to the religious values of his childhood. In March 1953, he writes of 'stumbling into sin' despite attending mass almost nightly. My notes on the diaries from March and May that year detail, respectively, how there is 'much, much less sex and much more religion'.

Another factor is that he is still living with his parents at this time, and his mother, ever the toxic personality, is always keen to point out his shortcomings – both in terms of his religion and his 'masculinity'.

25 November 1953 (Wednesday):

[Mr Lucas's mother]: *'You're ugly, dirty and half bald... your religion is very shallow... if you were half a Catholic, you'd be in the* [Knights of the Southern Cross – a Catholic organization] *or the B. Sacrament Guild* [Guild of the Blessed Sacrament], *not going to Marble Arch and places...'*

The early fifties find Mr Lucas curbing his sexual activities in an effort to square the two warring factors.

24 October 1953 (Saturday):

My meeting again with John last Sunday has restored me. That exquisite face, that character that, with all his defects, bewitches me, have afresh done their work, as they did last year and now I can go on. 'A charge I have to keep' – to observe, obediently, that command of perpetual chastity that God has laid upon me and, observing it, to win help and healing for those He has given me to love. This, as I see it, is the reason that justification for homosexual temperaments such as mine, that from abstinence from the smarts of wounded love, from the pain and doubt, inseparable from such love as mine, may be made at last, an eternal weight and glory.

The fifties are full of vignettes of Mr Lucas's attempt to reconcile sex and spirituality, 'perpetual chastity' not withholding. He still falls for handsome young men, of course, but these obsessions are always tinged with religious guilt. This tale from 1955 neatly sums up that turmoil – and his constant fear during that difficult decade at being fingered for a 'queer':

3 March 1955 (Thursday):

To lunch with J. S. Jasper, who observed J. Russell-Johnson and Alan very narrowly [all colleagues at the Board of Trade at that point]. *The coarse loutish young men were for some reason not there today. I left Jasper with the other two, as I had to be back in a reporting officers' course at 2 p.m. This lasted until 5.20 p.m., very tediously. On coming out of the lecture room, I found Jasper waiting for me, who – in the role of candid friend – lost no time in telling me that, after my leaving, Alan had confided in him that he found my fondness for his company suspicious and my society both annoying and disquieting, while J. Russell-Johnson said I was 'queer'. Home, with no light heart, reflecting on what I ought to do in this situation.*

The terror, fortunately, is short-lived, but stands as a constant reminder of what danger Mr Lucas is in, should his sexuality be revealed.

7 March 1955 (Monday):

Well, God's providence is truly wonderful. At lunchtime today, I walked disconsolate up to Hill's coffee bar behind Lucan House with no clear purpose in mind and no sooner was I there when, by the finger of God, I was met by Mr Russell-Johnson, absent for once from Alan, who was lunching with one of his Chatham friends. To him, by degree, I revealed some of my troubles, and Jasper's report. He was disturbed and said he would mention it to Alan. Sure enough, Alan telephoned me; and from a call box I told him the whole story. He was very angry indeed. He had, he explained, asked Jasper what, in his opinion, was the nature of my regard for him – questionable or otherwise – since my lavish Christmas present had caused an uncle of his to suggest there was some ulterior motive. He vigorously denied that he had done more than take the opinion of the only person he knew that knew me well. This was a mighty relief to me. I took the opportunity of explaining that my regard was wholly honourable, and had a long and illuminating talk with him, in the course of which I both spoke well of Russell-Johnson (for whom I do indeed feel sympathy) and warned him against putting any sort of reliance on so mischief-making untruthful a creature as Jasper. We parted more friendly than ever – this has indeed cleared the air. But what is one to think of Jasper – either he is a most detestable and deceitful fraud and humbug, or else (as I believe) potentially deranged, and as dangerous in social relationships as in official business. I thanked God, St Mary, St Joseph, St Victor as Alan's patron saints, in tears and kneeling, tonight.

You can see how religious Mr Lucas was at that point, his beliefs becoming a bulwark against society and the opinion of his so-called friends.

Returning to the late fifties, the search for Flannan O'Hehir remains futile, not least because the friend Mr Lucas has drafted in to help has his own legal difficulties...

19 January 1959 (Monday):

I went this rainy night to the Moo Cow [restaurant owned by Peter Austin, a close friend] *to see Austin and learn the result of his canvassing the rest of Wincott Street. To my dismay, I learned at his restaurant that he had been arrested there this evening and must appear at Marlborough Street tomorrow (presumably for his committing buggery with the lads from Leeds he told me about). Evidently, I was sanguine in thinking that, in all the circumstances, the police would not prosecute him for his one night with the unhappy lad.*

Austin is released on bail – after Mr Lucas very nervously, given his professional vulnerability, takes to the dock himself to guarantee a surety of £250 [£7,000] – and the search continues. But this time with success.

25 January 1959 (Sunday):

Returning home tonight, I learned, to my incredulous joy, that, at the very last house he visited in Wincott Street, a hostel, Peter Austin gained news of Flannan O'Hehir, who he was told moved from there on the 15th of January to take a live-in job at the 'Swan' public house in Blackfriars Road. I mean to go there tomorrow night – though I hardly dare to believe I shall see the lad's face again. Matters now must be handled with delicacy, of course. He is hardly likely to welcome a complete stranger coming as a reminder of a trouble now past, and I shall have to be discreet and rather reticent. Full disclosure of all I have felt for him will have to be deferred to a more suitable time. If meeting him, I am deeply thankful, but if unhappily it all goes awry, then I would accept any sadness and disappointments.

So to the Swan he goes, the following night, full of fear and trepidation – and much excitement.

26 January 1959 (Monday):

Tonight to the 'Swan', at the junction of Blackfriars Road and St George's Circus. I went into the saloon bar and at once saw 'that dear remembered face'. I could say little to the lad until closing time, since there were four people at the bar, all engaged in conversation by an elderly, racy Cockney woman, and it would have been too noticeable. But I did chat with him when all were gone, brief, but friendly, found that he comes from County Clare, and said I would see him tomorrow. It's not impossible he has some recollection of my face from the 8th of December last [at the court]. *He gave me several covert and speculative glances. Home in a state of extreme joy. I should never forget that walk across Blackfriars Bridge, and all down Blackfriars Road tonight, about 9–9.30 p.m.*

Popping into the Swan at lunchtime, and then returning in the evening, becomes Mr Lucas's regular daily routine, sitting quietly, sipping his half-pints of ale in the hope of snatching some brief conversation with Flann. As the days stretch into weeks, Mr Lucas drops enough hints for Flann to realize he has a friend who knows the backstory.

29 January 1959 (Thursday):

I've used Peter Austin's [arrest for buggery] *as convenient means of giving* [Flann] *an idea of my own views on such matters and have also mentioned my being at the Old Bailey earlier this month. He is too intelligent not to appreciate the meaning of this. I am, however, tortured by doubt and fear lest he turned from me, either from suspicion of my motives or dislike of having his past trouble known. But I pray that God will not soon take away what he has so kindly bestowed. That I'm in love with him, there is no doubt – I know the symptoms too well, now, to be mistaken. And so again, 'amo... et excrucior'* ['I love and it hurts']. *The saloon bar of a small quiet pub in the Blackfriars Road is become to me a shrine, love's Mecca, a place of pilgrimage, to be approached hesitantly with beating heart and a mind full of fear and hope and delicious expectation.*

Mr Lucas finally plucks up the courage to ask Flann out for a drink – and I love this diary entry, written with all the giddiness of someone falling hopelessly in love, even down to repeating the same deeply saccharine simile...

3 February 1959 (Tuesday):

I left at 10.30, a little elevated with liquor and full of the feelings of a schoolgirl looking forward to her first date. He has tentatively agreed to 'do the rounds' with me on Thursday evening. My heart is fluttering like that of a romantic schoolgirl looking forward to her first date.

That he is in love is in no doubt – and something he himself readily admits.

10 February 1959 (Tuesday):

I am as deeply in love with Flannan O'Hehir as I have been with anyone, including even Fred [his love in the late forties]. *My love now can feed daily on sight and speech and hope, as never before.*

Date night comes and Mr Lucas is nothing if not florid in his description of the evening. The 'giddy schoolgirl' is very much apparent.

12 February 1959 (Thursday):

After some little time in the 'Flowers of the Forest' opposite the 'Swan', we went to the 'Oxford Arms'. Here, discreetly and indirectly, I told him all; and we spent till 10.30 p.m. talking of his case. Adjourning for coffee and sandwiches in the Waterloo Road, we did not part till midnight. Flannan: 'I feel I've got a friend now I can talk to about everything.' He told me of how the police beat him up after his arrest, of his three appearances in court, refusal of bail, his seven weeks in Brixton [jail] on bad food, and the close of the long ordeal. Dermott O'Grady, manager of 'Mooney's in the Strand', has stood as good friend to him and gave him an excellent reference for his present job, which he started on Sunday 11th of January. He gets £6-10s [£186.47] a week now – his first money since July 1958 – and is still paying his debts out of it. Home in an ecstasy of gratitude and love.

They start to meet regularly, visiting pubs away from Flann's work and occasionally the cinema. What Flann truly thinks of Mr Lucas is lost to us. But if the diary entries are to be believed – and it is a big 'if' here – then Flann sees Mr Lucas as a confidant and a budding friend, despite their twelve-year age gap (which, to be fair, is not unusual in the gay world). Giddy schoolgirl that he is, Mr Lucas even writes to his mother about meeting Flann – although, given her past attitudes and opinions, I'm not quite sure what he was expecting in reply.

20 February 1959 (Friday):

A wounding letter from my mother to trouble me. In innocence, I had mentioned my friendship with Flannan to her. She has replied with angry reproaches that I should make a barman my friend, and so anxious is she to poison my mind against him that she declares most Irishmen to be thieves and criminals, (this from her!). This is painful and rather shameful – I fear it is more a kind of nauseous snobbery that angers her, rather than any real concern for me, however clumsy and blind. I replied as mildly as I could, urging her to look with clear eyes at life and people.

But while Mr Lucas is blissfully happy, Flann is becoming increasingly unwell. We discover he had been in hospital between July and November the year before for something serious – and that it has returned and is worsening by the day. There are two photographs of Flann behind the bar at the Swan taken by Mr Lucas at this time. Dark-haired, a little stout – or 'sturdy' as Mr Lucas would describe his favourite

type of man – he looks much older than twenty. Dressed in a dark suit and tie, a light v-necked jumper over his shirt, his hand on one of the pumps, I can see the attraction for Mr Lucas and his lust for the portlier young gentleman.

Things move pretty quickly. Flann passes out at work and is rushed to hospital, where Mr Lucas discovers the young Irishman had been admitted last year with a tumour on his hip. For many, this would have been treatable, but it very much sounds as if it's been caught far too late for Flann.

10 March 1959 (Tuesday):

I learned that, in fact, he is dying of a malignant sarcoma that has invaded his pelvis and iliac [lower body] *region, is inoperable and can only be palliated, not cured, by radiotherapy. A few weeks or so relatively free from pain can be expected if radiotherapy continues, but in due course he will need heavy sedation in hospital; and death will follow. He refuses to be admitted to Lambeth Hospital as an inpatient. The Royal Northern Hospital cannot treat him; he is most reluctant to stay with his brother-in-law and sister, Gerald and Mary McCabe, and is, in fact, anxious to stay with me. What is to be done? My only wish is for him to have a little comfort and consolation in his last weeks of comparatively active life, during which he may, as mercifully as possible, be told of his condition and make his peace with God. So, if he can stand the daily journey to Lambeth for radiotherapy, and if the medical authorities think it best, I will, humbly and devotedly, try to comfort him here.*

There are three further photos of Flann, taken by Mr Lucas at the hospital. The sturdiness is gone. Flann's face is grey – noticeably so even in black and white photographs – and pinched, the pain very visible in his tortured eyes as the cancer has obviously started to spread.

27 March 1959 (Good Friday):

At midday, Flannan and I had a conversation comforting to me. He understands how I love him and, I feel, likes me. I promised to help him always, wherever he was, and I think he had an idea of what I meant. The disease has evidently begun to affect the lungs and possibly the trachea. Flannan now has developed paroxysms of choking; his throat is irritated and his speech rather slurred. He is eating tolerably well, though, and the pain in his back is responding to codeine. But it looks as though the almoner of the Royal Northern Hospital was right and he will die from cancer of the lung. The thought of his dying away in Ennis [where his sisters want him to go] *pierces my heart, but worse, far worse, is the fear lest he has to suffer great pain.*

Death is approaching and Mr Lucas is a constant presence by Flann's bedside.

30 March 1959 (Easter Monday):

Arrived at [the hospital], I was told he was dying fast. He had fainted at about 4 o'clock, having got out of bed and gone over to the light switch before falling down. On his recovering consciousness, [the nurse] gave him some tea, a little of which he was able to drink, and at his request gave him his rosary. Later on, Dr Sewell came and saw that he had pulmonary congestion and pneumonia. Fr. Smith also came and gave him the last blessing; and sometime after 10.15 a.m. he lapsed into unconsciousness. I sat by him, holding his hand and praying until his father and two sisters arrived. Towards 3 o'clock, one of the sisters moved away from the bed and I resumed my place, holding his hand again. He opened his eyes once and looked at me and at the crucifix by his bed, closed them and began to breathe more slowly. At 3.30 p.m., he gave three slow gasping breaths, raised his head a little and died. I kissed his dead lips three times. May we kiss again in the resurrection at the last day and be together eternally. I'm glad I was by him as he died, wiping his face and holding his hand. May he hold my hand thereafter.

The poignancy of that last passage is almost painful to read – and palpably so for Mr Lucas to experience. All his life, he has been searching for a love that would be reciprocated; a relationship on equal terms that could be celebrated semi-openly on trips to the pub or cinema. And now he has seen those dreams die before him. The short life of Flannan O'Hehir – and even shorter friendship with Mr Lucas – will resonate throughout the remainder of his eighty-eight years, even to the extent of being raised with me on one of my usual trips round to 24 Mandalay Road, the memory as sharp as if it had happened a few days ago.

Just four months had passed since Mr Lucas first saw Flann's name on the court listings. One month of searching for him; another of becoming friends. And then, the last two months of Mr Lucas at his finest, both as a friend and diarist. The story, poignant and painful, also explains much of Mr Lucas's vulnerability as we head into the sixties and the extent to which he can fall in love suddenly, passionately, with an idea, as much as what was actually happening around him. Romantic? Maybe. A dreamer? Most definitely. Either way, it sets him up as easy prey for the chancers of this world, including one Irish Peter.

5

Irish Peter

17 November 1964 (Tuesday):

A good deal of the troubles and anxieties of the last few months have their origin in that afternoon, four years ago today, when, with the dusk deepening outside, the evening rush about to begin, I was walking round Piccadilly Circus underground at 4.45 p.m. and had my eye caught by a glance from someone standing by a shop window – a slim youth in a leather jacket.

It is November 1960, and the thirty-four-year-old George Leo John Lucas is on the cusp of an obsession that will span the sixties, lead him close to ruin and, ultimately, turn his mind to murder. It is also a relationship that provides the dramatic setting for a decade of incredible social change, as the UK moves from the dowdy post-war years of the fifties into a brightly lit decade of sexual liberation for women, increasing rights for people of colour and the partial decriminalization of gay sex.

But the sixties was also a decade riven with social strife as progressive ideas faced a backlash from a deeply conservative British society. Homosexuality – or, more exactly, gay sex – is still illegal in 1960 and Mr Lucas spends almost another decade dodging the police as he explores the queer subculture taking nervous steps into the mainstream. The law will shift in 1967 to partially legalize same-sex love, but society, led by a rampantly homophobic tabloid press, most certainly will not.

We do not have the exact details of the first few days and weeks after Mr Lucas's first fateful meeting with Peter outside the Swan & Edgar department store on Piccadilly Circus, as the 1960 diary did not survive the skip-strewn aftermath of Mr Lucas's death in 2014. But, ever keen to look back to the past, we can make some sense of the first tentative signs of the relationship, piecing together those early days through a series of flashbacks:

17 November 1964 (Tuesday):

In a moment, he was beside me and said 'hello' in a warm, soft Irish voice. After a few words, I asked, 'Are you gay?' and with a remarkably vivid smile he answered, 'of course'. That was the start of the liaison with Peter that has led me into some strange places and among exceedingly shady people, and placed my security, my privacy, the key to all those defences against the dangerous world outside, in the hands of this young man.

At times, I am dismayed and appalled at the imprudent folly of giving him the key to my flat, my telephone number, the invitation to come and go as he pleases. I am disquieted by thoughts of criminals, dividing their loot in my sitting room, of stolen property concealed in the wardrobe or under the bed, of [police] *officers calling with search warrants, then these anxieties subside. I recall his infrequent visits, and then only to go to bed* [in my flat] *with some young man he fancies.*

They first met on 17 November 1960, when Peter was a callous, street-savvy young man and Mr Lucas an older but certainly much more immature thirty-four. Even then, Peter is a man on the make, an aspiring wannabe gangster limiting himself at that point to rolling (or robbing) the occasional client and fencing (or handling) the odd stolen watch.

As we learn from the 1964 diary, when they first met, four years before, Peter was selling 'toy dogs in Regent Street' in central London.

9 August 1964 (Sunday):

I can foresee him doing jobs like this for the next forty years – postcards, hot dogs, balloons, toys and the rest, diversified by shady deals in stolen property, and no doubt spells in gaol. With the passing of his youth, I see his face growing sharp and pinched and lined, his charm coarsening, the vague inconsequent patches in his mind spreading, his wide intelligence becoming a short-sighted cunning. Living ever from suitcases jumbled in one drab room and another, sinking to the level of his associates, 'down in the stinking fosse' where no light comes, and ending a shabby, seedy, furtive old man, his opportunities and abilities trickled away to waste, and only evil memories left to him. Already he's gone more than a few steps down that road.

Peter – occasionally 'Irish Johnnie' or 'Irish Peter'; sometimes 'Miss Peter of the 'Dilly' – is not Mr Lucas's first love, but as passion turns to hate and despair over the decade, it is the most enduring and, ultimately, the most destructive. Hailing from Kildare, a rather beautiful historic market town an hour's drive west of the Irish capital, Peter first arrived in London as a teenager. Little is known about his earlier years, but the diaries tell us that, by 1960, alongside selling fluffy mechanical toys, he was working as a rent boy, 'treading the pavements of Piccadilly and standing opposite Green Park' – two notorious pick-up haunts at the time.

To read the early months of 1961 is to gain a picture of a budding friendship – with paid-for benefits – but the seeds of his obsessional love are already planted. The initial feelings he writes about are akin to his previous 'relationship' with Flannan O'Hehir. Mr Lucas writes that 'to be in love, with my temperament, is to be in hell. The pain varies in intensity of course but pain is in every moment.'

When they first meet, Mr Lucas is emerging from a long period of religious fervour brought on by disillusionment with gay London and the vapidity of the late fifties and early sixties scene.

5 January 1961 (Thursday):

Home with a cold and a bitter awareness of the almost inhuman greed and egotism of the boys round the 'Dilly and [Trafalgar] *Square – these add up to loneliness and depression. What I need is someone young and gay and conversable. I envy the lads I see in the Coffee-House* [a popular gay haunt in central London] *and such places with their friends... When I was their age, I was by no means so well-adjusted and sophisticated. An ageing queen losing hair and looks, and without much chance of manners, has little hope now of having what she missed then.*

It is a foul mood that stays with Mr Lucas in the early weeks of 1961, giving him ample opportunity to rail against the materialism of the gay world.

13 January 1961 (Friday):

To Town. A stout kindly queen, who works in Forte's at Charing Cross and to whom I had mentioned Ian McKenzie asked me this evening what [Ian] *was. I said that he was the senior* [waiter] *in the Pronto; and heard this shattering comment, 'Only a senior? Oh well he won't have much money – better to make friends with a manager!' Gross materialism, reduction of everything to l.s.d.* [pounds, shillings and pence] *can go no further.*

Having spent many evenings at mass during the mid- to late fifties, now, as he emerges back into the gay world, he is lonely and conscious that life is passing him by. Vulnerable and sick of meeting 'queens', with 'their loud cruel laughter and humour that has little of good nature in it', Peter is almost exactly the type of person Mr Lucas should not have met at this point in his life. By now, Flannan O'Hehir has achieved an almost saint-like status in Mr Lucas's eyes and there's a sense that Flann is looking after him.

9 January 1961 (Monday):

Ronnie saw that young student Larry last night, had sex with him with great pleasure, saying it was the first time. Meeting nice young people who are gay and civilized as well is a refreshing change... and I feel it is Flann who has helped to bring it about. 'I will always help you,' he said.

Peter is certainly photogenic, if bearing a disconcerting resemblance to a young George Osborne, Britain's former Chancellor of the Exchequer. The cover of the 1961 diary is missing, so it opens immediately with four photos of Peter smiling smugly to the camera 'at his room in Villa Road', a twenty-five-minute walk or so from Mr Lucas's house at 13 Kildoran Road in Brixton, south London, which he moved into in November 1959.

Peter at that point has a certain baby-faced innocence. He is also rather a dandy. Mr Lucas writes of his beau in February 1961 'with new blacked eyebrows, a mixture of Vaseline and shoe polish'. And a month later of how Peter has 'a new hairstyle, plucked eyebrows and powdered face'. It is easy to see why a lonely man in his mid-thirties, but mentally fast approaching middle age, should play out an age-old trope: an older man making a complete and utter fool of himself over a much younger crush. But the question remains whether, in those relatively early days, love was reciprocated or not. The answer is almost certainly not – and Mr Lucas is fully aware of this.

13 January 1961 (Friday):

When I met Irish Peter, I could not have been cooler. It may be of course that my violent reaction is simply caused by stinginess or a reluctance to spend money on sex... but I don't think so. Love, friendship, kindness, sympathy cannot be bought, and the sale of their simulacra is repulsive as simulated friendship, simulated love is repulsive. Reciprocity is essential in love, in friendship, in sex enjoyment itself.

20 March 1964 (Friday):

I remember my own second visit to him on the 27th of March 1961, when, having got his money, he was reluctant to let me feel his penis, avoided an embrace, and managed to elude more than one kiss by saying, 'There's a horrible stench from your breath.' This is quite understandable, of course; [anyone] *would find the clutching or caressing of an ageing man extremely distasteful.*

Peter himself is in love with a fellow Irishman, an eighteen-year-old called Billy Flynn, whom he is attempting to shield from a similar life of prostitution, something Mr Lucas finds both affecting and bemusing.

19 January 1961 (Thursday):

I'm intrigued by the mental processes of a Piccadilly male harlot solo, who is in love with an Irish lad, and has prevented him from adopting the same trade – how he can reconcile prostitution and affection, I don't know.

24 March 1961 (Friday):

[Peter's] *own sexual and emotional life is centred on this lad Billy Flynn, who apparently is not a prostitute, is in love with Peter and seems on the whole to have a good influence on him.*

These are the early days of Mr Lucas starting to pay for sex and mixing with 'professional' male prostitutes. One of the earliest references in the diaries to him exchanging money for sex has more of a feel of a favour about it, rather than something clinically transactional. It is 1958 and Mr Lucas is thirty-one.

17 February 1958 (Monday):

Cold. Tonight, a young Irish guardsman in plain clothes spoke to me in the 'Standard'. I had not intended taking anyone home, but he seemed so pleasant a lad, I yielded to his unexpressed but obvious plea [for somewhere to stay for the night]. *He turned out to be very agreeable – a nineteen-year-old lad from Enniskillen called Sean, a year in the Irish Guards on a three-year engagement, and now absent, who would like to be on the stage.*

18 February 1958 (Tuesday):

Sean had a hot bath this morning and left 35/- [35 shillings – now £50.20] *richer. I hope he was well-pleased as I was pleased to give him 35/-, which he deserved – pleasant disposition, sexual vigour and tolerably good looks justify some expenditure on them.*

For the first decade and a half of the diaries, sex is plentiful and for free. There are hints that others are being paid – or want to be paid – but for the time being Mr Lucas is behaving like any gay man of the fifties or today.

6 October 1949 (Thursday):

David has a girlfriend and was not at all responsive to my advances. He only has homosexual intercourse on a strictly cash basis. This liaison, too, like all others, will be sterile and joyless, although expensive.

Sexuality seems somehow more fluid in the fifties – or at least the horror of gay sex, perhaps damped by wartime dalliances, is not so extreme. Supposedly heterosexual men were more than happy to share their bodies with gay and bisexual men for a price.

5 May 1958 (Monday):

I was amused at [a] *remark* [by Mr Lucas's pick-up that evening] *that when he returns to his barracks room after a night out he is greeted by a chorus of 'how much?' by those guardsmen who have returned earlier.*

The early diaries are, perhaps unsurprisingly for a gay man in his twenties of any era or decade, awash with sex. Cottages, parks, prowling for pick-ups at Marble Arch in central London: the early photographs of the young Mr Lucas show a smartly turned out, dare one say almost handsome young man. Bespectacled and over-serious, certainly, but also with a certain rakish style and evident intelligence.

Now in his thirties, the hair, always precarious, is going and no attempt to massage it over his ever-expanding scalp will hide the fact that Mr Lucas is balding – and badly. Since 1953, he has been combing 'some of my back hair forwards and sideways across my bald crown; and very well it answered for a good many years, as photographs show'. It will be another few years until he finally concedes defeat.

18 January 1964 (Saturday):

Well, after eleven years, I've given up the struggle to conceal my baldness. But the strands have grown fewer. And last year I had to surrender the front of my head, and cover only the top (like Ian MacLeod, the ex-minister). Tonight, I at last surrendered to time and gave up the struggle, cut the few strands left and combed them back and hoped there'd not be too obvious a change.

Racked by insecurities about his looks and his status in the world – and no doubt still reeling from the death of Flannan O'Hehir – Mr Lucas doesn't stand a chance against the younger, much cannier man. And he knows it. As he looks back in 1964 to their first encounter four years earlier, he writes how he has 'supped full of horrors' throughout the car crash of his relationship with Peter.

Mr Lucas is the classic john, falling for the 'damaged' and 'desperate' prostitute; keen to save Peter from both circumstances and himself. Yet despite the obvious and painful depths of his feelings, the old fool is not a total fool. Even in these early days of their relationship, Mr Lucas is still very aware of what type of man Peter really is. Lust is tempered by caution, as he writes in February 1961, 'Miss Peter is, I fear, as dishonest a prostitute as the rest, to judge from what she was saying tonight.' And then in March of that same year:

24 March 1961 (Friday):

Johnnie – or rather Peter – is a prostitute with a built-in cash register who dislikes sexual relations with his clients and tries to bring them to emission and departure quickly.

But Peter is no wide-eyed ingénue, having fallen into prostitution because no other options are available. At nineteen he is already showing signs of how he will morph into one of the tabloids' favourite gangsters, a 'friend of Ronnie's', as Mr Lucas writes, just one of the many indications of Peter's connections to the Krays.

Mr Lucas is not the only one wary of Peter. The former doorman of Bobby's Coffee Bar in Soho – 'before it became a haunt of rogues and riff-raff', our diarist writes in April that year – has 'an extreme contempt and dislike for "Irish Johnnie", whom he called the "vilest thing in London"'.

Peter plays only a fleeting part in the 1961 diary. Mentions of him are kept curt: a meeting at his postcard stall; a tale of his being involved in a fight outside Ward's Irish House.

30 January 1961 (Monday):

I'm distressed to hear that Irish Johnnie was last night involved in an ugly scene outside 'Ward's', in which, according to one report, he was roughly handled by someone with whom he had been staying and from whom he had stolen a registered letter containing £5 [£137] and a new overcoat – no doubt the fine coat he wore for a few days last November. This nasty story is all too likely to be true – dishonesty in its meanest form is an integral part of the lads' ['Dilly boys'] *lives.*

We also hear Peter is off to meet a john in Jersey, before disappearing at some point in April or May to Dublin; given the police are conducting another crackdown in the West End, it is perhaps in the nick of time.

22 June 1961 (Thursday):

The police have recently made their usual summer sweep-up in the 'Dilly. Some of the rent boys and layabouts are not to be seen; some have migrated to the Square or to Marble Arch; one or two have taken casual jobs – selling glass figures or postcards – as camouflage; and most of the old regular male prostitutes are in the 'White Bear' and 'Wards' as before. 'The abominable Miss Peter' – or Irish Johnnie, prostitute, drug peddler, thief – is still, no doubt, in Dublin.

As Mr Lucas discovers years later, Peter had in fact been in Oxford, where he had attempted – rather amusingly to my mind – to blackmail his probation officer, accusing the official of 'homosexual advances'.

17 April 1964 (Friday):

Tonight, after spending the evening in the 'White Bear', I met Johnnie at 12.30 a.m., and went home with him on the night bus down the Brixton Road. We spent till six o'clock in conversation and records and drinks. He told of his friendship with Father Swain of Kildare, with whom he toured Ireland in 1959, of his being deported [back to Ireland] *early in 1960 and his troubles with the Oxford probation officer, by whom he was accused of demanding money with menaces and sent to Borstal.*

Mr Lucas had at first thought this admirable bit of chutzpah was no more than 'a piece of colourful romancing' on Peter's part, but it does neatly explain his absence in the early years of the sixties before he reappears fleetingly in July 1963. Again, the entries at that point are matter of fact, not revealing any depth of emotions for Peter – other than a nagging desire for the young man to have a taste of his own cynical ways.

2 July 1963 (Tuesday):

Irish Peter tonight knocked very much off his balance. His friend Billy, while 'blocked' (under the influence of Benzedrine and 'purple heart' tablets) has 'turned over the gaff' – that is, burgled someone's room – at Tachbrook Street and made away also with Johnnie's clothes and bank book. I could hope that for Johnnie to have a taste of his own medicine would do him good... but I doubt it. More probably he and Billy will soon be occupying some squalid room together and 'nicking gear' as occasion arises.

By this point in 1963, Peter's descent from the bushy-tailed young man outside the Swan & Edgar department store in

November 1960 to dead-eyed druggy is underway. We lose him again until February the following year, when he's working as an usher – in a plum and gold uniform – at the London Pavilion, a cinema in the centre of Soho. 'Returned, he says, from the remainder of his Borstal sentence,' Mr Lucas writes, with a hint of doubt as to whether Peter is telling the whole truth.

Outwardly, Mr Lucas is successful. In December the previous year, he had finally been promoted to higher executive officer at the Board of Trade, something he welcomes but also worries might displace him from his 'current comfortable office in Horse Guards Avenue'.

He remains at 13 Kildoran Road in Brixton; his tenants, the Hemsworths, humming along happily in the downstairs flat. Married with no children, they seem the perfect neighbours: quiet and not in the slightest bit inquisitive about Mr Lucas's night-time callers (or the young men, freshly bathed, leaving the following morning). And, overall, he seems – dare we say? – content. Happy would not be the word for Mr Lucas. In fact, a thorough search of my notes of the diaries over the years shows he never once uses it when describing how he feels. He talks of having 'free happy sex in the suburbs', looking back on his younger days of early adulthood in Chadwell Heath and his numerous trips to visit his mother (and the local cottages) in Clacton-on-Sea, but at no point does he ever say anything resembling 'I am happy'. Perhaps this isn't unusual for a diary. What are they at times other than the extended whines of the misunderstood? Contentment is probably the best we can hope for as 1964 opens.

Peter, on the other hand, is falling fast. 'Irish Johnnie is still, apparently, for hire, charging £4 for "car trade",' writes Mr Lucas in March that year. Car trade was a particularly dangerous form of prostitution that involved getting into a car driven by an unknown person. On the 'Rack' of the 'Meat Market', as the railing along the northern edge of Piccadilly Circus was known, any prospective punter can be sized up and evaluated properly.

He is also facing constant hassle from the police, arrested repeatedly for 'obstruction' for manning his postcard stall, presumably without a licence, in Piccadilly Circus.

24 March 1964 (Tuesday):

Peter's hatred of policemen is, to some degree, understandable. It must be maddening to be given summons for obstruction whenever a policeman on that beat feels inclined (and the laughs and jokery with which some large overbearing constable says, 'You're nicked, Johnnie', must be infuriating). This allegation of 'obstruction' is the most transparent fiction, a mere advice to mulct a street trader of money in lieu of the rent he's not paying for shop premises.

As Peter goes back and forth to Bow Street police station, Mr Lucas is with him, stumping up the 10 shillings (£12.46) or, at one point, £2 ('the maximum amount' – £50 today). And the feelings, at least from Mr Lucas's side, are starting to re-emerge with a vengeance. Now that Peter isn't in such a position of power, Mr Lucas believes he can do some good. Cynics would argue this is classic predatory behaviour. No doubt his behaviour seems distinctly unsavoury now. But is he exploited by the rent boys, Irish layabouts and guardsmen or is he actually the exploiter?

His actions feel more as if they're part of his street philanthropist persona, continuing to help rent boys financially and morally.

21 March 1961 (Tuesday):

A queen of my acquaintance – a butcher, I believe, often about the Square and the 'Welsh Harp' – told me on Sunday that a certain tall young Irish guardsman is to appear in court on a charge of theft this week. With the usual lack of intelligent curiosity – lack of gumption, indeed – he has not asked the lad for any details, so I know neither the venue nor the nature of the proceedings, nor indeed if the story is true. But in case it is, I have determined to help the lad a little, by going to the mission at Warwick Street every night this week and abstaining from any sexual enjoyment that may offer till the weekend.

There's a parallel here with the Church of England priest Harold Davidson, known as the 'Prostitutes' Padre', who was the rector of Stiffkey in Norfolk in the early twentieth century. Davidson, too, decided to help as many 'fallen women' as he could, before being defrocked for sleeping with the girls whom he was trying to prevent from turning to vice. His story was later made into the 1982 film *The Missionary* with Michael Palin in the lead role. Both wanted to help, while getting something in return.

30 March 1964 (Easter Monday):

This Easter Monday, I rose early at 8.15 a.m. and went to Bow Street [Magistrates' Court] *where Peter was to appear on a charge of causing an obstruction. The magistrate was C. R. Beddington, a quiet courteous man with a crumpled soft collar, who in the brief minutes it took Peter to plead guilty and be fined £1* [£25] *(rather steep for his first appearance, the innumerable drunks were being fined 10 shillings* [£12.50] *only) remarked, 'I think you'd better find another job.' It is not apparent to me why this advice should be given to a young man who sells maps and postcards in the open air. This whole business of charging postcard sellers and hotdog sellers with obstruction reeks of unfairness. Afterwards, over lunch and a couple of gins, we chatted and Peter mentioned that once, Michael Redgrave, drunk, had picked him up and gone to a hotel in King's Cross with him.*

The Oscar- and BAFTA-nominated actor Redgrave pops up a few times in the diaries, picking up rent boys by the clutch. He'd have been fifty-six in 1964 – and forty-three in 1951 when he first makes an appearance.

7 August 1951 (Tuesday):

This evening, I met the two [Scottish] soldiers – both in kilts – and spent the evening with them in a tour of various bars. One Private Kesson is a stocky lad from Paisley with a lively sense of humour, a comical little face and considerable sophistication. The other, Pte Craig of Berwick-on-Tweed, is taller, quieter and will probably end as a Marble Arch layabout. At one time he says he was 'going around' with a full colonel from the War Office. Kesson's clientele includes Redgrave the film actor and Stewart Granger.

Granger is a fabulous find. There have been arguments over the years about whether he was bisexual or not – he married three times (needless to say, to women) and had four children. The wonderfully titled *Hollywood Gays*, written by Boze Hadleigh and published in 1996, argues that he was, but, as we'll never truly know, this snippet from Mr Lucas is rather lovely.[1]

Meanwhile, as 1964 progresses, Peter brings 'lunch and a couple of gins' on many occasions and, by early April 1964, the boozy lunches have had their effect.

3 April 1964 (Friday):

There's no doubt, now, that I'm developing an infatuation for Irish Johnnie. I began to be sensible of it on Tuesday, and today I recognize the antica fiamma [ancient flame] *once more. It's not a high exalted passion, such as I felt for Fred Newton or Ray Allen* [two former pashes from the forties and fifties], *or strongest of all, for Flann. But it's the same kind, weaker certainly but recognisably love.*

This is dangerous on many levels – not least as Mr Lucas's social life is finally taking off and his less unsavoury options are growing. For the first time in his life, he attends a gay party, held in the distinctly un-chi-chi south London suburb of Tooting. The party is in honour of his sort-of friend David Hancock's twenty-first birthday. This is one of my favourite diary entries, mixing, as it does, a kind of awe at having been invited with Mr Lucas's usual heavy dose of sardonic realization of his minor-cog status in the queer world.

4 April 1964 (Saturday):

It was an enjoyable evening with about ten guests ranging downwards from about thirty-eight, some fairly personable, others like me; plenty of drinks (including a very nasty punch that smelled of face powder and a good brown sherry), cold snacks, continuous music and, after a while, alcohol and security produced their usual result. A good deal of mildly amorous kissing and cuddling, three queens doing a high-kicking chorus act and a quite amusing set of camp songs from Terry Madeley, during which I caressed David for a moment. The young man danced with his 'husband', a self-possessed friendly young man who resembles [a former friend] *Arthur Earney, as he used to be sixteen years ago. David is certainly double-jointed. I can understand John Sutton's remark that he 'captivated Tony with dancing in sexy postures'. It lasted till 2.10 next morning.*

But even while caressing David and noting how 'double-jointed' he is, his mind is elsewhere.

My thoughts were running all this time on Irish Johnnie even while tongue-kissing with a big young queen, very camp and floppy, who was once, he said, a female impersonator at the 'Review Bar' but is now a clothier's shop assistant... Home rather tipsy at 3.10 a.m. having walked from Tooting.

Peter, however, is not having much fun. He has been arrested and fined yet again, and Mr Lucas muses on whether to invite him to stay in Brixton (Peter's continuing residency in his own flat is under question), his mind befuddled by love – and anxiety that it won't, yet again, be reciprocated. As such, it leads to one of the most passionate – and heart-wrenching – passages in the diaries.

9 April 1964 (Thursday):

After the first exhilaration of a new love come the piercing anxieties, the gnawing fears and tremulous hopes I so well remember from before. There's hourly concern lest Johnnie again be summoned for 'obstruction' – concern sharpened by a better sense of injustice; there's the cruel sense of absence that every lover feels when away from his beloved... 'When I am from you, I am dead till I be with you,' as one wrote long since. There's the longing for the physical expressions of love, the kisses and embraces and yet closer intimacies, that are a world removed from those identical touchings that satisfy lust; there's the certain knowledge that all such contacts must necessarily be repulsive to him; and, beyond all these, choking the throat, misting the eyes and stopping the breath, is the total yearning of the whole person for that loved face and form and voice and mind. This is the grief of the widow in the newly empty house, or the mother for her son at the war... grief and yearning. In this state of love that all lovers feel, heterosexual and homosexual are terms fading into irrelevance. In this region, physical desire fades too, and copulation becomes sacramental, an interpretation of persons and not bodies alone.

Disarrayed by love, Mr Lucas retains some grip on reality. 'There's the certain knowledge that all such contacts must necessarily be repulsive to him,' he writes, the quaver in his voice almost audible. As the months tick on and Mr Lucas's love intensifies, there's no suggestion that the relationship was consummated ever again. If anything, it has returned to a financial arrangement without any sex despite Mr Lucas paying half Peter's rent each month even though he has suggested Peter move in. And the bills add up. By July 1964, he realizes he has spent '£100-7s-0d [£2,500] on Peter since I started to be in love with him on 30th March – not including money spent on drinks, meals, the cinema or loaned to him'. He is fully aware of the cost to both his wallet and his libido. 'I could have had 20 rent boys, at £5 [£125] a time, for this money.'

Peter is an expensive taste that will soon start to sour. He is still working on his 'board' – the postcard stall in Piccadilly Circus – but only as a front for his real job as a receiver of stolen goods. Peter is a fence and he is heading, ineluctably, closer to the sticky paws of true East End gangsters Ronnie and Reginald Kray.

20 July 1964 (Monday):

He consorts with thieves, blackmailers, fences and the like, is reckless and irresponsible, spending and squandering all the money he gets, taking the shortest of short views. The worst by far than all of these is a homosexual who poses as a male prostitute to ensnare other homosexuals, and then cheat or bully them out of their money. But in spite of this, I am reminded of the winning charm, that is also the silver crucifix about my neck [a recent birthday present from Peter] *which tells of his courtesy and flashes of thoughtfulness. I recall his moments of domesticity, buying air freshener, and soap and scissors. His real fondness for children, his intelligent comments, his taste for good novels, his capability of genuine feeling...*

Peter is growing increasingly reckless, at one point admitting to burgling a car belonging to Antony Armstrong-Jones, Lord Snowdon, husband of that other star of the sixties, Princess Margaret.

18 May 1964 (Monday):

About 9 o'clock, Johnnie was back on his board and displayed a cigar saying, 'Royalty has smoked some of these,' adding, 'at least, Antony Armstrong was the name on the driving licence.' I asked where the deal had been carried out and was told, 'in Kensington Palace Gardens. We needed a car to take all the stuff – a lovely mink coat and lots of polo gear.' The Welshman [the leader of the gang] *came by and stopped to whisper, 'Wasn't that a good tickle?' before getting an evening paper and running through it, looking first rather closely at the late news column.*

It's a lovely image – Peter swathed in the royal mink – but Mr Lucas is reaching his limit. He knows his personal security – and that of his job and his flat – is on the line now. Much as he might be in love with the young Irishman, self-preservation is also starting to kick in; he can see how this will end. A further anecdote from Peter about rolling some poor German tourist – in addition to two other examples of his callousness towards his clients – is the final straw.

31 July 1964 (Friday):

In bed tonight, I wrote to Irish Johnnie, telling him that our association must end and why. I mentioned the three instances of his treachery, that I knew from him – the affair on the road from Bray, the old man of Green Park and the bald-headed German – assured him that he'd always behaved well to me and said various friendly things about his good qualities.

The diaries do not contain futher details of these 'three instances', but we can see how Peter is morphing into a gangster. He might still be spotted with his board at Piccadilly Circus on occasion, but his evenings are spent honing his skills as a member of London's criminal underclass. As Mr Lucas writes later, 'If I were asked, "Why this change of attitude?" my answer, in a nutshell, would be "Because he's a mean dishonourable fellow who takes advantage of other people." But I'm not sure how far a desire not to spend any more money is mixed in with this.'

Love tempered by sense and a keen understanding of the financial necessity sees the relationship – and friendship – broken off temporarily.

Mr Lucas returns often to his earlier diaries, adding little notes in the margins and updating details of people since lost. But with Peter there is little updated or changed – as if he didn't want to tarnish or alter the memories. Where would Mr Lucas have been if he hadn't spent almost a decade chasing the idea, the ideal, that was Irish Peter? I'd like to say we would have seen a happier, more settled man, perhaps in love, perhaps more focused on his career. But I doubt it. There is something in Mr Lucas that draws him towards danger, towards the damaged. This is apparent when he attends the initial trial of the Kray twins – charged with extortion – at which Peter appeared as a defence witness.

22 September 1965 (Wednesday):

I think of how my heart bled and almost broke for this same young man, when he was appearing in court, how my mind was busy planning ways to do him good, of all the many ways I sought to please and benefit him. It would have been better by far if that first evening, nearly five years ago, when I went home with him, he had rolled me then and there.

Peter, increasingly entangled with the Kray twins, is physically attacked on several occasions, his face slashed. In *Surviving the Krays*, David Teale goes further: 'According to [the Kray Twins' manager] Les Payne (though his account gets a bit confused): "Peter became a member of the Kray gang, and one was not surprised to read in 1969 that he had been nailed to a wall in Soho and beaten with wires."'[2] There are no more details, either in the newspapers or published books, as to what happened to Peter after this. The diaries themselves are also silent.

Hard drugs, particularly heroin, were also starting to emerge on the scene at the time, with many of the vulnerable young men around Piccadilly Circus desperate for the next fix, something of which our diarist was only too aware.

12 February 1965 (Friday):

I met Harry this evening who asked me for 2s-6d [£3.11], understandably, since these lads never have money in their pockets for long. This young man is rather attractive sexually, and to some extent, socially. I mean to give him another turn shortly. Tonight, as we chatted, he told me of the effects of drug tablets that turn so many lads into vicious, though temporary, mad men. And of the 'pushers' who go to the clubs, homosexual and otherwise, and raise or lower the price of their sinister wares, according to the craving of the customer. From what he says, there's no doubt that, in fact, many of the silly lads and girls that take the pills, usually in the small hours, become addicted and then move on from pills to 'shots of intravenous cocaine, heroin or morphine injections'. This is the ugly world into which policemen and magistrates, clerical moralists and legislators are pushing the younger generation of homosexuals.

The scene is shifting – and hardening – both in terms of the people on the 'Meat Rack' and also their motives for being there. The swirl of available paid partners manning the 'Dilly morphs from guardsmen in the forties and fifties looking for a bit of extra cash to take their girlfriends out for the night into something far darker with the appearance of young men from broken backgrounds and rocky mental health.

IRISH PETER

But for Mr Lucas, the end of the affair with Peter, now increasingly world-weary, comes brutally one dark night.

22 September 1965 (Wednesday):

The trouble of this most unlucky day was added to, a little, by the hot clean sunshine, so that I was sweating with heat while shaking with fear and dismay. I was just about to take the first sip of coffee this morning when the doorbell sounded; and my private life blew up in my face. There was Peter with a woman, young, but I had no eyes for her. Up the stairs he went and sat her down in my sitting room, and I, all amazed, took him into the front room.

Coldly, with a hard smile, he said, 'I'm moving in George'; and though I persuaded him to dismiss the girl, and an ill-looking fellow that came ringing at the door a minute or two later, he was not to be shifted. At first he kept on insisting he was going to move in, adding with a sneer 'I know you won't mind if I get behind with the rent or come in at all hours, and my gear will be safe here.'

My agitation was visible and uncontrollable, but when all my attempts to get him to leave now and meet me this evening to discuss it had failed, he put a plain alternative to me – either I let him move in, now, at once, or he'd ruin me. I refused; anything would be better than having my home occupied by someone of this sort. So then he dropped his smiling air and showed the vicious, slightly mad, personality that he keeps so well hidden.

Threatening me with a complaint to the police, he went on 'and there's enough in your diaries to make a lot of charges stick, Johnnie Joyce told me that. If you won't have me in your flat I'll have you in a prison cell.' My mind was concentrated now on my diaries, unprotected, in the sideboard; and with dry mouth and trembling voice I tried to remind him of our friendship, of all I'd done for him, and how ill a return this was.

He listened with a hard sneering smile for a little while, and then cut me short with 'I'll strip you of every penny. I'll take your job. I'll strip this place clean and set it on fire.' Then, getting up, he proceeded to fill the old large suitcase (my parents', who never thought it could be put to such a use as this) with my records; taking my briefcase, he unplugged the automatic record player and took it from the front room, and then returned to my sitting room, and remarked 'and now let's have your money'.

Opening the sideboard drawer he took the £8-10s [£205] *that was in it, and £6* [£145] *out of my wallet (saying, 'that's for fares and lunches'; he left me £2* [£48.25] *– an echo of the similar scene in* For Those in Peril *[a 1944 war film]). I did nothing to stop him – Mrs Hemsworth, I knew, was below and, even in this extremity, I shrank from a scuffle and an upset that could compel her to come up. But more compelling than the desire to keep up appearances was concern for my diaries. Once I let him get his hands on those I was sunk indeed.*

So I stood still, and when he'd added the album of photographs of him to the contents of the briefcase, I thought he was going to go... but a thought struck him. 'And we'll have the diary too and the dirty photos Johnnie Joyce says you've got,' he remarked chattily; but my 'no, you won't have those' didn't seem to provoke him, and he left. I left with him, going to the corner of Lambert Road, walking under the sun in a daze of horrible anxiety as he casually said he had friends who would do what he wanted, 'Frank, for instance, looks on me as a brother' and he'd be back himself... 'this is only the first instalment'.

So I left him, and returned to my flat in what a state God knows. Then quickly, with trembling hands, to put the diaries and papers into the writing case, lock it, and out to deposit it at Charing Cross. It was ten years ago I was doing much the same, but with much less cause for anxiety.

At the office, there were two urgent matters that helped settle my mind as I wrote, so that I was able to put together a good plausible story to account for both late arrival – at 12.25 p.m. – and my horrendous preoccupied and very visible agitation. Before I left the office I wrote to Peter at his Kildare address reproaching him for this callous treachery and betrayal of me who has trusted him; and to John Joyce, telling him the consequences of him not keeping his eyes and tongue to himself.

About the West End and the Square tonight, uncertainly hoping to find help in my trouble, and getting some sympathy from Sammy Russell and Michael Rowland and Desmond O'Kelly, not gone back to Dublin yet, and ending by asking me to buy 9 penn'orth [90p] of chips; and then home, sick in mind and stomach, pondering on what I had best do.

It is very certain that all courses are full of trouble and inconvenience and expense.

If I brave it out and stay here I may involve the Hemsworths in some unpleasantness of broken windows or burgled premises or even arson. And to stay here means to live under a shadow, not knowing from one moment to the next if the doorbell is going to sound. To leave means going through all the wearisome nerve-wracking toil I experienced six years ago, with little chance of selling my present property at a price anywhere near – let alone greater – than that I'd have to pay for something as good, or nearly so. Either course is daunting.

Suicide has come to me, too, as a solution of all the problems – but I am afraid of what may come after. And through all this murk of fears and anxieties and perplexity comes a flame of anger at this vicious young psychopath, that returns me to all this from all that I've given him. If he drives me into a corner I might perhaps put an end to him; if I could get him inside my flat I might even do it safely.

This is not the first time Mr Lucas's thoughts have turned to murder when it comes to Peter – not even the first time this month:

3 September 1965 (Friday):

A dark day with last night's heavy rain continuing to stream down without ceasing. Most other European cities are being drenched. I read much about murderous rage but little about murderous fear. I think fear is a greater inducement to murder than either anger or malice. If I could safely destroy this Peter and these young men, in particular, who menace my security [various rent boys whom Mr Lucas does not trust to have his home address], *I believe I would do so readily. I begin to sympathize with those maligned rulers, spiritual and secular, who have resorted to massacre when faced with threats to their positions.*

These are not random thoughts. Through bitter experience, Mr Lucas has formed a clear idea of how to deal with this – even three years later.

13 December 1968 (Friday):

A bitter cold day, to match the ice of fear on my mind. All day, in the intervals of official business, I was pondering how to get out of this trap I am caught in. I have left the selling of my house over-late; I cannot evade him [Peter] that way. Only his death, or mine, can free me from this persecution – there's no help to be got from the police, that's certain. And I am not going to die before my mother. So I must try to end his life, that's of no use to anyone. It would scarcely be murder, morally at any rate; one is entitled to use deadly force against an unjust assailant of life or valuable property, and Peter is certainly that. He's a real and present threat, not a remote one. I think I would be justified in conscience if, when he was in my flat on his own, I used a steak knife in his throat, suddenly. Disposal of the body is the main problem, but to be living on one's own is a help – in a large metal trunk (metal is fairly odour-proof) his body ought to lie for years, till only bones and skull and withered tissue were left.

Passion turns to love turns to hatred: the trajectory of any relationship is very well-worn. However, for Mr Lucas, those initial heartbeat flutters outside Swan & Edgar in 1960 have led directly to a pair of scissors held close to his face, when he was viciously robbed in his home in January 1968. Was it the grand passion of Mr Lucas's life? Yes, in many ways, as it coloured everything and everybody subsequently. One-sided it may have been – unfortunately like all of his relationships – but it scarred him, almost physically that horrific night in his flat, but definitely emotionally ever since.

Murder, abuse and jail: only the second ever came true for Mr Lucas in terms of his relationship with Peter.

Barfly rumours come and go, but Peter somehow survives, despite his increasingly rackety lifestyle.

25 February 1966 (Friday):

[An acquaintance] *tells me that Peter has already been tried and given three years for buggery. This may be true – one cannot rely on newspapers to report these cases. I wonder how long it will be before he escapes. I hope that he doesn't come ringing at my door again.*

Peter disappears once more from the pages of the diaries, slipping out of sight until the night Mr Lucas is robbed in his flat by three young men, one of whom he presumes is his nemesis. And then, nothing for months – until September that year. Peter has moved from a little light fencing into a much, much darker world of murder and torture.

9 September 1968 (Monday):

I was thinking of my visit to Dublin when the front page of this morning's Daily Mirror *startled me with a story – the only one on the page – of 'a bearded street trader called Johnnie the Irish' found yesterday morning beaten, whipped and wounded in Soho. I was sceptical at first, the details of four men forcing tranquilizing tablets down his throat 'to deaden the pain', and one hand being nailed to a piece of wood, sounded much exaggerated. But there's no doubt Peter has been assaulted – my regret is that his assailant should have been so half-hearted, and neither put him out altogether nor disabled him from doing more harm. So long as he has eyes and hands and tongue, he is dangerous. The evening papers carry 'Soho Torture Gang Sought'. I hope I'm not disturbed by any spreading ripples from this dark and direful pond in which Peter moves – dark and evil as the lake before the gates of Moria* [a *Lord of the Rings* reference].

6

England on Trial

THE EARLY SIXTIES was a time of witch-hunts, high-profile court cases and a quite startling number of pretty policemen. Who knew the police at that point had so many eligible good-looking young male recruits, eager to act as bait for supposedly predatory homosexuals cruising the public toilets of central London?

It is a wonder that any other crime was solved between 1961 and 1963, as Mr Lucas reports time and time again that the police are out in force and every cottage – or public lavatory – seems to have been visited by a pair of handsome male officers (always in pairs, presumably just in case they were overpowered by rapacious 'queens') at least twice a week. As the mood in the country started to move towards the eventual partial legalization of gay sex in 1967, it seems the police and the media did not get the memo.

Shadowing everything in the early sixties was the Profumo Affair. The forty-six-year-old Secretary of State for War,

John Profumo, had been caught in a relationship with nineteen-year-old model Christine Keeler, somewhat callously dismissed by Mr Lucas in his diaries as 'a brainless strumpet'.

While the affair might have passed off as a minor note in political history, Profumo's subsequent attempt to lie his way out of the mess – and mislead parliament – would almost bring down Conservative prime minister Harold Macmillan's government.

But the 'unlucky Profumo Affair', as Mr Lucas writes in August 1963, did more than reinforce a general distrust of Establishment figures, it also gave 'the bigots the opportunity they wanted' to embark on a moral crusade, he adds. Gay men were subsequently rarely out of the news or the courtrooms. Three cases in 1963 in particular – all diligently recorded by Mr Lucas – are critical: the trial over the murder of former Labour Party chairman George Brinham; the resignation of Charles Fletcher-Cooke, a Home Office minister who was forced to quit over his relationship with an eighteen-year-old man; and the trial of journalist Laurence Bell, accused of nine counts of indecency with assorted guardsmen.

Mr Lucas also writes of the arrest in 1962 of John Vassall, accused of spying for the Soviet Union. Vassall pleaded guilty and thus avoided a trial, but the affair – and subsequent public tribunal – further swayed both public and official opinion against gay men, at a time when Britain was still reeling from Guy Burgess's defection to Moscow in 1951 as part of the Cambridge Spy Ring scandal. Both cases provided further ammunition for the widely held view that gay men represented a security risk simply by dint of their sexuality. Now, thanks to Vassall and Burgess, they stood accused of being traitors.

Here, Mr Lucas comes into his own as a diarist, never quite at the centre of things, but always on the periphery; either knowing some of those directly affected or moving in the same social circles or bars and pubs. His diary moves from the events of the time to the feelings among his fellow 'queens' on London's gay scene and on to the general mood of the country, as detailed in the national and regional newspapers.

He'd come across the journalist Laurence Bell many times in the low-lit world of the capital's gay bars and private clubs, which were buzzing, despite the frequent crackdowns. He knew Charles Fletcher-Cooke by reputation and through friends of friends; and George Brinham, a TUC organizer and Labour Party activist, more directly, as someone he'd occasionally catch a half-pint with, if only to write disparaging things about him later.

These early years of the sixties reveal a deeply homophobic society, whipped up into righteous hysteria by a spiteful tabloid press. Mr Lucas, as he reaches the midway point of his fourth decade, has already faced arrest numerous times and been held in a military prison in Germany.

As 1961 opens, danger lurks everywhere.

19 January 1961 (Thursday):

Much plainclothes police activity around Piccadilly Circus and several of the boys taken up, I hear. May God frustrate the police and deliver all their victims! The 'Dilly boys in some dismay.

20 January 1961 (Friday):

Piccadilly Circus is lousy with plainclothes police these last few days, and five of the lads, 'on the game', have been arrested so far. It is galling to think that police who are so well paid out of our taxes to preserve life and property should devote themselves to the easier task of prosecuting harmless people. And male prostitutes, if not exactly the best type of youth, are harmless enough.

The country is still reeling from the two trials in 1953 and 1954 of Lord Montagu of Beaulieu. The first had been a charge of buggery against Montagu brought by the Director of Public Prosecutions (DPP) on behalf of two boy scouts. He was eventually acquitted, but a charge of indecent assault, introduced late in the trial by the DPP, led to a hung jury.

The second trial saw peer of the realm Montagu arrested alongside landowner Michael Pitt-Rivers and *Daily Mail* journalist Peter Wildeblood and charged with 'conspiracy to incite certain male persons to commit serious offences with male persons'. Found guilty, Montagu received twelve months, with Pitt-Rivers and Wildeblood both getting eighteen.

But the Montagu trials and other high-profile cases, including actor Sir John Gielgud, caught soliciting in 1953, had one benefit: the establishment of what came to be called the Wolfenden Committee under the leadership of academic and former public school headmaster Sir John Wolfenden.

In 1957, the Departmental Committee on Homosexual Offences and Prostitution published what has since become known as the Wolfenden Report. In a groundbreaking move, the committee recommended that 'homosexual behaviour between consenting adults in private be no longer a criminal offence'.[1]

The law was set to change, yet there were many who remained reluctant to see it happen, not least the police. While the upper echelons of society, long used to tolerating gay and lesbian friends and family members, if not quite accepting them, were preparing to push through legal reform, attitudes among the more working-class rank-and-file members of the police force remained fixed.

A man trying to extort money from our diarist in Trafalgar Square simply presumes Mr Lucas would not turn to the police for help. 'He followed me into the post office,' Mr Lucas writes on 31 October 1961. 'And when I threatened to tell a policeman, he sneered, "Someone in your position wouldn't want a court case", which is painfully true.'

Still plagued by this 'queenie-looking man... at last I plucked up my courage and, going on to the Square, did approach a policeman, and asked him to, "Get rid of this man." The policeman's manner was cold and distant.'

But while he may have lost his aggressor, Mr Lucas has also just run the risk of attracting the unwanted attention of the police. 'After telephoning for advice, I suppose, the policeman told me in a distinctly hostile manner that I was to go back to the Board of Trade,' he continues. 'And so I arrived at my room white-faced and shaking. It's not surprising: no homosexual can be in contact with police without fear and trepidation, even when his reception is less hostile than mine was.'

This encounter happened on Halloween, 'when all evil things are loose', Mr Lucas writes. And that includes the police, out in force that night with an eye to round up vulnerable homosexuals.

31 October 1961 (Tuesday):

I saw two obvious detectives (that had been at Piccadilly Circus at lunchtime) lurking about the York Place cottage. And in due course they pounced on a victim, taking him off down the Strand to Bow Street [police station], *one holding each arm.*

Gay men lived under a climate of fear and prejudice that would, as we'll see, lead to lives ruined and, in at least one instance, murder with impunity.

The events start with the death the previous year of Mr Lucas's occasional drinking buddy, George Brinham. Brinham is a bit-part player in the diaries. He pops up a couple of times in 1961, rather a drink-sodden miserable type. By day a trade union activist, by night he frequents the same bars as Mr Lucas: the Welsh Harp, the White Bear and the Golden Lion – the Bermuda Triangle of gay bars at the time. Brinham's tale is a classic working-class kid made good. Having left home at fifteen, he took up an apprenticeship to become a joiner before becoming a member of the local union, climbing the ranks and eventually ending up on the national executive committee and then chairman of Britain's Labour Party.

Mr Lucas is not a fan, blaming the behaviour of 'Hungry George Brinham' – named not so much for his appetite for booze as for young men – for the general sleaziness of the times, railing against him in particular for being responsible for the crackdown by the Coffee-House on its regular rent-boy clientele.

9 December 1961 (Saturday):

The owners of the Coffee-House, not unnecessarily, have instructed the manageress to move on all obvious rent boys and such like. Much of the blame, though, must go to those who try to turn an agreeable gay coffee bar into a pick-up point, where rent-queens and pimps operate, where such predatory queens as Maurice Mullens and Ian Ball and Hungry George Brinham seek a new piece of flesh. These people are really ashamed of homosexuality, or guilty, and cannot understand the feelings of other homosexuals such as myself, who do not want the seamy side of sex to be brought into our own congenial meeting places to these guilt-haunted people.

Whether full of shame or guilty of something else, Brinham's 'hunger' would lead to his brutal murder late on the night of 17 November 1962. The story hit the papers the following week with the arrest of sixteen-year-old Laurence Thomas Somers.

No one comes out of the trial well. Not Brinham with his hankering for young flesh; not the judge, Justice Gilbert Paull, who would eventually move to order the acquittal of the defendant; and certainly not the murderer, Somers himself, who would go on to sell his story in the most salacious – and presumably profitable – way possible. 'Union chief is found beaten to death,' screamed the headline in the *Daily Herald* on 23 November 1962. 'Mr George Brinham, a former chairman of the Labour Party, was found battered to death in his London flat yesterday. Last night, a sixteen-year-old youth was accused of unlawfully killing him.'[2]

Accompanied by a photo of a gap-toothed rather guileless-looking forty-six-year-old Brinham, the *Herald* reported with some glee that the body had been found in his basement flat in Kensington. 'He had been dead for about two days,' the reporter added.

The *Mirror*, a long-standing Labour-supporting newspaper, splashed with the news on the front page.[3] Somers had been stopped by the police on suspicion of driving a stolen car. 'The young man climbed out and said: "I've killed a man",' the paper reported. There is no hint at this stage that this was a sexually motivated crime. But that would soon change as the newspapers picked up the scent of a juicier scandal. 'A 16-year-old youth accused of murdering George Brinham, a former chairman of the Labour Party, had said he hit him over the head with a decanter after Brinham had made an improper suggestion, stated the prosecution at Marylebone, London, Juvenile Court yesterday,' reported *The Scotsman* on 11 December.[4]

This bit – the 'improper suggestion' – is crucial and will play a central part in Somers' eventual acquittal. The so-called 'gay panic' – or guardsman's defence, as it became known – is now frowned upon by British courts. Guidance from the Crown Prosecution Service (CPS) of England and Wales now advises it cannot be used as the basis for a defence based upon 'provocation'.

But deep in the early sixties, it was common for a defendant to try to mitigate the length of their eventual sentence by attempting to prove they were the 'victim' of an unwanted sexual advance. Mitigate or – as happened in the Somers/Brinham case – gain an outright acquittal.

Justice Paull directed the jury to find Somers not guilty of murder, saying in court that as Brinham 'attempted to make homosexual advances... I think that is about as clear a case of provocation as it is possible to have'.

'This is a shameful business,' writes Mr Lucas at the end of the trial in January 1963. 'We [gay men] are indeed *hors la loi.*'

22 January 1963 (Tuesday):

We now have it from an eminent judge that for a man to put his arms round a youth and to say 'give us a kiss then' is provocation sufficient to justify killing him. Few homosexuals then, are really safe – indeed, it seems that many queers may be killed with impunity if the killer is fairly young. It is rather painful to realize that we are still, not merely subject to criminal prosecution ourselves, but virtually outside the protection of the law... in fact, if not legally, outlaws.

Somers leaves 'the Old Bailey grinning and swaggering', Mr Lucas writes, 'as much to say "How clever am I! I've killed a queer!"' The defendant was also subsequently found not guilty of manslaughter, leaving him free to sell his story to the *News of the World*, which quoted one woman who had written to the murderer to say, 'Have no regrets, you are a hero.' The story even made the international press, with a banner front-page headline in the US paper *The National Insider* reporting with relish: 'I killed him when he tried to kiss me: It made me feel sick.'

Somers drifted off into a life of obscurity after this early flush of infamy, dying in 1999 in Derby at the age of fifty-two. It's clear – and admitted – that he belted the former trade unionist over the head with a glass decanter until he was dead, but whether it was murder or actually self-defence is anyone's guess.

Brinham's low-key funeral – for such a formerly influential Labour Party figure – was held on 4 December in Brixham, a picturesque harbourside town in Devon, where he was born in 1916. More than forty floral tributes were delivered, the newspapers faithfully reported, including one, Mr Lucas noted, 'from the National Executive of the Labour Party and many from the Amalgamated Society of Woodworkers, of which Mr Brinham was president at one time'.

Somers' trial can be seen as the logical next step in the security services' crackdown on gay men in their ranks that had begun the previous year, as we've seen, with an eighteen-year jail term for John Vassall, the gay British civil servant caught spying for the Soviet Union. Vassall had been blackmailed into working for the Russians after getting drunk at a party in Moscow in 1954 and being photographed having sex with several men. Sentenced to eighteen years in jail, he served ten and was released in 1972, going on to publish *Vassall: The Autobiography of a Spy* a few years later. In it, he claimed he was drugged by a 'fur-clad mystery man' at the Hotel Berlin in Moscow before compromising photographs were taken of him in bed with three other men:

Not until 1963, nine years later, was it suggested to me that the wine I had been given must have been drugged. After dinner everyone seemed to drift away, leaving three of us and the one who had brought me to the dinner party. One of them said I did not look well, and it might be better if I lay down on a large divan which was appropriately placed in a recess. When I got to the bed I could hardly stand up. I was asked to take off my clothes including my underwear. It all seemed beyond my control. I did not know where I was or what was going on or why it was happening. I can recollect having my underpants in my hand and holding them up in the air at the request of others. Then I was lying on the bed naked, and there were three other men on the bed with me. I cannot remember exactly what took place. I saw the skier's friend standing in the room taking photographs.[5]

In its 1996 obituary, the *Independent* was having none of this and was scathing of Vassall's motives, character and his final days:

Vassall was certainly the smallest of beer compared with the Cambridge Five: Burgess, MacLean, Philby, Blunt and Cairncross. Unlike them he had scant ideological regard for Communism. He had operated entirely under threat of blackmail and also for greed. Victim of historical circumstance as much as anything, he might in another age have found a vocation as a gay cleric. As it was, he changed his name to John Phillips and spent his declining years in total anonymity and obscurity in St John's Wood, north London.[6]

Vassall had admitted his crimes the previous year and, as 1963 opens, the Vassall Tribunal into the repercussions of the affair is in full swing. Homosexuals and the risks they posed to national security were very much in the public eye at the time. But Mr Lucas remains unimpressed.

21 January 1963 (Monday):

So far in its public sessions, the Vassall Tribunal has provided no more than a dreary procession of journalists either refusing to disclose the sources of their stories or admitting that the sources were inside their own head.

One fact sticks out for Mr Lucas, one that plays very much to his own situation at the Board of Trade. Here, Roy East, 'crime reporter to the *People*', is giving evidence to the tribunal:

This creature's further statement – that he had been told by someone in the Admiralty that the late Mr Rickard [an Admiralty official] *had been instructed to report on any homosexuals he might come to know about who were in official positions – is disquieting. I remember how the last time I met Peter Morris at, of all unsuitable places, the 'White Bear', he greeted me with a very audible, 'And how are things in the Board of Trade?' Which is the sort of remark, silly but not malicious, that could be quite damaging.*

Loose lips sink ships. And this is why the case of Home Office minister and M.P. Charles Fletcher-Cooke is so dispiriting: no fool like an old fool.

In 1961, Mr Lucas welcomes the appointment of Fletcher-Cooke as an Under-Secretary at the Home Office as a possible sign that the 'penal laws [against gay sex] will be less rigorously enforced against us'.

13 November 1961 (Monday):

This barrister M.P. not only voted in favour of the Wolfenden reforms last year, but I remember John Wood told me that he gave a gay party in his flat in [the central London district of] *the Temple at which Mr Wood himself was present. Presumably Fletcher-Cooke is himself gay or half-gay.*

Presumably gay or half-gay indeed. Fletcher-Cooke's high-flying ministerial career came to a crashing end in 1963 when the newspapers received a tip-off that he was living with an eighteen-year-old former Borstal boy. At first, Fletcher-Cooke, who had entered parliament in 1951, attempted, like Profumo and many politicians before and after him, to brazen his way out of a deepening scandal. However, the news that he is in trouble does not come as a surprise to Mr Lucas – or probably many other gay men on the scene in London at the time.

18 February 1963 (Monday):

Knowing what one does of Mr Fletcher-Cooke, the present Under-Secretary of state at the Home Office, one wonders what lies behind the report in today's newspapers that a lad named Anthony Turner, aged nineteen and lately released from a detention centre, was stopped for speeding yesterday in the minister's car, and was found to have been given the use of it by Mr Fletcher-Cooke.

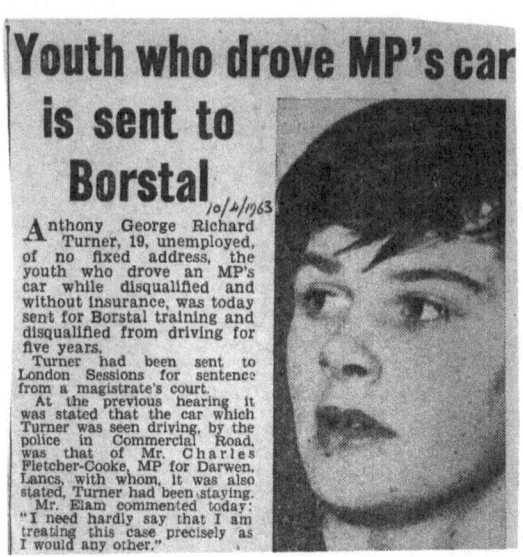

Youth who drove MP's car is sent to Borstal 10/4/1963

Anthony George Richard Turner, 19, unemployed, of no fixed address, the youth who drove an MP's car while disqualified and without insurance, was today sent for Borstal training and disqualified from driving for five years.

Turner had been sent to London Sessions for sentence from a magistrate's court.

At the previous hearing it was stated that the car which Turner was seen driving, by the police in Commercial Road, was that of Mr. Charles Fletcher-Cooke, MP for Darwen, Lancs, with whom, it was also stated, Turner had been staying.

Mr. Elam commented today: "I need hardly say that I am treating this case precisely as I would any other."

The facts of the matter are straightforward – and, to more contemporary eyes looking back sixty years at a middle-aged man shacked up with someone more than a third his age, pretty obvious. Either way, Fletcher-Cooke had to go, particularly in the wake of the Vassall spy scandal. Rather amusingly, in his resignation letter, Fletcher-Cooke attempted to justify the presence of an eighteen-year-old in his house, as Mr Lucas tells us, 'through his interest in the after-care of delinquents, which may well be true'.

It may indeed be true, but it strikes us now as highly unlikely and, frankly, ludicrous. Indeed, just how many people were there in the sixties claiming to be street philanthropists? But the resignation of Fletcher-Cooke has a greater significance than the self-immolation of a once-promising ministerial career. 'He's a loss from the homosexual point of view,' notes Mr Lucas. 'He might have been of very great help at the Home Office.'

Did his resignation set back the cause of gay liberation? Might the government have moved to legalize gay sex earlier if it hadn't been for Fletcher-Cooke and Vassall? We'll return to this, but first let's look deeper into 1963 and the one further scandal that ties them all together.

In June 1963, as the world marked the death of Pope John XXIII, Laurence Bell, a twenty-six-year-old freelance journalist who had sold stories to the *Daily Express* and *Daily Mail*, was arrested for nine charges of indecency with guardsmen. He is an acquaintance of Mr Lucas's, 'a man [I've] rubbed shoulders with for years in the "Welsh Harp"', and someone for whom he has the utmost dislike. His hatred stems from Bell's role in Fletcher-Cooke's downfall. Mr Lucas is in court to watch the opening remarks before Bell's case is adjourned until later in the year.

19 June 1963 (Wednesday):

But not before Raphael Tuck of [defending] *counsel had declared that Bell was the victim of a 'political frame-up', having embarrassed the government by bringing about the resignation of Mr Fletcher-Cooke, exposing various scandals about the guards and having provided information about [John Profumo], the Secretary of State for War, [society osteopath] Dr Ward and Miss Keeler. If this line of defence is run, the pot of scandal will be kept-a-boiling merrily, and Bell will cut the figure his perverted mind desires. I hope, though, he's convicted in spite of it all and gets a really heavy sentence, if only for his part in forcing Fletcher-Cooke out of office (I believe it is quite true that he discovered and informed the newspapers of Tony Turner's using the then-undersecretary's car).*

This leads Mr Lucas to write one of his more shocking sentences: confronted with the dilemma of justice versus supporting one of his own, he – perhaps unsurprisingly given the high moral tone he adopts throughout the diaries – plumps for what he feels is morally right: 'It's surprising to find myself welcoming a prosecution for homosexual intercourse – but this is one where it is fully justified.'

Bell characterizes himself as a martyr, if not to the cause of gay

'NO' TO BAIL FOR A JOURNALIST
24/5/1963

Bell ... remanded

LAURENCE BELL, 26, journalist, of Preston-drive, Wanstead, was remanded in custody until May 27 at Bow-street on Monday.

He faces four charges of attempting to commit unnatural offences with other men, one of committing an unnatural offence with a man, and one of importuning men for immoral purposes.

Det. Chief Insp. James Graney, objecting to bail, said on the day Bell was arrested he was with one of the witnesses.

"I fear that inquiries by himself and his friends may interfere with witnesses," he equality, then to the higher ideals of truth and justice in the face of an attempted Establishment cover-up. The case reopens in October, when Bell admits he is gay, 'and attributes this,' Mr Lucas writes, to being '"interfered with by the lodger when he was nine".' The quote marks around the comment about the lodger clearly indicate Mr Lucas's views that these remarks are risible.

8 October 1963 (Tuesday):

[Bell] says that his activities have been inspired by a belief that 'scandals in high places' should be exposed.

In this instance, 'journalist' seems more likely to have been cover for quasi-blackmailer, with Bell's inky fingers smeared all over many of the gay and straight scandals of the early sixties.

8 October 1963 (Tuesday):

His own behaviour has been more sinister than I had imagined. He had insinuated himself into [gay] society and so practised on young Turner (the nasty brat who seems to have spilled on poor Fletcher-Cooke to Bell, who got £166 for the story); he told Marcus Lipton, M.P., about Lieut. Commander Peck of the Admiralty, whom Lipton asked a parliamentary question about; he sent anonymous letters to the police about Stephen Ward...

> *and received from newspapers some £672 in the first half of 1963 for his pieces of information.*

Peck had resigned from the Navy in early 1963 after being accused of, according to the *Birmingham Daily Post*, 'unsatisfactory conduct in a youth organization'.[7] Stephen Ward – memorably described by Mr Lucas as the 'osteopath-ponce-procurer' – had been at the centre of the Profumo Affair, the man long suspected of introducing the minister to the call girl.

But that sum of £672, the modern-day equivalent of almost £12,000, is not to be sneezed at and does allow Bell some credibility to claim his profession as journalist, if very much a tabloid muck-raker. In his defence, two relatively senior national newspaper reporters testified to the accuracy of Bell's tips at the trial. Clifford Luton, a former *Daily Express* reporter working at the BBC, said he had known Bell for 'about a year'. 'Mr Luton said Bell had always been an accurate informant,' the *Guardian* newspaper noted. '"In 14 years in Fleet Street, he is the first informant of whom I can say that",' Luton told the paper.[8] The former BBC journalist faced his own charges in 2013, accused of abusing young boys in the seventies and eighties, until procedures were halted due to the then eighty-nine-year-old being deemed unfit for trial.[9]

So, whom to believe? Laurence Bell with his trusty sword of justice and shield of fair play or Mr Lucas with his ink-scrawled pages of righteous moral fury? If Bell is going down, he is going down screaming – and fully intends to take half the Establishment with him.

10 October 1963 (Thursday):

Under cross-examination at the Central Criminal Court [CCC – also known as the Old Bailey], Bell has turned nasty. As well as declaring, 'I know that Mr Fletcher-Cooke is a homosexual' he has insisted on relating a tale of going with a guardsman 'to the flat of a well-known Communist' where 'a minister in the present Cabinet, a minister closely connected with nuclear weapons' had sexual relations with other guardsmen in his presence.

Whomever Bell is fingering here, his intentions to squeal will have alerted Britain's security services, rattled by the quick succession of Establishment scandals. And a few days later, perhaps what we, sixty years on, might view as inevitable comes to pass.

16 October 1963 (Wednesday):

The incredible has happened. 'There ain't no justice' for once is true. Bell – Bell the informer, Bell the cheat – was this afternoon found not guilty of all nine charges after the judge had directed an acquittal on one, had ruled that there was no corroboration in five and, when leaving the remainder to the jury, suggested quite strongly that Bell's allegation that he had been framed was not absurd or even unlikely.

Referring back to the judge's earlier acquittal of Somers in the Brinham murder trial in January that year, Mr Lucas writes of how 'it's perhaps sinister that earlier this year Paull J. [Justice] strained the law violently to secure the acquittal of the murderer of a homosexual and now McKenna J. has done his best to protect an informer on homosexuals'.

Now, Mr Lucas continues, sleazeball Bell is free to 'get good fees for his lurid revelations in some gutter-newspaper and might even appear on a Moral Re-Armament [the spiritualist movement that campaigned for greater morality in public life] platform as a reformed homosexual – rather like the "ex-priests" who used to flaunt their apostasy from Protestant platforms sixty years ago'. Indeed, that very night, on the evening of his acquittal at the Old Bailey, Bell is spotted by Mr Lucas, out on the town, celebrating.

16 October 1963 (Wednesday):

Tonight, I saw Bell in the 'White Bear' with his dark glasses and the homosexual naval officer that is, I suspect, his informant on naval matters. He seemed hugely elated, as well he may be. I don't envy Charles Fletcher-Cooke or anyone else Bell fancies he'd like to vent his malice on.

And so the self-styled 'Captain' Bell is free once more. Five years later, Mr Lucas hears the former journalist is as sleazy as ever.

8 December 1968 (Sunday):

In the Café Roché, I heard that Bell is now established in a Knightsbridge flat and beginning his old furtive hunting out of matters that can be turned to his advantage. With him back in Town, there's one further peril to be wary of... though, with their short memories and lack of information, most of my fellow queens seem to have no clear recollection of Bell in his days as a pseudo-captain.

These three separate events matter because they coloured the thinking and acceptance of homosexuality at every level of society. The unfortunate George Brinham ties together the political left and the working classes, who, spurred by the tabloids of the time, rallied to the defence of the sixteen-year-old Laurence Somers.

Then there is the case of Charles Fletcher-Cooke, the archetypal Establishment figure, again enamoured – and no, we won't give him the benefit of the doubt here – with another working-class youth. And then finally, the case of the journalist Laurence Bell, who taps into every stratum of society, scooping up titbits of information for the papers and who knows what other purposes.

There are other notable cases in 1963 that add to the moral climate. In February that year, M. W. Bennitt, the assistant secretary – or a senior civil servant – at the Ministry of Public Building and Works 'was arrested for importuning at midnight at the Prebend Street cottage at Islington', Mr Lucas tells us. 'Whitehall man on immorality charge' shouted the midday papers on their street placards the following day.

February was a bad month for gay men but particularly fruitful for tabloid scoops. The exceptionally dopey Mervyn Horder, the second Baron Horder, was arrested for sending 'some pictures of himself naked to the Danish magazine *Male Models*', Mr Lucas tells us. 'They can hardly have been very exciting pictures – Mervyn Horder is tall, thin, bespectacled and untidy – but they shocked Mr Powell the magistrate very much.' According to Horder's 2011 *Independent* obituary, there is no doubt that 'his true sexual orientation was firmly homosexual, with leanings towards exhibitionism'.[10]

These events might seem faintly amusing now, but they were tragic at the time for their protagonists and the greater cause of gay liberation. Gay men were reduced to criminals or figures of fun with all the attendant notes of tabloid disgust and disdain. And society was taking note. The Coffee-House was cracking down on a certain type of clientele and finally closed its doors in June 1963. 'The militant puritan reaction gathers strength,' writes Mr Lucas in October that year.

10 October 1963 (Thursday):

The bishop of Coventry, in most things a rather advanced prelate, last week complained of increasing sexual laxity and said that homosexuals condemned by the courts should not be regarded as martyrs. But while the ecclesiastical pronouncements do not influence young lovers, the boys and girls at whom they are directed, they do enable magistrates and policemen and other moral inquisitors to cloak their frigid malice under an affectation of Christian zeal.

Frigid malice indeed. The high-profile arrests, court cases and tabloid splashes all fed into the growing hatred of homosexuality in society, the law and the press. Mr Lucas's 1961 and 1963 diaries are awash, as we've seen, with reports of heightened police activity. And their methods are becoming ever more sinister.

9 December 1961 (Saturday):

The Coffee-House plainclothes policemen have been sitting in there, noting who comes and goes, and with whom; and they have employed a stool pigeon, a nark, in the shape of one tall unpleasant young queen who has been passing information to Savile Row police station, and has had more than one arrested for soliciting. (Just so, in the religious persecutions, have the police employed spies to discover where mass is said, for example, what priests are about, who harbours them, and so on.)

While the bishop of Coventry might be keen not to turn gay men persecuted and prosecuted by the law into martyrs, Mr Lucas sees himself and his friends as facing the same levels of oppression as Catholic priests under English Protestant rule.

Yet despite the constant crackdowns, gay life, particularly around Piccadilly Circus, memorably described by a judge in another trial in 1963 as 'the marketplace of the bugger-boys', is relatively thriving. The Coffee-House might be keen to go upmarket, but other venues, notably the Golden Lion, the Welsh Harp and the White Bear, are heaving.

Society's censure has extended to the guardsmen as well. Various 'Gay Romp Shockers', to borrow the language of the red tops of the eighties – my own childhood – has seen them banned from certain pubs, including the Welsh Harp and the Lemon Tree, another popular gay-ish bar at the time.

Yet despite this, British society was shifting in the early sixties. Following the Profumo Affair, the tabloids ceased to be so deferential to politicians in particular. Gay and straight sex scandals, the meat and drink of the red tops in the seventies and eighties, were becoming fair game – as were Establishment figures.

'The Profumo Affair was not only a body-blow to Macmillan's government. It was the death-blow of an England that was deferential and discreet,' Richard Davenport-Hines writes in *An English Affair: Sex, Class and Power in the Age of Profumo*.[11] 'Until 1963, newspapers protected politicians who were detected in adultery, or caught in the bushes with guardsmen. After 1963, Fleet Street's emetic brew of guilty joys, false tears, nasty surprises and dirty surmises seemed limitless.'

Fleet Street was becoming more and more vicious. But as we leave the early sixties and the courtrooms behind, who, really, is to blame for the fall of Charles Fletcher-Cooke and the murder of George Brinham? Certainly, they bear some of the responsibility for their own actions, but as Mr Lucas notes in February 1963, so does the wider society.

2 February 1963 (Saturday):

It's society that has turned you and every other queer into a hunted criminal, that has crushed you and driven you underground.

7

A Brush with the Krays

As the first trial of the notorious gangsters the Kray twins, charged with blackmail, opens in 1965, Mr Lucas is caught up in a tale that darkens by the minute. Brothers Ronnie and Reggie, both thirty-one at the start of 1965, had risen from the rubble of the bombed-out East End after the Second World War, to become nightclub owners, blackmailers, murderers and – who wasn't, it seems in the sixties – friends of celebrities, royals and peers of the realm. They owned bars and clubs frequented by stars of stage and screen, popping Champagne corks with the ubiquitous Princess Margaret and faded politicians who should have known better. Now they stood accused of demanding money with menaces and all of London is agog, wondering if this is the end of the celebrity gangsters.

Mr Lucas has a more intimate connection: Irish Peter, who will be called as a defence witness. As the year begins, he and Peter have broken off contact; Mr Lucas opting to sever ties for the sake of both sanity and security. But his memories of first meeting Peter remain strong, if somewhat bittersweet. Here he reminisces after hearing that Peter himself has been robbed.

3 January 1965 (Sunday):

It is a mere coincidence that today, four years ago, I went with Irish Johnnie (not well known to me then) to his room at Villa Road in Brixton, for an hour's not disagreeable, rather platonic, dalliance; but it reminds me what kind of lying cheating whore he was in 1961. I would be very pleased to see his actions beginning to return to him. It is always refreshing to see the biter bit, the robber robbed, the poisoner given a dose of his own medicine. Peter's past baseness disqualifies him from any claim to sympathy, and I feel none for him.

While Mr Lucas still bears the emotional scars of that relationship, the picture is about to become much bleaker – and more dangerous. 'The world [Peter] moves in is a cannibal one and its denizens prey on each other,' he writes presciently. Exactly how Peter first came across the Krays is not recorded by Mr Lucas, but one can presume that for a petty thief and chancer becoming a member of the Firm would represent the height of their achievement. Peter's involvement also shows how deeply the Krays' claws were wrapped around London's criminal underclass. Even lowly scam artists had to answer to someone.

Mr Lucas is still living at 13 Kildoran Road in the slightly down-at-heel suburb of Brixton. He has changed roles at the Board of Trade – now responsible for overseeing the papermakers and board makers industry – and is being kept busy. 'I have not had such full days, so much business, so much waiting still to be done at day's end in all my time before,' he moans in January.

Kildoran Road facing the west

Outside the diaries, time passes, not least marked by the death of Winston Churchill at the age of ninety. 'Sir W. Churchill's lying-in-state continues to attract very great crowds of people to pass the catafalque in Westminster Hall, despite bitter winds, sleet and a very long wait in the long queue,' Mr Lucas writes in January 1965. But, as ever, the diary entries dwell more on his emotions, thoughts and feelings, than great moments of state importance.

We've seen how his feelings for Peter cooled over the course of the previous year, as the extent of his former paramour's crimes became apparent.

24 May 1964 (Sunday):

This evening, the iridescent soap-bubble love that has blown for six weeks past collapsed. I was talking to Irish Johnnie on his board and, somehow, I can't recall how the conversation came round to a point at which he said, 'I've rolled [robbed] *hundreds of clients. Yes, hundreds' and recounted how he'd been driven to Bray one evening, 'and on the way back,* [the man] *stopped the car and said he had to make a phone call. He'd left his wallet in the car, and it must have had £150* [£3,750] *in notes in it. I made a mistake there. I only took two fivers* [£10 = £250], *out of the whole lot.' This came as a most horrible shock to me – evidently his 'I've never betrayed anyone' in the Pronto when I first saw him this year was as untrue as 'no one gets hurt' about the stolen goods he buys.*

But now, perhaps fortunately, Mr Lucas has his eye on someone new. John Joyce – 'a former boy soprano [who] now has a rather good tenor voice' – has returned from Glassilaun in West Ireland, famed for its beautiful white sandy beach, and is moving into Mr Lucas's life in more ways than one.

9 January 1965 (Saturday):

Up at 4.30 and out before 6 in the darkness of a mild January morning to meet John Joyce at Euston. He arrived at 7.25 pretty tired after the journey from his home at Glassilaun that began at 8 o'clock yesterday morning. I took John and his heavy case to my flat. After some chat, he went to bed (in my bed, as the other one has been unused for so long), slept for three hours till 1 o'clock and, after some records played and coffee, went down to Croydon by bus leading me to reflect on his attractive qualities, and to recognize with some alarm that it is I who am developing a tendresse for him.

Joyce first features in the diaries a year earlier when Mr Lucas pops into Ward's Irish House for his usual half-pint of ale. The bar is still notorious today – although long closed. Journalist and author Peter Popham, writing in the *Independent* in 1994, sums up Ward's 'appeal' perfectly. 'It all went wrong when they closed down Ward's Irish House in the 1980s: the big, dingy, labyrinthine pub in the bowels of the London Pavilion, with zinc counters, Dublin standard Guinness, gruffly amiable service. Underground, it was a sort of sanctuary, a club for the unclubbable. Nothing like that left now.'[1]

Mr Lucas was a regular there throughout the sixties.

8 May 1964 (Friday):

In 'Ward's', we met a pleasant young man called John Joyce, a countryman of Terry Sweeney's, who is a plasterer living at Bromley and gay. It transpired that he knew Nipper Wales, the barman in the 'Music Box', and once had sex with him. Frank Brady was rather épris with the young man and eventually went off to the 'Huntsman' with him.

And with Peter replaced by Joyce for now, life continues easily, and passion grows for the lad soon to be in the spare room.

11 January 1965 (Monday):

Full of thoughts of John Joyce tonight. I'm beginning to fall in love again, I think.

Things move quickly, even to the extent of the usually solitary Mr Lucas inviting Joyce to move in with him.

15 January 1965 (Friday):

To meet John Joyce in 'Charlotte's Bar'. I had been feeling a good deal of anxiety, wondering how he'd take the suggestion he should take a room in my flat and wondering, too, if, once again, I am letting desire outrun discretion and giving up my cosy seclusion for the sake of a passing fancy.

Joyce, a somewhat innocent young man, is oblivious to Mr Lucas's feelings towards him, happily bringing back other men to the flat and gleefully hinting at the horrors of a man in his late thirties sharing a flat with a man in his twenties.

21 February 1965 (Sunday):

For once, John was up after me and got his overnight bedmate out very unceremoniously. The poor man had to wash under the bathroom geyser and was not permitted to come into my sitting room at all. Over lunch, John described him as 'boring' and said it had been a frustrating night, even though he had buggered this nervous, rather gauche Southampton man twice with the man's nervous grunts and lip noises, 'It was like sleeping with a horse,' he commented.

Even on his best behaviour, though, Mr Lucas was never going to find it easy to live with someone after so long on his own. And so the arguments start.

21 February 1965 (Sunday):

Petulant ill-temper, childish emotions, fluid and shallow and an egocentric fickleness seem to characterize pretty well all the younger homosexuals I know.

Joyce remains on the scene for several months before, perhaps inevitably, falling out with Mr Lucas and being asked to leave.

He pops up occasionally in the later diaries, but mainly as the target of simmering resentment from Mr Lucas for supposedly abusing his hospitality – or, more evidently, just being a terrible house guest.

So far, so comic – and so harmless. But there is danger brewing outside this attempt at cosy domesticity. Mr Lucas takes up the tale of the Krays on 8 January 1965, scratchily making notes in his usual A6 Challenger notebook. At that point, he is broadly sympathetic to the Krays, seeing them as apex predators ensuring some sort of order in the wilds of the capital's rundown eastern boroughs.

8 January 1965 (Friday):

I see that the two Kray brothers, who were concerned in the Boothby affair last summer, are taken up and charged with demanding money by threats. This sounds bad, but I suspect they've merely been squeezing 'protection money' out of club proprietors and such like vampires feeding on ghouls. I believe they've made some generous gifts to charity from their takings. And in any case, one must feel sympathy for anyone shopped by the Daily Mirror.

The Krays may have been 'shopped' by the tabloid, but it would prove a costly mistake for the paper. On 12 July 1964, the *Sunday Mirror* – sister paper of the *Daily Mirror* and one of Britain's top-selling newspapers with a readership of more than five million – had splashed with the headline 'Peer and a Gangster: Yard Inquiry'. 'A top-level Scotland Yard investigation into the alleged homosexual relationship between a prominent peer and a leading thug in the London underworld has been ordered by Metropolitan Police Commissioner Sir Joseph Simpson,' wrote reporter Norman Lucas.[2]

The *Sunday Mirror* was at the forefront of many of the homo hysteria stories in the tabloid press at the time. The previous year, when the paper had changed its name from the *Sunday Pictorial*, it ran a particularly notorious two-page spread still shared regularly on X, formerly Twitter, today headlined: 'How To Spot A Possible Homo', complete with a list of the signs to watch out for in a possible gay man, including 'a fondness for the theatre' and 'an unnaturally strong affection for his mother'.[3] Unsurprisingly, the Kray twins' trial, with its air of menace and hint of homosexuality – Mr Lucas writes that even then rumours swirled about Ronnie Kray's sexuality – was pure catnip for the popular papers of the time.

While the *Sunday Mirror*'s journalism was undoubtedly homophobic, their reporting was spot on. Lord Boothby, a former M.P. and parliamentary private secretary to Churchill, had indeed consorted – or, let's be more accurate here, attended sex parties – with the Krays. According to a 2015 BBC report, quoting declassified MI5 files, concerns over Boothby's connections to the Krays went right to the very top:

An association between Conservative peer Robert Boothby and London gangster Ronnie Kray was the subject of an MI5 investigation, documents have revealed. The men went to 'homosexual parties' together and were 'hunters' of young men, declassified MI5 files claim. Allegations in 1964 about the pair's relationship caused such concern within Downing Street that the then head of MI5 was summoned to the Home Office. The government feared a scandal greater than the so-called Profumo Affair.[4]

Neither the peer nor the gangster – Ronnie, in this instance – were named in the front-page story. But in a pre-emptive strike, Boothby gave an interview to *The Times* in which he denied he was homosexual and explained he had only met Ronnie Kray on several occasions for 'business', a wonderfully loaded term.

Boothby sued the *Sunday Mirror* for libel, with the paper eventually forced to pay £50,000 in damages – more than a million pounds today – alongside printing a grovelling apology that also named Ronnie as the Krays had been threatening the journalists involved:

We now wish to apologize to Mr Ronald Kray, whom some people identified as the other person concerned, and to state that the allegations contained in our reports were without foundation. We express our regret to Mr Ronald Kray for the embarrassment and distress our reports caused to him.[5]

The case was indicative of how homosexuality was seen at the time, and of how the Establishment moved to protect its own. The evidence was all there, particularly one notorious photograph of Lord Boothby, Ronnie Kray and Boothby's chauffeur and then lover, the rather pale-faced and scrawny Leslie Holt (who would die fifteen years later after an ill-fated operation to remove a verruca on his big toe). Boothby knows he's been rumbled, suspicion and fear leaking out of his drink-sodden face; Ronnie, looking straight to camera, is arrogant and confident: he knows the value of a photograph with an English peer.

This is how the Krays operated – and how their criminal enterprises were able to flourish so successfully throughout the sixties. Despite the efforts of the police – some of whom were on the Kray payroll – the twins in the early and mid-sixties were too close to power to suffer more than the occasional slap on the wrist. That would change as the decade approached its end, but for the time being the Krays are untouchable.

The 1965 trial in which Peter was called as a defence witness stemmed from an attempt by the twins to strong-arm their way into part-owning the Hideaway Club in London's West End. It had been opened the year before by baronet's son and general sleazeball-about-town, Hew McCowan – sometimes also known as Hugh McGowan – in Soho's Gerrard Street. In the fifties and sixties, the street was at the heart of the capital's hopping underground scene, home to the West End Jazz Club in the basement of number 44 where 'beatniks, Soho layabouts and art school students' took part in the first 'all-night raves', according to legendary jazz musician and Soho barfly George Melly.[6]

McCowan needed investors for his new venture at number 16 and brought in the Krays to provide doormen for the club in return for a stake in the venture. Reports suggest McCowan had initially offered them a sizeable slice of the club in return for the bouncers, but later reneged on the deal – leading the Krays to ramp up their threats. Mr Lucas picks up the thread in his diary in March 1965.

7 March 1965 (Sunday):

The Mr 'M.' whom the Krays are charged with demanding money from is in fact the Hugh McGowan I've heard so much about in the past three or four years, and whom I must have seen, but certainly don't know even by sight. This McGowan is said to be very rich, youngish, homosexual, promiscuous and was a member (some said owner) of the Music Box club. The club involved in the present trial is The Hideaway in Gerrard Street, a basement that in essentials is the same as the Huntsman or the Tiptoe [two other gay clubs of the time]. *This McGowan bears no very good reputation and is an associate of thugs and shady fellows, though himself a man of good family. My sympathies remain with the Kray twins – 'a couple of steamers', as* [my friend] *Noel Ryan called them. I hope they get off.*

As yet, Mr Lucas is the passive observer, devouring the accounts in the papers and soaking up gossip in the bars, keen to hear how his former love, Peter, is associated with these thugs. Indeed, all of gay London is alive with rumours about the upcoming trial, with almost everyone our diarist meets keen to either give their take or stake their claim to knowing the protagonists.

9 March 1965 (Tuesday):

At lunchtime, as I was passing through the 'Dilly underground, a young man beckoned me and with a great air of importance confided that he was 'a witness for Hugh McGowan in the Kray case', a witness apparently to the fracas in the Hideaway that is the not very solid foundation of the charge. He told me there were five defence and five prosecution witnesses. I was a little sceptical of course, but he may be telling the truth. He was certainly right in saying that the Krays are being tried before the Recorder of London [most senior circuit judge at the Central Crown Criminal Court].

A better theory, posited by Mr Lucas himself, is that the police – and the *Sunday Mirror* – were looking for revenge on the Krays after the Boothby debacle the previous year, and had persuaded McCowan to testify against them. 'My own opinion is that quite possibly the libel action brought last summer by the Krays against the *Daily Mirror* owners and not yet heard, lies behind this attempt to discredit and jail them on this hypothesis, Mr M. is as much a willing tool – no more – as the police.'

He is incorrect in presuming that the Krays were suing the *Mirror*, though there were many reports that they had threatened journalists. But while this would seem a relatively easy case for the prosecution – the Crown versus two well-known thugs – the problem is the Honourable Hew Cargill McCowan himself. Just how believable or trustworthy a character is he? Mr Lucas and others have their doubts.

10 March 1965 (Wednesday):

This evening in Forte's at Charing Cross, a chat with Ian, a young man who has been around for quite a while now and, from being street trader and magazine stall holder and one of the rent boys of the Square, has passed to being an usher at the Dominion cinema. He says he knows Hugh McGowan well and stayed with him in Jersey. He thinks that wealth has bred an extreme arrogance in the man (though, of course, these aren't the words he expressed his opinion in) and brought him to prosecute the Krays for some undisclosed motive. 'I don't suppose any of it really happened,' he added. 'McGowan is well within the law,' he said,* which accounts, no doubt, for their being refused bail for three months while the police dredged around for more evidence and apparently got none.

---

* I'm interpreting this in the sense that Mr L. means McGowan/McCowan is a party to the police action, rather than acting legally.

The Honourable Hew McCowan, in Mr Lucas's eyes, is flashy and common, despite his aristocratic pedigree. 'A man who dispenses five-pound notes in "Ward's Irish House" like Lady Bountiful and will get a lad who attracts him with an open bid of a "40-guinea Savile Row suit" is a crapulous vulgarian for whom one can feel little but distaste,' he writes, the disdain dripping off the page.

But there is a flash of the danger underpinning the case, not least for the main witness for the prosecution. Should the Krays win, McCowan had better get out of town and pronto. The twins' reputation for extreme violence was well known even then, ramped up by the first appearance of Peter in court. To the delight of the tabloids, Peter takes the witness stand with a large bandage on his face, having been the victim of a knife attack several nights earlier.

Peter's ravaged appearance is seized upon with glee by one of the red tops, which splashes with the headline '"Slashed man" shown to witness at Kray trial'. Peter is being set up for his future 'career' as a tabloid darling, the go-to gangster for the popular papers. The story continues:

Another man called into court for identification purposes was Peter – whom [manager of the Hideaway Club] *Mr Vaughan said he knew as Johnny. Mr Paul Wrightson Q. C., defending Reginald Kray, asked Mr Vaughan: 'Did McCowan ever tell you what had happened to Johnny?' Mr Vaughan replied: 'McCowan never told me.' 'Have you heard, in fact, that Johnny was slashed one night?' – 'Yes.'*

Mr Lucas is shocked, but also suspicious. Are Peter's injuries connected to the trial or simply the result of his criminal past catching up with him, he asks.

3 March 1965 (Wednesday):

I was surprised to see in this morning's paper a short news item saying that ex-nightclub owner Peter was pounced on when he returned to the Lyle Street flat last night, tied up and gagged and then cut with a razor. My first thought was that Nemesis had called on him again, and that he was paying with interest for past roguery.

'Ex-nightclub owner is an imaginative way of describing an employee of the Tiptoe café,' scoffs Mr Lucas. 'Probably he telephoned the story himself [...] and will get a couple of guineas for it.'

At this point, Peter is a jumped-up barman, having graduated from his postcard stall on Piccadilly Circus. This is almost certainly how he came across the Krays in the first place. The stall doubled as a means for Peter to meet fellow rollers and housebreakers in need of fencing stolen goods. Mr Lucas's diaries show that this was inordinately common. 'The Tiptoe Club is closed and no wonder, with one of its co-owners, Joe Cook, arrested for receiving and the stolen goods including a safe and a television set,' he writes in January 1965. A chance encounter with Peter a few nights after his first appearance at the trial leads to more questions – not least about Mr Lucas's

Polaroid camera that had gone missing from the young Irishman's room in January during a supposed robbery. The fresh-faced man Mr Lucas met in 1960 is long gone.

14 March 1965 (Sunday):

[Peter] looked rather grey in the face, had a plaster on his left cheek and seems to have lost another tooth. He was in fairly good spirits, though, and promised to phone me later. He did and our conversation was, on his side, so cordial and friendly, but I begin to doubt it if he has stolen the camera after all. He says he's not only been cut to deter him from giving evidence for the defence, but £40 [£710] worth of damage was done on Friday night to the counter and display stand of his café in the Roman Road at Bethnal Green.

Most people would be content to watch the trial unfold from afar, picking up gossip in bars and happy to criticize newspaper coverage. But Mr Lucas, driven as much by interest in the trial as lingering love for Peter, attempts to be in the courtroom when Peter is giving evidence – although not with much luck on his first attempt.

15 March 1965 (Monday):

Away from the office for most of the afternoon to hear something of the trial, and perhaps see Peter in the witness

> *box. So I would have had not a slack-faced Irishman in a soft hat and two hard-faced Irishwomen of the embezzling manageress type forced their way ahead of me as the queue was letting in and took the last vacant seats in court number two. I had to sit for a while in court three where the common sergeant was trying five men for showing obscene films, and then went out and up to the hall of the Old Bailey.*

Where, fortunately for us, he bumps into Peter once more in the corridor.

> *Here, as I was looking at the list, Peter tapped me on the shoulder, took me down to the Old Bailey cafeteria, about the only human normal place in the whole ghastly pile, and over coffee chatted away with five gins inside him. He remarked that 'there's a lot of making up on both sides, and I'm contributing my little bit too'. The police have called at his former postcard stand where Frank Stack is selling cards as a change for coffee club-running, and said that, 'If Irish Johnnie ever comes back here, he will be inside at Savile Row* [police station] *in thirty seconds.' They are not at all pleased with him for giving evidence on the Krays' behalf (the two brothers do, no doubt, squeeze protection money out of the club owners, but of course the police with their 'club raids' and the like are little better). He thinks that the twins will be acquitted, as I do, unless Carl Aarvold* [senior judge at the CCC] *is more persuasive with the jury than the prosecution evidence can be.*

The Krays and the police for Mr Lucas, and many other gay and bisexual men of the time, were not at the moral polar opposites they might have been for his straight contemporaries. For many queer men – and the few exceptionally brave trans women – the police were very much the enemy; criminalized due to their sexuality or gender identity, one can understand the sympathy and perhaps greater understanding they had for fellow outlaws such as the Krays. The diaries are full of poignant tales of lives ruined, but this is a particularly affecting example; the image of a forlorn Anthony Kelly, in the dock in last night's blue dress, brings angry tears to my eyes.

30 May 1964 (Saturday):

Two pansy queens were given six months in gaol by Barraclough the magistrate for 'perfectly appalling public behaviour'. They had been soliciting in female dress, presumably to perform fellatio or masturbation on men who thought they were girls and would have gone away quite satisfied. One, Anthony Kelly, aged twenty-one, was still in blue frock and nylons and looked more girl than youth. The other, Leslie Ward, aged twenty-five, was in male clothes and is in fact a queen I have spoken to when he was in [Mr Lucas's friend] *Vivian McCormack's company.*

Back at the Old Bailey, Mr Lucas is taking a risk by associating with Peter so openly – one that he is aware of and one that will become more apparent and much riskier as the trial progresses. 'I hope that my conversation with Peter at the CCC was not noticed by any henchmen of either gang,' he writes. 'I should intensely dislike being held accountable for Peter's appearance or non-appearance!' We are left in no doubt as to what that exclamation mark means. The Krays were already notorious for leaving a trail of bodies across the East End, ensuring there were no onlookers who could live to have their day in the witness stand. As an acquaintance of Mr Lucas – 'Ray, the socialist speaker' – tells him over tea in the Pronto as the trial continues, 'They're not nice people – they can put petrol bombs in your flat.' But despite his misgivings – and rising concerns for his own safety – loyalty to friends comes first and, the following day, he finally makes it into court for Peter's appearance for the defence.

16 March 1965 (Tuesday):

I was able to get into number two court this morning, and though one can't see the witness box at all, and the dock only with difficulty, I heard all... Then came Auerbach, a young stammering and very muddled solicitor, who was clear enough in his recollection of a meeting with McCowan and young Vaughan, who was the manager of the Hideaway Club, at which McCowan had been so keen to get the Krays to organize and launch a gambling annex, that he brushed aside the solicitor's objections to the uncertainty of the lease. This was about all he was clear on and fumbled and floundered very much on all other matters. Still the general impression he left was an eager McCowan anxious to get his new club on a profitable basis and willing to have the Krays as his partners with their expertise in running a casino.

At the heart of Mr Lucas's concern is his love for Peter, but he is also fully aware that he is not alone in his pursuit. He has a much wealthier competitor for Peter's affections: a rich Scottish businessman called Colonel Davidson. This connection worries our diarist, as it represents another instance of how Peter's activities are encroaching ever closer upon Mr Lucas's professional life.

14 March 1965 (Sunday):

It is surprising how one's official and emotional lives can interlock in unexpected places. For weeks past, I've been working on the brief and speech notes for the President of the Board of Trade's attendance at the annual dinner of the British Paper and Board Makers Association (BPBMA) on Thursday at which the new president, a rich Scottish paper mill owner, Colonel Davidson, will be installed. I had wondered if this would possibly be the same Peter Davidson that is Peter's patron host at the Mirabelle, partner in Champagne drinking at the Savoy and so on. And tonight, a couple of questions on the telephone confirmed that he is and has mentioned his new office to Peter. This should add piquancy to my official dealings with the BPBMA.

Piquancy indeed. Colonel Davidson was the owner of Mugiemoss Paper Mill, based just outside Aberdeen until it closed in 2005. Having served in North Africa and Italy during the Second World War, in 1961 Davidson became Deputy Lieutenant – or the deputy representative of the British Crown – for Aberdeenshire in eastern Scotland. He had also fallen hard for Peter's charms.

'The retired lieutenant colonel has property in Aberdeenshire and entertains him lavishly,' Mr Lucas writes, with more than a slight air of jealousy. 'He has opened an account for him at Barclays on the Strand with a handsome initial deposit and is talking of buying an apartment house to provide the young man with a home and income.' As the trial progresses, Peter is increasingly worried about losing this lucrative meal ticket, particularly when the tabloids pick up on his previous criminal record for blackmail.

17 March 1965 (Wednesday):

Two papers carried reports of Peter's evidence, the former under the headline, 'Witness for the Kray brothers admits blackmail offence'; the latter saying, 'he admitted having previous convictions, including one for blackmail'. Newspapers have to condense the word-for-word accounts of what is said, and one could not reasonably expect Peter's indignant rejection of the statement that he had been convicted of 'blackmail' to be printed in extenso, but it's a pity, all the same, that this affair should suddenly come to life after three years. I hope that Colonel Davidson doesn't get to hear of it.

Which, of course, he does. 'I don't suppose he'll speak to me again,' Peter wails on the phone to Mr Lucas later that evening. But there are more pressing matters afoot for our mild-mannered civil servant, not least the extent to which he is prepared to put his professional life on the line for the sake of his ongoing friendship with Peter. Most commentators had expected a speedy resolution to the trial, an acquittal after simply half an hour's deliberation. But instead, the jury is split, returning for a second and third time to admit they can't reach a verdict. 'Everyone in the public gallery with me was surprised and one or two were angry at this most unexpected end to the nine-day trial,' Mr Lucas writes. But as a result, Peter's testimony is thrown into doubt – mainly as it was a pack of lies to start off with.

25 March 1965 (Thursday):

Peter went on to ask about the Music Box club: was it on the ground floor or in the basement, how large it was and so on. I told him and remarked that he seemed to know the club well when he was giving evidence of overhearing Mr McCowan boasting of a forthcoming O.B.E. in it. 'So, I was right on target was I?' he chuckled. 'I was so scared in case he asked me to describe it.' So that's one piece of embroidery identified – a very convincing artful piece it was too. There's no denying my fondness for Peter in spite of all I know of him, including perjury.

The messy end of the trial outrages both the police and the tabloids and Peter is being lined up to be the scapegoat.

4 April 1965 (Sunday):

When I phoned Peter this afternoon, he sounded a little worried. And with some reason, if it's true that Earle,

> *East and Garrett, three reporters from the* People *and the* News of the World, *have called on him and tried to persuade him into making a statement that he'd been forced by threats to give his evidence at the CCC. When he refused they threatened to 'get you two years'; and the photographer with them took pictures of both the café and the proprietor.*

Yet despite the additional press scrutiny, Peter continues his cosy relationship with the Krays, telling Mr Lucas two days later that he was 'in good spirits and said he had dinner last night with the Krays' family'. But the calm was not to last. On 10 April, 'the two reporters who threatened Peter last week, may be as good as their word. He telephoned me this afternoon to say that he was going to be arrested for perjury, adding that there was a piece about him in today's *Daily Mirror*, and a photograph in later editions.' Panicking, Peter turns to Mr Lucas for help.

12 April 1965 (Monday):

> [Peter] *tells me that, according to Devlin, of the firm of solicitors advising him, his only chance of getting out of a charge of attempting subornation of perjury is to show* [how one of the prosecution witnesses] *had been influenced by Mr Hew McCowan. So, to my horror and dismay, he asked me if I'd make a statement that I saw the two of them in deep conversation one Sunday night in 'Ward's', three weeks ago.*

Mr Lucas starts to see his professional life slipping away from him: the price of getting too close to Peter and his associates. 'I don't want to be dragged into it,' he writes, the terror evident from the scrawled words of that day's diary entry. 'Apart from the disagreeableness of giving evidence for the defence, there's the glare of newspaper publicity to fear. Even a short paragraph about Mr George Lucas, a civil servant, would be pretty embarrassing, pretty damaging...' Mr Lucas can see what the tabloids would do to him.

12 April 1965 (Monday):

There's worse to fear that [reporters] *Gabbert and his fellow ghoul East might pounce on the chance of yet another 'official scandal' story and do an article on 'twilight man is still in government department' with much horror and dismay that a civil servant who frequents the West End haunts of male perverts, known thieves and male prostitutes – and was dismissed from the army in 1950 for an indecent offence – is still in government service. I could almost write the article myself.*

Mr Lucas is still scarred by that dismissal and well aware that it would not only be the Board of Trade that would be furious.

There is, too, the faint possibility of Mr Hew McCowan's deciding that someone so often around the West End, who dared to get in his way and give evidence for an enemy of his, should be taught a lesson. I don't relish the thought of a razor slash or a beating up or a petrol bomb through the Hemsworths' front window.

The tabloids have also done a number on Peter. His lies in the witness box were easily shredded by journalists looking into the case.

[Peter] gave evidence for the defence in the first trial. He appeared in court with a large plaster on his left cheek. He said four thugs had broken into his home in Lisle Street, Soho, in the early hours of one morning and beaten and slashed him because he refused to give McCowan certain information connected with the police. Police could find no evidence of any forcible entry at the Lisle Street address. Today, we can reveal why [Peter] concocted the story. [Peter] hoped to bring a private action against McCowan after the Kray trial and claim damages for the attack. In fact, he approached a man named Raymond Jennings and asked him to give false evidence to support his claim.

With the focus growing on Peter – one paper runs a photograph of him on its front page – Mr Lucas is in turmoil. As he paces around Trafalgar Square over the next few days, desperately trying to think of ways to say no to Peter, he sees McCowan 'prowling about in a fawn overcoat, darting a gorgon glare at me'. Peter himself is attacked again, phoning

Mr Lucas at 1 a.m. one night to tell him that 'two bricks were just thrown through the window of his café' in the East End. Danger is everywhere – from the police, the tabloids, Hew McCowan and last but certainly not least, the Krays – and Mr Lucas is caught in the middle. And then, to compound an already dire situation, Peter accuses Mr Lucas of writing to Colonel Davidson with the details of Peter's sordid past. The colonel had planned to buy the young Irishman a bar in a small village near Dumfries, if we believe everything that Peter tells Mr Lucas, but that is now firmly off.

2 September 1965 (Thursday):

The repeated shrill buzzing of the doorbell got me out of bed this morning and Peter pushed past me and was up the stairs and sitting in my armchair in an instant. Angrily, with an evil look, he said I had been telling people he had stolen things from me and robbed my gas meter, so some 'camp young slag' on the Square had repeated to him. Someone had told the police where he was living and they'd come yesterday, 'turned the gaff over, looking for a ring', and got him turned out. Nobody knew where he was living except me. And someone had written to Colonel Davidson at his private address telling him something – what, he didn't know – that caused the colonel to say it was too much of a risk to have anything more to do with him. Nobody except me knew Colonel D.'s home address at Kinellan. Someone, too, had written about [Peter] *to his mother, and nobody but me knew his own home address. I was a good deal staggered.*

Mr Lucas knows Peter is dangerous, but this is the first time that he has felt physically afraid of him. 'I had a sick feeling that it is perfectly possible that, behind that soft voice and sweet smile and game manner, I may be dealing with a cold unscrupulous mind without warmth or pity,' he had written earlier in the year. But now he is starting to realize he is dealing with a psychopath and, as we move deeper into the decade, the obsessional nature of Mr Lucas's feelings for Peter will start to unravel once more as we've seen, giving way to feelings of fear and loathing – and ever-present danger. For now, life must go on – and Mr Lucas's diary is his only friend, the only place he can confide his fears while presenting an unflappable face at work. Like many gay men of the times, Mr Lucas is forced to live a lie.

7 September 1965 (Tuesday):

Who at the office, seeing but his public face, the sharp-tongued talkative official of humorous speech with ready chuckle and busy pen, would guess that Mr Lucas about Town or going home wearing his private face is this nervy terror-haunted person imperfectly masking fear with the front of genial courtesy?

The trial ends in a rather scandalous acquittal for Ronnie and

Reggie, both of whom were guilty as hell. It would be four years until they were finally jailed following what the *Guardian* called 'the longest murder hearing in British criminal history':

> *The verdicts, all of which were unanimous, were in order of declaration: Ronald Kray (34), of Bunhill Row, Islington, guilty of the murders of Jack 'The Hat' McVitie, a bookmaster's clerk, in a Hackney flat in October 1967, and of the murder of George Cornell in the Blind Beggar public house, Whitechapel, in March 1966. Ronald's twin Reginald Kray, guilty of murdering McVitie and of being an accessory after the fact to Cornell's murder.*

As a witness for the defence at the first trial in 1965, Peter has cemented his place in the Firm, but, as far as we know, avoided further prosecution for perjury. The Krays were the main target for the authorities at that point, leading up to their eventual arrest and jail four years later. But Mr Lucas, not someone I'd describe as naturally resilient, does carry on – and finds life beyond Peter in the bars and clubs at the time.

8

Out on the Scene

LONDON'S QUEER SCENE has changed beyond all recognition since Mr Lucas's heydays of the fifties and sixties. The nineties saw Soho flourishing once more as the centre of queer British life. Almost thirty new venues opened over the decade, and Old Compton Street became a mecca for gay people, not just those in London but from around the country.

Today, most of those bars and clubs have closed. The sexy rough edges of the scene I knew and loved in the nineties have been smoothed by neon kiss signs and £14 margaritas. Dating apps such as Grindr or HER have further removed the 'need' for queer-only spaces. A 2017 report from UCL Urban Laboratory revealed that 'since 2006, the number of LGBTQ+ venues in London has fallen from 125 to 53, a net loss of 58 per cent of venues'.[1] The research, which looked at the overall number of bars and clubs in the capital from 1986 to 2016, showed that the fall-off in LGBTQ+ spaces was markedly higher than for general nightlife venues. The authors' figures show that, between 2005 and 2015, the number of UK clubs declined by 44 per cent, and between 2007 and 2016, 35 per cent of London grassroots venues closed. A comparable statistic for UK pubs shows that 25 per cent closed over fifteen years to 2016.

But to be fair, I have happily been part of that move into the mainstream and remain a gleeful part of it. Writing this book is to understand that my experiences are only a small part of a much longer and richer history that goes far beyond my bar-hopping years – and indeed those of Mr Lucas. It is not so much a lament for a lost queer London as a celebration of a scene evolving and changing.

Mr Lucas's world revolved around the Golden Lion – or, as he would refer to it in his diaries (along with every other name of a pub), the 'Golden Lion' – always in quote marks.

The bar, first opened in 1875, is situated neatly in the heart of Soho – the centre of Mr Lucas's post-work life. Just off the main drag, the Golden Lion is an unprepossessing pub compacted over two floors. Today, the layout remains pretty much as it was sixty years ago. As you enter, there is a short staircase on your left, leading to the upstairs seated area, with almost ten tables arranged neatly across the floor.

Downstairs, several free-standing tables punctuate the space in front of the bar, which curls round to a nook on the left – the perfect place, slightly away from the crowd, for Mr Lucas and his fellow barfly and frenemy, the incorrigible Mr Niece, to sit and entertain the latest array of sailors and soldiers, all out to make £3 (about £70 in today's money) to take their girlfriends out later that evening or the following day. By the late sixties, however, the inimitable Mr Niece is getting on in years and the evenings don't always go the way they are intended to.

8 February 1969 (Saturday):

Mr Niece spent a long while shilly-shallying outside the 'Golden Lion' – his sight is grown so bad, the tall guardsman he'd meant to take home had gone while the old gentleman's eyes were fastened on another he mistook for the first one; the lance-sergeant hanging about to be hired did not please him as a substitute, and at last he made off on his own.

The Golden Lion is no longer a specifically 'gay bar' – or queer bar, in today's more inclusive language – but when I popped in one recent Friday night before heading to see *Mother Goose*, a Christmas pantomime starring Sir Ian McKellen in the title role (yes, it was a very gay night), there was a very beautiful man – or perhaps non-binary person – at the bar with rather gorgeous glittery eye make-up and ravishingly well-painted fingernails. Soho might have lost the old demarcations between straight and gay, but it certainly remains very queer – whichever pub, café or restaurant you might happen to wander into.

Here's the Welsh painter, novelist and journalist Molly Parkin, herself a noted Soho habitué of the sixties and seventies, talking to the *Guardian* in 2015:

One time [the renowned British artist Francis Bacon] *took me to the Golden Lion in Dean Street. Homosexuality was still illegal at that time, but this was the place all the gay boys would go to when they arrived in London to meet kindred spirits. I remember Francis throwing all these £5 notes into the air and all the boys were scrambling for them, shouting: 'Francis, Francis!' I've never seen such adoration.*[2]

The Golden Lion also has a darker history. As Bill Waddell details in *The Black Museum: New Scotland Yard*, it was the haunt of serial killer Dennis Nilsen who is thought to have killed fifteen gay men in the early eighties, many of them picked up in Mr Lucas's favourite pub.[3] Indeed, a few years ago, one could even join a horror walking tour that took in the Golden Lion. Nilsen took the rest of his dark secrets to the grave in 2018, dying at the age of seventy-two at H.M.P. Full Sutton. But, as with the Krays in the sixties, crime and the gay scene were still inextricably linked right up to the eighties.

For Mr Lucas, finishing work at the Board of Trade at around 6 p.m., the Golden Lion was his first destination on his nightly stroll around Soho. But, to begin with, he was not a fan.

20 February 1961 (Monday):

A drink with Willie Davidson this evening in the 'Golden Lion', a gay pub I detest – its atmosphere of sleaziness, brassy coarseness and 'rent' puts my teeth on edge.

In the earlier years of the sixties – Mr Lucas is thirty-four in February 1961 – he does not always have to pay for sex. Most of his hair still in place – or just about – he can still rely on wit and charm to bring men home. Indeed, the 'attractions' of the big city are exactly the opposite for Mr Lucas, still carrying fond memories of frequent and hurried sex in the cottages and Raphael Park. He sees the capital, with its nasty rent-boy pubs and bars, as a corrupting influence.

13 June 1961 (Tuesday):

An evening's argument with Maurice [occasional barfly friend] *on the morality of homosexual acts. This Catholic queen who believes homosexuality is unnatural and homosexual intercourse wrong, yet spends much time chasing young men, is an interesting case. He is forty-two now and until about five years past, though conscious of homosexual inclinations, did not indulge them, but stayed at home with his father, occupying his leisure with carpentry and conversation, the church choir and the cinema. When his father died and he lived on his own, he entered the gay world – and what an introduction to it he had! He went to the 'White Bear' and the 'Golden Lion', meeting rent boys and roughs; and in consequence all his thoughts on homosexuality were tainted by the unsavoury atmosphere of these places as I have told him. He has never known free happy sex one gets in the suburbs, when like-minded people get together. For him, all has been prostituted from the street. It is small wonder he finds his homosexual indulgences troublesome to mind and conscience. I am thankful my own background is so different.*

The action, such as it was, was mainly upstairs at the Golden Lion; veteran LGBTQ+ activist and former seventies and eighties rent boy Julian Hows picks up the thread: '[The first floor was full of] rent boys, long-term drinkers, punters – the West End riff-raff is what I call it,' he told me. 'It was always upstairs, as that was the gayer bit to a certain extent. You could slip upstairs and, once you were up there, you were out of sight to most people. It was almost as though the public of the time wanted that sort of thing to go on upstairs.'

No one I've spoken to can remember Mr Lucas at the Golden Lion. And who, really, is surprised by the fact that the grey, balding civil servant in his dark suit faded softly into the background and out of people's memories? Retired BBC studio operator Martin Hazell was eighteen in 1968, drifting from the Golden Lion to other pubs as London's nascent gay scene took off. 'There were lots of [people like Mr Lucas] and more of the more conservative sort,' he told me. 'The more flamboyant types were very much out of the style of the place. Marble Arch was more full of "ordinary guys".'

The scene at Marble Arch was fading at that point; it had been the main cruising ground in the forties and fifties, awash with guardsmen and their fanciers. 'It may seem paradoxical to suggest that the existence of a benevolent creator might be deduced from the guardsmen at Marble Arch,' writes Mr Lucas in November 1949. 'But the inference seems valid. For could any but a spirit unlimited by time and space design such perfect forms, or any but a benevolent God grant to our eyes the vision of such beauty?'

As the sixties progressed, the social strata started to break down, particularly within the gay world. It was a time when high and low society mingled, and the common denominator of one's sexuality meant that you would rub shoulders with stars of the stage and screen as you ordered your pint or gin and lime. 'I always think of John Gielgud who you would occasionally catch on the scene – and he'd been done for cottaging,' Martin added.

Renowned Shakespearean actor Gielgud, knighted in 1953 for services to the theatre, was caught four months after the announcement of the coronation honours list, cruising for sex in a public lavatory in London. Eventually fined, Gielgud imagined that his career would be over, that the public would disown him. In *Binkie Beaumont: Eminence Grise of the West End Theatre, 1933-1973* biographer Richard Huggett describes fellow actor Sybil Thorndike urging Gielgud to come onstage with her during a production of *A Day by the Sea* in Liverpool soon after the news had come out:

She grabbed him and whispered fiercely, 'Come on, John darling, they won't boo me', and led him firmly on to the stage. To everybody's astonishment and indescribable relief, the audience gave him a standing ovation. They cheered, they applauded, they shouted. The message was quite clear. The English public had always been loyal to its favourites, and this was their chance to show that they didn't care tuppence what he had done in his private life... they loved him and respected him dearly. It was a moment never to be forgotten by those who witnessed it.[4]

There are even times when Mr Lucas writes of pop stars who are alive to this day – ones who cannot be named for obvious reasons – including one who had a song out in 1963 with a rather, shall we say, leading chorus:

30 January 1963 (Wednesday):

There is a charming irony in the latest successful song of that attractive young 'pop-star' [censored]. Called [censored] it has the refrain [censored] which – as the cognoscenti appreciate but his millions of adolescent fans don't – comes very appropriately from the vivacious queen with a fondness for 'butch boys' that [censored] is.

Given the small nature of the scene at the time, everyone knew everyone else's business – this is a tabloid dream made real in pub gossip form.

So many of these stars who make teenage girls swoon – and who are talented young men producing good songs and lively tunes – are gay: [censored], of course, Rock Hudson, the American actor who plays tough 'he-man' roles (and some years ago had a romantic affair with a grenadier in London), Russ Conway, the pianist (a sado-masochist who likes being thrashed and beating the other young man), Frankie Vaughan and so very many others. The impresario Larry Parnes, of whose homosexuality Godfrey Coe told me years ago in Romford, where he and young Mr Parnes had known each other, has grown rich from his 'stable' of young pop-singers... whom he presumably selects on the basis that if a young man appeals to him, he will appeal to the teenage public.

Forgive the censorship, but several of the protagonists from the sixties are still with us – and remain notable public figures. But while awash with gossip and rumour the gay scene might have been, 'people looked after each other', Martin told me. 'They kept an eye on the people who were active and looked out for the ones who had disappeared, who didn't turn out one weekend. Quite a lot of them were civil servants,' he added. At times, I'm sure, that was true. But the scene has always been a place for sniping queens and evil bitches. 'Peter Shaw and Fred Forman were in the Café Roché. I observed how much backbiting is coming from these queens,' writes Mr Lucas in April 1968. 'Fred and Charles Niece phone each other and invite each other to tea – yet their feelings for each other are of dislike, contempt and distrust.'

In essence, though, the crowd at the Golden Lion was Soho in microcosm. Yet even in the early sixties, driven by constant police crackdowns and media hatchet jobs, the LGBTQ+ scene was starting to shrink in on itself. 'Since 1957, the "Bunch of Grapes", the "Standard" and the "Rainbow Corner", all the better-known places of resort, have ceased to exist, as well as various ephemeral backstreet coffee bars,' writes Mr Lucas in July 1961. 'The effect is to mix up the quayside criminal, the rent boys, the military and the rest in one place – at the "Golden Lion" in Dean Street, for example.' The level of casual crime, even by those who worked there, was notable.

25 January 1969 (Saturday):

The 'Golden Lion' none too pleasant – crowded, and with that mean-faced cadging guardsman roving about. Dodging him kept me from any manoeuvre. The young man from Kirkcaldy was here, but Mr Niece was piqued at his casual nod of greeting and took that talkative Cornish guardsman off quite early on. Dr Hughes-Jones related, without any disapproval, a mauvaise histoire of the scrawny old potman, who escorting that drunken old clergyman home (wherever 'home' may be) stole £40 [£825] from his wallet and was chuckling at the old person's failure to remember anything of being escorted home or by whom. Had anyone told me of such roguery, I'd have felt insulted at the implied assent to this behaviour. Hughes-Jones seems to have regarded the tale as nothing, not remarkable.

While Mr Lucas's Soho life mainly revolved around the Golden Lion, he was also regularly seen propping up the bar – with his standard half-pint of ale – at the White Bear and the wonderfully rough Ward's Irish House. Here, Barry McKinley, author of *A Ton of Malice: The Half-Life of an Irish Punk in London* describes the delights of what was a complete and utter dive: 'Ward's was a legendary basement pub. It had once been a public toilet connected to the Underground and the counter was always lined with hard men and rent boys. It was like drinking in a submarine that smelled of porter, pee and pine disinfectant.'[5]

David Parker was a semi-regular at Ward's in the seventies. 'There were a very mixed bunch of people,' he told me with masterful understatement. 'But there was obviously quite a lot of trading [renting] going on there. They got away with it because the police actually never went down. Anything that erupted tended to be contained by virtue of the steep stairs to get up to the surface. It was kind of a controlled explosion whenever it went off.'

It was the type of bar, as Mr Lucas writes in August 1968, where even the straightish barman was potentially for sale. 'We went on to "Ward's", and observed this fetching young barman Pat. He is much engaged in conversation by Lonegan and other homosexual patrons, and though himself entirely heterosexual, is said to have gone home with someone and submitted to his embraces.'

At times, Ward's and other 'gay bars', and I use the quote marks to show that there really weren't any official LGBTQ+ pubs or clubs then, were also too open for Mr Lucas. As a middle-ranking civil servant, he was always aware of the possibility of being exposed and potentially blackmailed. Homosexuality might have been partially legalized in 1967 in England and Wales, but that didn't mean he could be in the slightest bit 'out' at work or to his colleagues.

2 April 1968 (Tuesday):

There was a curious, mildly disgusting episode in 'Ward's' when a tall heavily built spectacled young man that had squeezed himself behind Donnelly at the bar finished his drink and suddenly leaning over enquired – in an Irish voice – 'what brings someone from I.M.3 [a reference to a division within the Board of Trade] *down to "Ward's Irish House"?' and repeated 'I.M.3' several times before going. Though I don't remember his face, he must be someone that was in I.M.3 two years or more ago – and who has presumably left the Board of Trade now. He is an oafish fellow, whoever he is.*

Mr Lucas was not a big drinker; his was more the half-pint of ale or – earlier in the forties and fifties – a gin and lime before bedtime. Any more than that, and he would suffer from 'penile discomfort', something he comes back to time and time again in the diaries as a possible prostatic ailment. Here he is in August 1968: 'Some penile discomfort again tonight, though I supped but half a glass of beer in the "Golden Lion".' But it did mean that his memories were captured with still clear eyes and an unfuggy brain once he was home or very first thing the next morning. The moans about a sore head in the morning are mentioned, but only rarely. There he stood at the end of the bar, half-pint in hand, watching others make fools of themselves while he remained apart and aloof.

Food for Mr Lucas was a utilitarian affair and usually consumed alone. The diaries contain lots of references to him sharing a drink with friends, associates and assorted rent boys, but nothing on dining out with someone like Mr Niece, for example. I can't find a reference to Mr Lucas cooking anything at home other than buttered toast, a favourite comfort food of his particularly when the weather turned cold. 'This cold snowy weather calls for buttered toast,' he writes in February 1969. 'Contrary to what I resolved, I bought a loaf and more Irish butter; the Irish is sweeter and smooth beyond any English or Danish butter.'

For lunch and dinner, our diarist always ate out, perhaps not unusual as he grew up in a household where the domestic chores would have been left to the women. Kathryn Ferry in her book *The 1950s Kitchen* writes of how, 'Cooking was very much women's work, and the kitchen was generally their domain. Even men who enjoyed cooking might do so only in a weekend or evening capacity, away from the regular routine of the family kitchen.'[6]

Ferry goes on to say that 'men were no strangers to the kitchen', but it is highly unlikely that Mr Lucas had a clue as to how to make a simple meal for himself. 'Some men did cook for themselves, especially if they were single or living alone,' she writes. But not Mr Lucas. Although he does look back in 1982, marvelling at just how much these gendered roles were hardwired within him.

6 January 1982 (Wednesday):

Looking back twenty-five years, I am surprised that at turned thirty I should still have believed 'twas necessary to have a woman, aunt or mother, to live in my house and clean and cook for me.

Certainly, the very few meals I ate with him – the soup and fish at the Green Man & French Horn pub whenever we would meet in the West End, rather than at his house – were never ever, and perhaps fortunately for me, cooked by him. His coffee, when I first met him back in 1994, was frankly undrinkable.

6 September 1994 (Tuesday):

Greenhalgh's response to my initial 'would you like a drink?' was that he'd 'love a coffee'... and I was amused to see that, like everyone else I make coffee for, he left it untouched after the first sip.

The Pronto Café and the Trafalgar were where he took lunch and dinner during the sixties. Both are now long gone, neither leaving much of a trace in terms of details of the available menu. But we know from Mr Lucas's diaries that the Pronto was next door to Ward's, both beneath the pavement of Shaftesbury Avenue. But even as a regular at the Pronto, he was never truly at home.

15 January 1961 (Sunday):

The Pronto less pleasant this evening. A horrible pansy queen, with a hard face and a foul mouth, seller of postcards, in there chatting with Ian [an acquaintance]. *One disadvantage of having a queen in the Pronto is that all the repulsive evil queens of the West End tend to come in too.*

12 April 1961 (Wednesday):

The regime of Mr Marks, the manager, has worsened the amenity of the Pronto very much – no rolls prepared at 1.30 p.m.! – and only Gordon actively serving, with the counter and shelf littered with dirty crockery.

Mr Lucas is dining at the Pronto when he hears about the assassination of U.S. president John F. Kennedy, one of the few occasions when the outside world disrupts his very orderly and ordered routine. Yet even the disruption itself is not without its perils.

22 November 1963 (Friday):

Tonight in the Pronto, at about 8.30, I heard from [the manageress] *Mrs Stone the news of President Kennedy's assassination, which I hardly believed at first. In 'Ward's', I perceived a man reading a special edition the* Daily Sketch *was putting out with news of the assassination. An unpleasant incident occurred – one of those incidents that show the savage jungle, the world of violence and thievery and malice that lies beneath the film of civilization in the West End of London. I went out of 'Ward's' to get one of these special editions and was followed by a stocky dark-haired barrel-chested young man that hangs around the 'Dilly and whom I'd seen earlier in the 'White Bear'. He wanted £1 [£25], or else he'd make an accusation: 'It's only your word against mine.' I made some negative-sounding replies and inquired if he knew where the papers were being sold. He tried to persuade me down into the underground to get a paper, and then trotted beside me, now demanding 'half a dollar for a drink, or else I floor you with a right uppercut', flourishing his fist the while. I was as much disgusted as alarmed and simply said, 'Why do you have to carry on in this mean, nasty way?' By now we'd reached the Corner-House in Coventry Street where I struggled into the crowd and so lost him.*

Even inside the Pronto, Mr Lucas is not safe from abuse: 'In Rayner's tonight with Frankie and then on to the Pronto,' he writes in June 1964. 'Desmond Kelly, Dave from the Eros, Frankie and I were chatting when I became aware of a muttered background commentary from a sharp-faced youngish man, and a rather dirty-looking layabout behind me, mostly directed at me, and on the theme of "I hate poufs. Look at that fucking old pouf. That's Queen George works for the government, the fucking old queer".'

One by one, as the decade ticks on, the bars, cafés and clubs start to close – or turn 'straight'. Despite the supposedly liberalizing atmosphere in the run-up to decriminalization, the bars' owners and managers are under increased scrutiny by the police.

9 December 1961 (Saturday):

The persecution continues after a lull in London. At any rate, recently there has been a spate of arrests at two south London meeting places, the cottages of 'Grove Tavern' at Camberwell, and the 'Hanover Arms' at Peckham.

A new manager at the Welsh Harp, for example, spells disaster for its usual clientele.

5 July 1961 (Wednesday):

Gossip tonight with M. Mullen, etc. The 'Welsh Harp' very quiet. There is a new manager in his early forties who is said by various queens to disapprove of the particular amenity of the house. If the man is foolish enough to turn all the guardsmen-fancying queens away, I'm sure his trade will decrease. The guardsmen certainly will. The former manageress, Mrs Howe, a peaky painted woman with blue hair and a mild pansified husband, is installed at the 'Round House', not far away and opposite the 'White Swan', that was pretty gay when Peter Morris and I first came to the Square and is now a dull enough tavern. If the 'Welsh Harp' ceases to play its accustomed tune, it is to be hoped its customers – and their customers – will move to the 'Round House'.

I love that phrase, 'its customers – and their customers'. It sums up neatly the appeal of these types of pubs at the time: one did not pop in only for a drink and one absolutely hoped that one would not leave alone.

5 January 1969 (Sunday):

Mr Niece in the 'Golden Lion' was in talk with the tall baby-faced ex-Welsh Guards young man and another, more rugged of feature but seemingly as amiable. The old gentleman had thought better of his last night's guardsman and gone home alone. They had both wanted to accompany him – and I vividly recalled the two Scots guardsmen that Peter Morris and I picked up in 'Ward's' twelve years ago or so back and were near being rolled by.

Charles Niece, old Mr Niece, is the almost perfect Falstaffian comic foil for Mr Lucas's over-serious Prince Hal. A bawdy, larger-than-life figure – indeed at six foot-something, he is at times an overwhelming presence whom we first meet in March 1961 when Mr Niece is fifty-eight. 'Tonight, I observed stout red-faced Charles Niece – a post office security officer, a good-natured guardsman-chase with a fixation on large penises.' And, it is fair to say, Mr Lucas is fixated on Mr Niece's fixation, returning to it time and time again – here in 1965:

24 January 1965 (Sunday):

Like Charles Niece, Mr Dolphin is a phallomaniac and, like Charles Niece, is engrossed with the size of the penis. Phallomania is, I suppose, comparable to the breast-fixation of large proportions of the heterosexual world, with their gloating contemplation of female mammary development.

Peter Dolphin was a minor actor of the sixties, perhaps better known for becoming the face of many C&A and Marks and Spencer clothing campaigns in the seventies. But, if perhaps little remembered today, he did give rise to a quite spectacularly brilliant headline in the *East Kent Times and Mail*:

PETER DOLPHIN OF DOLPHIN SQUARE GETS A DUCKING – IN THE DOLPHINARIUM

His name is Peter Dolphin. He lives in London's exclusive Dolphin-square. So where-else [sic] *would Peter go when visiting Thanet on Tuesday than the Dolphinarium at the Queen's Hotel, Cliftonville. Dark-haired good-looking Peter, well-known for his TV and film appearances, got a ducking from one of the 'aqua stars' but that didn't stop him appearing in the fashion show at the Winter Gardens organized by Marks and Spencer in aid of the Royal National Lifeboat Institution.*[7]

Mr Niece is a figure of great distaste for Mr Lucas, sometimes 'old Mr Niece'; other times described as 'good-natured and boring', despite the fact – or maybe because – he's one of his closest friends. Yet I wonder just how much of this comes from jealousy. Mr Niece is absolutely driven by his earthy passions – for guardsmen, sailors, you name it – and seems entirely unapologetic and someone who genuinely enjoys life.

26 October 1968 (Saturday):

The 'Golden Lion' extremely crowded. I could not force my way to the bar without more exertion and embarrassment than I cared for, and left again after a brief word with Mr Niece, a little tipsy with a group of guardsmen hanging on to him – tall straight-backed Colin among them, that has not been seen for a good while. I was stung by the greeting, 'Hallo, it's Parson George' from one of this circle of spongers – not a guardsman, this, but the cocky marine that Mr Niece picked up at Southsea.

17 November 1968 (Sunday):

I did not stay long in the 'Golden Lion' – there were no young men of interest, and that odiously camp and vulgar little man, France, the undertaker, was talking so loudly and lubriciously as to discompose an elderly married couple who had strayed in, and on whose departure Mr France did not fail to comment. I find this bad-mannered buffoonery a little less embarrassing when directed against other people than when I am the victim. This little group – Niece, France and others – were distasteful on other grounds, too. It is rather sickening to hear them discussing the 'lovely hairy legs', penis, etc., of Niece's guardsman of last night in so unreticent a fashion.

Very much unlike our morose, introspective diarist, Mr Niece knows how to enjoy himself. Occasionally, the 'professional' jealousy does slip out: 'Mr Niece is a corpulent slow-moving man of sixty-five, with no great intellectual capacity or conversation, and I am twenty-three years his junior, with a livelier and better-furnished mind and a quicker tone,' Mr Lucas writes in April 1968. 'He has an endless supply of satisfactory and safe young men, and I am starved of even those hired and paid for.' And indeed, the diaries abound with tales of Charles Niece on the prowl – and sometimes at Mr Lucas's expense.

15 April 1968 (Easter Monday):

I did not stay long in the 'Golden Lion'. One tall, hard-faced guardsman came over to Niece and chatted awhile, and on leaving suddenly turned, pinched my cheek, hard, and sneered, 'Goodbye Curly'. With the contemptuous condescension of the guardsmen on one side, with the treachery and spite of layabouts and rent boys on the other, I am squeezed indeed.

27 April 1968 (Saturday):

In the 'Golden Lion' this evening I noticed how indiscreetly Mr Niece was behaving, feeling a tall young guardsman's penis through his trousers – the same guardsman that he took home in full uniform some weeks ago, and tried for size in a lighted shop-doorway.

19 January 1969 (Sunday):

Mr Niece was moderately well-pleased with the Kirkcaldy ex-gamekeeper, whose sexually passionate responses included acceptance of tongue-kissing. Yet, because his penis is not as large as Mr Niece likes, the old man was not disposed to have him to bed a second time. I must try to taste his charms as soon as I can.

It's fair to say Mr Lucas was not a fan of big penises – or indeed, as he moves into his late thirties and early forties, that much into penetrative sex. Even in his twenties and thirties, when he was regularly picking up young men and taking them home, Mr Lucas was always – like Sir John Gielgud and many a Shakespearean knight, I'm sure, after him – much keener on a quickie in the local cottage or public loo. The word 'cottaging' is simply one based on semblance: many of the public lavatories of the time looked like little cottages dotted around London and the suburbs. The end of the sixties started to see the closure of many public amenities and, with it, the door closing on a way of life and sex enjoyed by gay and bisexual men for centuries.

31 January 1969 (Friday):

Home by way of the Embankment, where I see the Westminster Council's spoiling of public lavatories goes on. Having spent much money on the indecent bowls and greenish daubed walls now put in Leicester Square and Irving Street and York Place, they have now shut up the Embankment lavatory for the same treatment. The city engineer must be bribed by ceramic bowl makers; I cannot think that any man, not being either bribed or perverted, would spend so much public money on these unnecessary alterations. Putting glass panels in the W.C. closet doors is another fad. One must sit visible in outline through the glass, and the coat hook is so placed one can't drape one's coat across. Still it's encouraging to see graffiti appearing on walls and doors again. I saw 'Besame les cojones, gerl' ['kiss my balls, girl'] *in a Leicester Square closet – some lecherous Spaniard, no doubt. Home, very sleepy to eat buttered toast by the fire.*

Even at the start of the decade, the passing of time is evident as the local London authorities start to crack down on nocturnal activities. In January 1963, Mr Lucas notes how 'the cottage in Dove Mews (where Sir J. Gielgud was caught) is now closed – yet another of our houses gone'. However, as we reach the end of the sixties, Mr Lucas is fully aware of the passage of time and how it brings the destruction of the world he has known so well for decades. In 1968, we can see him already thinking that the end of the scene is near. In July that year, he writes of going on to Ward's, where 'Tommy O'Connor summed up my own feelings in a sentence, "It will be a pity when there's no Ward's or the White Bear or the Pronto. We'll miss them."' In perhaps one of his most moving and memorable passages – worth quoting in full for its elegiac beauty – the passing of time is mixed with the move towards gay liberation and how the expected benefits of partial decriminalization have not come to pass. The piece marks the end of the decade and is Mr Lucas at his most honest, raw and lyrical.

31 December 1969 (Wednesday):

A bitter cold day, powdery snow driven before a biting east wind. Out to dinner at 8 o'clock, with many young fellows on the train bound for the West End to see the New Year. After dinner, I saw very many gathering in Trafalgar Square and the usual street vendors beginning to do a trade in comic hats and squeakers. I was home again by 10.15 p.m. to listen to a watch night service from Bangor. Drank a glass of curacao as Big Ben chimed out 1969 and chimed in 1970. The last years of each decade have been pivotal for me and now 1969 sees me moved into a Clapham Park flat. In those ten years, changes have been many – television is now as much a part of daily life as electric light and its influence, bad. Everywhere is sex, nudity, 'frankness'. All of the old reticences are gone or almost gone and the general mood of the country is one of feverish frivolity. The whole character and spirit of the Wilson administration is implicit in the M.B.E.s given to the sniggering, mannerless Beatles, the O.B.E. for Mary Quant, the fashion designer whose life's ambition is to devise a costume that will enable women to expose their pudenda as they walk and sit. The sexual life of London – the 'gay world' – has changed enormously. When I moved to Brixton, there were four public lavatories around Clapham North; now there are none, no place where the homosexually inclined may indicate their inclination and discover like-minded partners. Marble Arch, once the grand open-air meeting place, is dead, the public houses and coffee bars nearby, demolished; its thronging guardsmen and Irish layabouts vanished. What is left is a few rent boys and a handful of guardsmen in the West End, a few Household Cavalry troopers in a Knightsbridge bar, a gaggle of pansy young men in Earls Court. The legalization of homosexual intercourse in 1967 has been a relief to me personally, but has come at a time when the opportunities of such intercourse are lessening. What, in the fifties, would have been the 'Open Sesame' to a treasure house, has unlocked the door of Mother Hubbard's cupboard.

Now, at the end of the decade, I fear that my capacity for sexual enjoyment is beginning to be withered at its source. I am like someone who has longed to taste the sweet fruits of some orchard, but found the gates locked and keepers patrolling, so that it was only windfalls that came his way, so delicious-sweet that he would sometimes dare dogs and keepers and, poised perilously on the orchard wall, reach in and grasp some apple or plum from the nearest trees. But, at last, after years of squabble and contention, the orchard is thrown open and he passes through the gates to find the trees dying, strangled in mistletoe and ivy, the fruits few, crabbed and sour, or else succulent enough, ripe and exuding juice, but almost tasteless, all the old remembered tang and sweetness gone...

9

The Slow Train to Ireland

THE AIR IS sharp as I join the rush-hour commuters cramming into Euston train station, squeezing past a clutch of committed morning smokers. There is no discernible increase in the police presence, despite a drive-by shooting over the weekend, just yards away from the station's main entrance. Euston is a dank low-slung building punctuated at the front by four limp Union Jacks and a host of dark grey and black air conditioner units. There is ice on the benches and tables in the forecourt on this January morning. Double-decker rows of bicycles arranged on racks opposite the six lanes of Euston Road traffic. As I arrive, traders are just setting up their stalls; artisanal bread kept fresh by the frosty air.

For years, I used to live just round the corner, a few blocks over in Thanet Street in Bloomsbury. But, as a cyclist, I have rarely been to the train or Tube station, preferring to pedal into work rather than suffer the daily commute. Many years ago, the Euston Tap, a pub carved out of one of the two

Victorian gatehouses facing each other as you come into the station, used to be a lesbian bar with a strict women-only entrance policy. But, armed with long eyelashes and a decent hoodie, I used to sneak a drink there sometimes with female friends before it closed in 2008. Looking closer now, I see that the names of destinations, some long lost to travellers from Euston, are carved alphabetically in columns up and down the portico framing the double-height wooden doors: Dewsbury, Dudley, Dublin.

Almost fifty-five years ago, Mr Lucas was also here, making the same journey I'm embarking on today: the train to Holyhead and then a ferry across the Irish Sea. I'd like to say the station remains unchanged, but the history of London's first mainline station, opened in 1837, is a chequered one, spotted by malign municipal planning and general neglect. The Victorian grandeur, crowned by the famous Doric Arch designed by Philip Hardwick, has been lost long ago.

But for Mr Lucas, who had been 'up betimes and left for Euston at 7.30 of this sunny clear morning, arriving at 8.15', the station would have been relatively new, having been rebuilt in 1966 from the remnants of that Victorian engineering success, a modern station for a modern era.

Rather uncannily, I'm also here at 8.15 – almost on the dot – and the morning misery on people's faces as this cold January day starts is evident. Both of us are off to Ireland, Mr Lucas on holiday – and me? Well, I'm going in search of memories, bars lost and pubs still going, and to see if I can track down any memories or traces of the Ireland that Mr

Lucas writes about so acutely: just how much of the lost queer Dublin remains?

Mr Lucas and I are on the train – if more than half a century apart.

10 September 1968 (Tuesday):

The Irish Mail was at platform six and people were passing through the barrier, so I went through at once and found a better seat than I had reserved, with one but elderly woman in the carriage till Crewe, when a young mother and her two alert, well-spoken sons of three and five years came in, and two old women after. The children were active and questioning, but untroublesome and I could observe the passing Cheshire and North Wales scene undisturbed.

I settle in for my three-and-a-half-hour journey with a large camomile tea and a lukewarm pasty. There is frost on the fields as we whizz past the cream-coloured Ovaltine factory in Kings Langley. As we curl into Wales, I start to count the caravans pockmarking the pebble beaches. They remind me of past holidays in Marazion, a little Cornish town famed for St Michael's Mount, the castle home to the St Aubyn family since the seventeenth century. We'd take our cat Kim with us much to my delight as our white Austin Allegro crept at the demanded – my mum was an excessively nervous passenger – 30 miles an hour along the A30.

More memories fizz and bubble up. There's something about three-hour journeys that ruins me. In the early noughties, I worked in Georgia as a TV presenter and travelled frequently when I was based in Batumi, a post-Soviet oil town on the Black Sea and capital of the southwestern region of Adjara. I'd have finished my usual bottle of wine at the Princess Café, a few doors down from the TV station and thought, 'Bugger it', grabbed my passport and hopped a cab to the Turkish border, only a twenty-minute ride up a steep winding mountain pass, dodging roaming cows in the darkness. A quick $10–20 bribe for the Russian border guards to allow me to slip through quickly (alongside the TV station, I also worked for the regional government after all), I'd then slump alcoholically on the back seat of a local taxi for the next three hours as we'd bump our way along the Black Sea to Trabzon and then a flight to Istanbul for the weekend.

Now, as we arrive at Holyhead, my back creaking from spending too little time in the pool this morning during my daily swim, I stagger off the train and head straight to the closest pub. Some things, it has to be said, never change. A dead ringer for the one in *An American Werewolf in London*, an audible hush falls as the door creaks open and I tiptoe nervously, if distinctly gayly, to the bar.

And then, two pints later and a quick dash back to the port, we're off. It is the shuddering, an underfoot tremor, that marks the start of the ferry's three-hour journey; followed by a rattling that shakes the windows and the gin bottles behind the bar. Part of me is excited; more memories of childhood flood back: taking

Brittany Ferries from Plymouth to St Malo in the late seventies and early eighties with my parents and brother, heading for the southwestern tip of France and the cheapest holiday possible.

And then with an almost imperceptible glide, the ferry pulls out of the harbour. The sea is still, unlike many of those Channel crossings my family took more than forty years ago; one particularly memorable voyage during a Force 9 gale. With the ship lolling and lurching, we'd gone to the front to find something to eat – and met lettuce-strewn mayhem, the smell of vomit heavy in the air. Aged six or seven, I was cock-a-hoop, watching the waves splash against the windows as the bow crashed gleefully up and down, up and down.

Today, I sit back with a pint and the *Irish Times*. The boat shimmies and shudders a little more and then settles back into its regulated drift to Dublin, the sun blinding against the sea.

Everyone in the posh bit – the Club Lounge, for which I'd paid an extra £18 – is assertively white and aggressively middle class. I catch the eye of a woman in her early forties, and we smile together, furtively, knowingly. About what, I haven't the faintest clue. The man behind me repeats, 'The point is…' into his mobile phone. 'The point is, the point is…' echoes as we head deeper into the Irish Sea.

10 September 1968 (Tuesday):

Dark clouds and heavy rain set in at Chester, but the sun shone at Holyhead, and I stayed on the deck of the S.S. Cambria for most of a pleasant three-hour crossing of a sun-bright blue and green Irish Sea. I found my usual lunch (put up for me yesterday by Chaudhuri [a waiter in his regular café, the Pronto]*) very acceptable. On this journey, I had more leisure to look about and observe; and noticed that there's but thirty minutes between the last rocky promontory of Wales going out of sight and the first glimpse of Howth appearing, with Ireland's Eye and Lambay close by… at 4 o'clock this was.*

More than fifty years later, the islands remain unchanged, but the view – enhanced in my opinion – is now dotted with hundreds of white swirling wind farms fading fast on the darkening horizon.

Dublin is bitterly cold; snow is forecast. To my frozen hands and nipped ears it feels like minus a billion. Who wouldn't come to Ireland for a gay bar crawl in the middle of what feels like a Siberian winter? As I struggle onto a bus into town, Mr Lucas has settled into his hotel and is already moaning about the food.

> *I had dinner at Moran's Hotel – 6s 6d [£7.02 today] for egg and sausages of more diminutive size than I have seen since my last visit. It is as well there is an abundance of bread and butter to eke out the meal. I was nervous this clear sunny evening, and to my fearful fancy a couple of men hanging round the Burgh Quay lavatory had a villainous cut-throat look. I noticed a tall youngish man in a pink shirt in talk with a man – not a visitor; he reminded me of that ex-guardsman Murray that was at the Pavilion four years ago when Peter reappeared, and that Peter had said Murray had stolen from him. I believed the tale, then.*

Moran's Hotel is no more, a victim of the coronavirus lockdowns I'm told by a woman who comes to the door to ask why I'm taking pictures through the windows of the redbrick four-storey building. I can just see through to the bar, a sign for spirits looks as if it's unchanged since Mr Lucas's stay. Otherwise, the hotel has become a temporary centre for the homeless.

The Migration Policy Institute (MPI) notes that 'net emigration [from Ireland] was particularly high in the "age of mass migration" (1871 to 1926) and in the post-World War

II era (1951 to 1961). Traditional destinations included the United Kingdom, the United States, and Australia.'[1]

London, at the time, was the most popular destination for Irish immigrants; certainly, reading the diaries, it would seem that almost two-thirds of the men who Mr Lucas either met on Trafalgar Square or the 'Dilly were from various parts of Ireland. Emigration, 'caused primarily by Ireland's lagging economic development', according to the MPI, would continue right up until 1996 when Ireland would become the last European Union nation to report net immigration. Ireland's 'Celtic Tiger' economy of the late nineties created jobs as the country saw unemployment plummet from approximately 16 per cent in 1993 to about 3.6 per cent in 2001.[2] Figures vary, but estimates from the Central Statistics Office of Ireland and the UK's Office for National Statistics suggest that about 500,000 Irish people emigrated to Britain between 1951 and 1961. This is quite remarkable given that the population of Ireland was just 2.8 million in 1961.

Ireland today bears no comparison. Dublin is thriving once more. But most of the queer landmarks of Mr Lucas's day are long gone. The underground toilet at Burgh Quay was demolished during the redevelopment of the riverside in the late 2000s, when Dublin City Council sought to remodel the derelict industrial buildings and warehouses lining the river into something more resembling a cultural and economic hub. I'm not here long enough to attest to whether that has worked or not, but the city certainly hums with activity. Morning joggers bounce along the wooden and metal walkways abutting the Liffey. Dog walkers dodge tourists – including myself – snapping pictures of the waterfront buildings, now home to international banks and consultancy firms. The ornate Victorian gas lamps that marked the entrance to the lavatory have also gone, presumably parked in a basement of a museum somewhere. Mr Lucas most assertively would not have approved.

Well-known gay rights campaigner and Irish senator David Norris remembers the spot well: 'Burgh Quay was a very popular spot because it was close to the station,' he told the *Irish Times* in 2016. 'And it was a very easy mark because if a [police officer] wanted extra points for promotion, he could knock up a few arrests there easily.'[3]

Gay sex – for both men and women – was not decriminalized in Ireland until 1993, mainly as a result of a campaign by Norris and the Campaign for Homosexual Law Reform, whose members included future presidents of Ireland, Mary Robinson and Mary McAleese. Civil unions for same-sex partners would only be legalized on 1 January 2011, and full marriage equality not until 2015 – two years after England, Scotland and Wales. Northern Ireland would finally follow suit in 2020. But for Mr Lucas, visiting in 1968, any sort of same-sex activity was still deeply illegal.

Speaking in 2018 to mark the twenty-fifth anniversary of the decriminalization of gay sex, then Taoiseach Leo Varadkar backed a motion before the Irish parliament calling on the Dáil to issue an apology to men convicted before 1993. Varadkar – Ireland's first openly gay prime minister – referred to research that revealed that an average of thirteen men were jailed a year between 1940 and 1978 for gay sex offences. The Taoiseach added that there had been 455 convictions between 1962 and 1972. 'In the three years before I was born in 1979 there were 44 prosecutions in this country,' Varadkar said. 'It's not that long ago. For every conviction there were a hundred other people who lived under the stigma of prosecution, who feared having their sexuality made public and their lives destroyed.'[4]

Back in Dublin in the sixties, Mr Lucas is assuming his usual position at the bar, watching and noting all that is happening around him. Gay sex may have been partially decriminalized the year before in England and Wales, but for someone who had lived so long under the shadow of arrest, Ireland's current laws are no matter for his diaries. Mr Lucas is more interested in whom he can see and write about.

10 September 1968 (Tuesday):

To Rice's bar and sat awhile over a lager, noticing that the rather unwelcoming barman of two years ago is gone; and then to Davy Byrne's, striking up courage with two whiskies and water and a good cup of coffee, served by the sandy-haired apprentice I heard called Paddy. Like every apprentice barman in Davy Byrne's, he looked out of spirits. Bartley Dunne's was crowded as I remembered it... but I saw only little tubby Bert the head barman and Mr Bartley Dunne's own somewhat spectral figure that I

> *recognized. Back at 11.15, a little tipsy – dilutoir might be a better word – and not lingering by the green urinoir in Eden Quay.*

Again, most are now gone. All except Davy Byrne's. Rice's was lost in 1986 when the Stephen's Green Shopping Centre was built; Bartley Dunne's was demolished in 1990, first transforming itself into the Break for the Border pub and now a whisper of the past remains in its current incarnation as Bartley's, the signs above the door promising tourists that it is 'Open for Food & Drinks' as well as the ubiquitous 'Cocktails'. But in the days Mr Lucas visited, it was renowned in Dublin for its cosmopolitan air and clientele.

'It was an Aladdin's cave to me, its wicker-clad Chianti bottles stiff with dribbled candlewax, tea chests covered in red and white chequered cloths, heavy scarlet velvet drapes and an immense collection of multicoloured liqueurs glinting away in their bottles,' David Norris told the *Irish Times* in 2016.[5] The landlord, Bartholomew Dunne, is worthy of his own book. The *Irish Times* wrote a particularly glowing obituary of Dunne and his eponymous bar when he died in 2016. It is worth quoting here at length to gain a real flavour of how it might have once appeared to Mr Lucas, braving the rain to pop in for his usual half-pint of ale:

> *Presiding over this cosmopolitan throng was the suave and ebullient Bartholomew Dunne and his older brother Gerard. Barmen wore long aprons, waiting staff crisp*

white jackets, and the soundtrack was jazz, Al Bowlly, vocalist with the Ray Noble band, giving way to Edith Piaf, beginning and ending with La Vie en Rose... *The clientele was eclectic: advertising 'suits' from nearby Harcourt Street, students from Trinity College, actors and stage staff from the Gaiety theatre, doctors, nurses and porters from nearby Mercer's Hospital... And there were gay men too. The word 'gay' was not used then. Male homosexuality was a criminal offence, so discretion was essential. At Bartley Dunne's there was a place for everyone. If there was a house rule, it was that.*[6]

And Davy Byrne's? I was in Dublin in 2019 and went to have a look and, at that point, the décor and layout would have still been familiar to Mr Lucas. Now, however, the famous writers' and artists' haunt is the archetypal trendy wine bar, home to €17 [£15] sourdough club sandwiches and €19.50 [£17] Wagyu beef burgers. With chipper staff in red waistcoats and white shirts nipping back and forth, pens behind their ears, it is firmly on the tourist trail. Andy, one of the current barmen, tells me it had been fully refurbished about three years ago, presumably not long after my last visit. I avoid the cocktail of the week – Shangri La – and plump for a quick glass of Sauvignon before heading out once more in search of Mr Lucas's lost queer Dublin.

As the time ticks on, I do the only thing that can be expected of me (both as a journalist and a happy homosexual): I get drunk and try to chat up guys. To be fair, I am actually after some insight into what the scene was like if not quite in Mr Lucas's time, but at least twenty or thirty years ago. Soon, I fall into talking about the past with fifty-eight-year-old community development worker Richie Keane and filmmaker and cinematographer Noel Connellan, aged fifty-two.

'I remember going into Rice's because I'd been out shopping with my ma and she suggested we go in there,' Richie told me as we sit in the wonderfully named Pantibar in Capel Street. 'I must have been about sixteen or seventeen and didn't know it was a gay bar – or a "mixed bar" in those days. I remember all the looks we got,' he said, laughing. 'But I didn't clock it at the time.'

Richie subsequently went on to be involved in grassroots politics and activism. 'I joined the Workers' Party when I was eighteen and everyone was pro-feminist, pro-gay rights and anti-war, so it was an early safe space in Ireland for me.' With his then-boyfriend, he'd go to the George and the Parliament pubs. 'It was like we were cleaving together,' Richie remembered now. 'We were all in the shadows and at the bar, there would be a barman, a doctor, a docker and a barrister all drinking together; the scene would cut across all social classes.'

For Noel, 'the bohemian crowd and the arty crowd and the gays were all lumped in together – just like in Soho in London. It's just the same now, to a certain extent,' he told me. The same now, but also different, to my mind; the bars and clubs of all our – mine, Richie's and Noel's – respective youths shuttered and long gone, and those of Mr Lucas even more long past. Yet the scene in London and Dublin still survives; the bars I went to that night – and the club I eventually ended up in – were busy, even for a cold Tuesday night. The same, but different indeed.

But while the queer scene might have changed beyond all recognition, the city would still feel familiar to Mr Lucas, who tried to visit at least once a year in the sixties. And Ireland was it – no other travel abroad, other than his ill-fated appointment with a German military jail in 1950. This was relatively unusual, even in the sixties. A debate in parliament on removing the £50 [£1,200] foreign travel allowance that British citizens were able to take abroad – down from £250 in the fifties – revealed the extent to which people were starting to travel abroad.

'In 1965, there were 4.9 million United Kingdom visitors travelling overseas. They spent £290 million outside the sterling area. In 1966, there were 5 million people travelling abroad. They spent £301 million. The estimate for 1967, again from the British Travel Association, is 5 million visitors travelling abroad, and the total expenditure will be roughly the same at £300 million.'[7]

Mr Lucas is in Dublin for the first time in two years – and with good reason. His last trip had ended badly, to put it mildly. But even then, in 1966, he is a reluctant tourist.

27 October 1966 (Thursday):

Another faintly misty grey day; rather cold. I did not get up till past noon and as I lay warm in bed I thought of my visit to Dublin that for seven weeks I've been looking forward to now. That it is almost begun, I'm unwilling to go. Had I not already bought my ticket I think I'd cancel the hotel reservation and spend a weekend at home. It's not only the £9 10s [£220] spent on fare and room that deters me, though I can ill afford it in present circumstances, nor is it wholly the embarrassment of having to dodge Christopher Flanagan while I'm in Dublin, lest I hurt his feelings by not having taken up with him. His offer of a bed at Crewe may have been motivated by the coldest calculation of profit with no feelings to be harassed, but I can't be sure it wasn't a spontaneous friendly gesture that ought not to be spurned. No, what most puts me off is the fear that I may have cut a ridiculous figure before Bartley Dunne's barman that in their eyes and mouths I may be 'that stupid bald-headed English queer, that threw his money around'. I have always feared ridicule more than blows and the thought of a barman's concealed – but not quite concealed – sneer, the glimmer of amused contempt in their eyes, their too friendly friendliness, is trouble to me.

Reading back to the previous entries covering this, I find nothing to justify his fears – other than his ever-conscious hyper-awareness of his appearance. He is in Dublin to satisfy his lust, quite frankly – even at the expense of his own discomfort on a night ferry from Holyhead.

28 October 1966 (Friday):

The train sped through the Midlands under a false moon with ghostly ground mist very thick in places though the ship was not at all crowded. This was the most wearing journey I have made by water. I think because I sat in one place and dozed. The light was too poor to read by and my feet swelled and grew painful as they pressed against my shoes. So uncomfortable did I become and so alluring was the thought of my own bed in my own home, that I made up my mind not to stay out of it a day longer and to return on Sunday night. My thoughts as the four hours between Holyhead and Dun Laoghaire [a small town just outside Dublin] *dragged by, were not of the most inspiring kind. I meditated on how my attraction to Irish*

youths – I share the blood, but neither the morals nor the crudity – has brought me grievous injuries to both mind and pocket. Peter, McGinnis and now Brady have robbed or swindled me, while others have taken much and given nothing. They are a shabby lot on the whole, those I've met, possessing sexual appeal but nothing else.

But on he goes, intent on leaving as soon as humanly possible. Of course, the barman, George, at Bartley Dunne's was as charming and welcoming as ever – and doubtless only had a faint memory of who Mr Lucas was.

29 October 1966 (Saturday):

My call at Bartley Dunne's this midday checked annoyance for a while – George, the barman, was amiable enough. His manner reminds me very much of Sam McCrum; he has the same hesitancy for just the word he wants, the same tendency to use what he fancies is the better word ('a beverage', instead of the usual 'a drink', for instance).

But as the evening progressed, it is clear that Mr Lucas should have indeed stayed in the relative safety of his London home.

I walked slowly back down Grafton Street and decided to have a look at the cottage on St Stephen's Green, intending to relieve myself there before going back to Bartley

Dunne's. There were a few people about, someone standing on the kerb some distance off, and two people who came out of the cottage as I went in. It was about two minutes later, when, having checked my loose silver and made sure I need not break into a note or not yet, I was buttoning my trousers; I heard a step outside and someone came in and, suddenly, I was aware of the impact of two heavy blows on my head, all went black for my eyes for a single instant and, in that crack of time, my mind registered the fact that someone had struck me on the head twice from behind. Even as I turned, in the moment of turning, a moment measured in milliseconds, the thought came into my mind wordless, but formed and clear: 'This is someone who hates homosexuals, who has struck me because I am homosexual, and standing in a public lavatory. People would think him in the right.'

This was a disabling thought. I had turned by now and saw my assailant starting back with a length of wood raised in his hand, a short man with light hair, spectacles, a small beard, a dark-coloured coat who cowered back as I grabbed at his stick shouting in my fear and amazement, some such words as, 'Stop it. What the hell are you up to? Stop hitting me!'

He let his stick go and dodged past me. And, as I came after him, said in deprecating tones, 'Now, don't be hasty. Let's talk it over.' I was confounded, dazed, frightened, and when he scurried across the road, made no attempt to pursue him.

> *Still clutching the stick, I walked up to two taxi men who were chatting 25 yards away at the cab rank by the park gates, quite unaware of what had happened. I must have startled them considerably with blood running down my head. And face in a red stream (though of this, I was quite unaware), holding a length of wood and saying in terms of surprise and petulant anger, 'What do you think of that? A man suddenly attacks me for no reason at all and hits me on the head.' One of them stood for a moment as well he might, and then 'Look, you want to go to a hospital, your head is hurt. I'll drive you around. It is not far – get in.'*

Seven stitches later, Mr Lucas is back at Moran's Hotel, feeling sore and, as ever, wondering what the hospital staff might have thought of him.

> *I knew that they were thinking that this was an English queer, who had made some indecent approach and got banged on the head for his rashness. 'Did you do something bad to him?' asked one of the nurses as he stood and contemplated me before the doctor's arrival.*

I've got in front of me – as well as Mr Lucas's ticket stub for the train to Holyhead (he really did keep everything) – two little photobooth photographs taken in London a few days later, after the bandage had come off, and you can see how the wound follows his receding hairline on the right of his head.

Deep, the stitches clearly visible in black and white, it was a serious attack and no wonder he arrived at the hospital with the blood flowing freely through the fingers of his hand clasping his injured scalp. Unsurprisingly, he leaves again for London the next day, not willing to be seen in public with 'a bandage looking rather like one of those turban-like hats one sees Italian merchants wearing in the fourteenth-century paintings'.

My own trip ended the following morning too, but with no such drama. I'd toyed with heading to the cruising grounds for one last look the night before, but then the snow started to fall heavier and heavier and, with my feet already unsteady on the side-slippery streets, my hotel called strongly and sensibly.

For me, the visit had been a success – or at least my attempt to tread in Mr Lucas's footsteps had provoked my own memories, now mingling happily with his; the two of us writing our own accounts almost fifty years apart. And so I wended my way along the slushy streets the following morning as the snow fell softly 'on the crooked crosses and headstones, on the spears of the little gate, on the barren thorns'. And headed back to London again, reluctantly leaving the living in pursuit once more of the dead.

10

Sex, Money and Death

HIS FIGURE LOOMED large above me. Like a furry pear drop, his face red and sweaty as he attempted to cum, I lay back and watched: cold-eyed and calculating, remaining firmly in control as he attempted to lose his.

It was 1992, a luxury flat in Edinburgh and I was a teenage rent boy. It's not something I'm ashamed of or embarrassed about; before coming to write this book, I'd not thought about it for a long time. But it's time I set down my feelings about what happened and how I feel about it now, particularly as I look back at Mr Lucas's exploits. Our diarist is good at capturing his own experiences, his own feelings, about paying for sex – but we rarely hear from the men on the other side of the equation. Here, the curtain parts slightly, to give us an idea – but refracted through Mr Lucas's personal lens – of how those who are paid for sex actually feel about it (as Dermot Byrne, shown in the example below, has been known to accept the odd punter, according to later diaries).

20 August 1968 (Tuesday):

At Leicester Square underground I was greeted by little Dermot Byrne, off to work, as he put it, and hoping to earn £5 [£108] or £10 tonight. It is not a pretty account he gives of his life as a fraudulent tout for non-existent blue films, but it does confirm that one may do very bad things before one has become a very bad man. Byrne rejects the idea of having sexual relations for money, and declares he'd feel ashamed of himself; he regards his nightly cheating as a job, an occupation he doesn't and oughtn't to feel ashamed of. He has a strong financial incentive, too, 'where else would I earn £30 a week?' he observed, adding that he couldn't live on less. Yet Byrne himself is a friendly, unmalicious young man of twenty-two, wishful to be married as soon as he has enough money saved, and quite honest except in his chosen career of fraud.

I have been paid for sex – only by one man – but that experience itself, and its rather sordid aftermath, gives me an idea of the transactional nature of prostitution and its emotional and psychological impact. But I digress. Let me take you back to where it first began.

Aged nineteen and studying at the University of Edinburgh, I realized I couldn't cope with selling kitchens and bathrooms over the phone in the evenings any longer. I'd been in the same sort of job since I was sixteen. A year or so earlier, my mum, in the middle of a nervous breakdown following the recent departure of my dad, had told me she couldn't afford to support me anymore and I had to move out.

So out I went. I spent a couple of months sleeping on my dad's floor in his house share in the centre of Exeter before finally getting my own room in the same house. And, well, I had a whale of a time. My first emancipated decision was to drop Further Maths as an A level and plough on with English Literature, Maths and Russian. But I had no money – and nor did my father. Devon County Council refused to believe I was living independently and would only cover half my rent. So every weekday night off I went to a light industrial estate on the outskirts of Exeter to sell kitchens and bathrooms over the phone for Therm-A-Stor, which itself would go bust the following year, turfing out me and about 800 others up and down the country.

I joined another telesales company run by friends of my dad's and then signed up to another one when I moved to Edinburgh to pay the rent. But by then, I'd had more than enough. So, one happy evening, I got up just before the half-time break in the usual three-hour session and announced I was quitting – literally skipping down the hill to join friends in the pub. I already had a plan for what I'd do next.

I'd seen an advert in *Gay Scotland*: 'historian seeks researcher for various duties' and thought, 'Yeah, right. I know exactly what you're after, mate.' I applied and a week or so later sat down over coffee with Alan Wilson, principal history teacher at James Gillespie's High School; I was nineteen, he was forty – and it was clear from the outset that my presumptions were spot on. He was my furry pear drop and I was determined to remain in control of the situation, which, considering what happened to Alan later, was absolutely the right course of action.

And so, for the next few months, we established a pattern. I would go over to his flat at some point during the week, we'd motor our way through three bottles of wine and then go to bed. But fortunately – and yes, deliberately on my part, pouring glass after glass – he couldn't get it up, so the sex we had was pretty vanilla. In the mornings, as I would always stay the night, I would get up before him and ask to 'borrow' some money. Waved towards a drawer on the side, I'd pluck out six or seven £10 notes and escape gleefully into the day and back to my university classes.

Then things changed and I realized I had to get my somewhat rackety life in some sort of order. Earlier that year, my then-boyfriend Will and I had answered an advert to help LGBTQ+ rights organization Stonewall bring a test case against the British government at the European Court of Human Rights over the gay male age of consent in the UK, then twenty-one to the straight male sixteen.

The summer had been relatively quiet after an initial flurry of publicity at the launch of the campaign at a press conference hosted by Sir Ian McKellen. But now things were really starting to take off with Will and I travelling around the country giving speeches at town halls, student unions and various debating societies – and doing round after round of media interviews for radio and telly as we went.

I soon realized my little renting on the side had the potential to backfire massively and derail our squeaky-clean image. Will was fully aware of what I was doing – we had an open relationship anyway – if not exactly supportive, but if the tabloids had gained a whiff that one of Stonewall's age-of-consent bunnies – there were three of us including nineteen-year-old LSE student Ralph Wilde – complete with our chinos and blue button-down shirts, was a teenage rent boy, all hell would have broken loose.

So I dropped Alan pretty pronto and committed to the campaign – and to my relationship with Will. He and I had actually broken up just before the launch of the European Court case, leading to panic at Stonewall, who convinced us to keep going in a 'media marriage' – not the most ethical decision, it has to be said. Fortunately for all concerned, Will and I got back together a month or so later, so all the onscreen, town hall and student union pronouncements of love and our relationship were actually true – in the end.

The campaign lasted for about eighteen months, culminating in a free vote – so M.P.s were allowed to vote according to their conscience rather than along party lines – in February 1994. We lost. In a classic British fudge, the M.P.s opted for eighteen rather than equality at sixteen and the baton was then passed to two younger and, to my mind, much braver guys (as Ralph and I might have been nineteen, but we were already at university and on our way; and Will was twenty-four and already starting his career in television), Euan Sutherland and Chris Morris, who battled on until we were finally granted equality in 2001.

Back to Edinburgh I went for my final year and, having been on the road for more than eighteen months, faced doing two years' studying in one go before finals nine months later. Needless to say, the idea of getting a part-time job was completely out of the question. So a quick phone call later: 'Hi, is that Alan…?', back I went: three bottles of wine; desultory sex (never penetrative); and mornings spent 'borrowing' money. And so it continued until the very last day of my time in Edinburgh when I spent the night with him with an eye to having enough money to fly down to London (I was a rent boy, I wasn't going to take the sodding train) for the last time and leave Alan and Edinburgh far behind.

Or so I thought. We never met again after July 1995, but I borrowed his flat one Christmas when he was away – spending a week in bed with a very cute guy (now, rather amusingly, a senior cleric in the Canadian Anglican church) in Alan's luxury apartment on the Royal Mile. Not so shabby, I thought. And so I drifted back to London and let Alan finally fall happily out of my life. I never really liked him; he always struck me as a total sleazeball – but then, as a former teenage rent boy, who was I to judge?

It seems his tastes ranged younger, something I'd been unaware of when I knew him, and he was arrested for sexually assaulting three of his sixteen- and seventeen-year-old students. His modus operandi was horrifyingly similar to my own experience: he'd ply them with wine and then pounce. He was jailed for eighteen months in 2000.

Then the story took an even darker turn. I remember

reading about this in horror at some point in the mid-noughties, when I looked online to see where he was and what he was up to. Alan Wilson was dead. He'd been murdered after his release – a former cell mate had cut him up into five pieces and left them in wheelie bins around Edinburgh. It seemed Alan had 'tried once too often to come on to [his former cell mate]' and Ian Sutherland, then thirty-three to Wilson's fifty-one, had discovered Alan in bed with him after a heavy drinking session, snapped and strangled him.[1] There is an even more grisly post hoc addendum. I'll let journalist Stephen Khan, writing in 2004 in the *Guardian*, pick up the baton – in a story appropriately headlined 'Horror tale stranger than fiction':

Wilson was more than a sexual predator who met a grisly end, however. He was a connoisseur of grisly ends. He had worked part-time as a macabre tour guide, regaling visitors with tales of the body-snatchers [William] *Burke and* [William] *Hare. He could describe in minute detail how Burke was skinned and hanged. Wilson even wrote a number of books on the city's violent past, with titles such as* Haunted Edinburgh. *Now he has entered the realms of Scottish folklore in the most chilling way possible. His interest in local history and his sexual predilections led him to skip between respectable and underworld Edinburgh, experiencing the Jekyll and Hyde nature of the city on a daily basis.*[2]

And so ends that particular tale. I'm not sure it could have ended in a more macabre fashion, but I'm afraid I don't feel much – if any – sympathy for Alan. No one deserves to die in such a horrific way, but he was a predator, more than willing to exploit my vulnerability and try his luck with his younger pupils. I'd heard he'd hired several more guys after me and perhaps they were better at being rent boys than I was in terms of actually putting out, but there is no excuse for his crimes. My experience, however, does give me an insight into whether Mr Lucas was exploited – or whether he was the exploiter.

The men – all over the age of eighteen – who Mr Lucas paid for sex were usually damaged in some way. Or if not damaged then desperate for cash – and willing to do anything to get it. Just as Alan Wilson preyed on me, did Mr Lucas prey upon the men he slept with? I was more than willing to sleep with Alan for money – to be fair, the sleaziness of it was actually quite a turn on. But, even as I opened the third bottle, I never felt out of control. I never felt as if the balance of power lay wholly with Alan. Of course it did: if he'd turned violent or threatened me as a very weedy, skinny nineteen-year-old (and later as an equally puny twenty-/twenty-one-year-old), I'd have been defenceless. My illusion of being in control was just that: no more than an illusion.

But why do we pay for sex? I have, just once, in Istanbul sometime in the mid-noughties. I was living in Georgia, in Batumi, and quite happily abstaining from sex. Well, happily for about two months at a time and then, usually on a Thursday night, I'd find myself in my usual restaurant, the fabulous Princess Café, ploughing my way through my second bottle of Georgian red, and realize I was bored stupid. A quick nip to my flat to grab my passport and by midnight I'd be bribing my way across the border into Turkey.

Jumping into a taxi, the third bottle of red tucked into my rucksack, I'd wend my way to Trabzon. Once there, a quick hop up to Istanbul and I'd book myself into the Pera Palace for $90 a night and stagger to the Mata Hari suite before sleeping until dinner and a night out on the town.

Usually, my strike rate was pretty good, but not that night, and staggering back along İstiklal Street at 3 a.m., I remembered a gay brothel just off the main drag.

I can't remember how much I paid (but I do remember they took Amex, which struck me as very civilized), but three minutes later, I found myself in a sauna-like cubicle with two extremely handsome Turkish guys in their mid-twenties who dodged kissing, but not much else.

We'll draw a veil over what happened next, but as I left I remember feeling quite disgusted with myself. I mean, the sex was great. But the fact of paying someone for sex was something I felt immediately uncomfortable with. To go back to the word control I used with Alan, the two guys were very much in control and very clear about what they would and wouldn't do. It was definitely my party, but they were pouring the booze.

But I didn't like myself for what I'd just done. I've been poor, I've been a rent boy. I should know better – I should have known better. Volition is a wonderful word to bandy around, but I still think what I did stinks. There's no easy way round it: I exploited them. I was financially in control; I shouldn't have done it. I'd like to say I carry the guilt around with me today. But, let's face it, that faded as quickly as the following day's hangover. I was a punter – a very happy punter – and that's it.

So is it any different for Mr Lucas? Can we – should we – apply the same guilt-laden principles, if one can call them that, to our street philanthropist? I'm not sure. The range of rent boys Mr Lucas picked up were layabouts, the unemployed, drifters, drug addicts, several of whom had distinct and obvious mental health problems.

3 December 1968 (Tuesday):

Maher is a wild schizoid, of course, and following his talk is like piecing a jigsaw together. There are numerous lacunae, and to get at sense one must supply the continuity of thought oneself. In extreme cases of schizophrenia, this discontinuity is more marked.

24 January 1969 (Friday):

On the Square this evening, I was greeted by Kevin Farrell, that young Irishman with the history of mental instability that Ian Hall introduced me to. He's visibly a mild latent schizophrenic, if his features are any indication, and I should say that part of his trouble is an uneasy balance between homo- and heterosexuality.

But while he can come across as the cold dispassionate onlooker, Mr Lucas does seem to care about his wayward charges – and those of others. He is aware that the damage done to the rent boys on the Square can easily be undone – if only people would be willing to make the effort. And, at times, people do step up.

21 September 1968 (Saturday):

Kevin Farrell chatted awhile with me in Duncannon Street. There's a strain of quiescent schizophrenia in him, to judge from the configuration of jaw and cheekbones, but it's not surprising – an orphan from Waterford brought up in the Dominick Street orphanage in Dublin, he came to London and might have gone downhill far had not Hall's ancient patron Mr Dale picked him up and got him medico-psychiatric treatment.

There is a difference, though, between Mr Lucas and the average punter that does soften the exploitation charge, even if it doesn't completely get him off the moral hook. And that's the type of sex he had. Mr Lucas was a watcher. He describes himself at one point as being a 'pornologophile' – or someone who gets off by listening to the filthy tales of others while wanking himself into happy voyeur heaven. The tales he prefers most are those of what his supposedly heterosexual paramours get up to with their wives and girlfriends – and the more obscene the better.

2 May 1963 (Thursday):

At my flat, he put on my record player, chatted, had a little sherry, and had sex with me in the kitchen by the faint light from the radio. Though he says he doesn't really like homosexual intercourse, he does enjoy and wants to have active sodomy, and attempted to bugger me. I came to emission by getting him to say 'I want to bumfuck you' and similar expressions (it's curious that this word should have so strong an erotic effect on me).

17 July 1968 (Wednesday):

I must keep in touch with Doherty and have him back here in the near future. He's one of those, like Derek Tilford and Michael Flanagan, whose proven complaisance and willingness to provide the verbal titillation I most enjoy outweighs any lack of novelty; and though I suppose he will require coffee and the playing of a record or two, his subsequent performance should be worth the tedium.

17 January 1973 (Wednesday):

To Victoria after an early dinner and sat down in the dim 'Windsor Castle' bar to await Moran, not much wishing him to appear. But appear he did, and for a time I made conversation while he imbibed his pint of beer; and then with him briskly to Charing Cross and the journey home. He was docile enough, and quite well-behaved, described his sexual experiences and repeated obscene phrases as I directed; and finished off the cherry vodka I bought before Christmas and found undrinkable. His £5 [£79] fee was fairly earned, though on a weekday evening I am a bit too tired out to enjoy any sexual dalliance. With Moran seen into the Alexandra, home sleepy and rather thrown out of my accustomed routine; and after falling into a heavy doze, to bed.

It's amusing on many levels, not least the fact that Mr Lucas is constantly bemoaning the fact that the media is awash with crass sexuality, even the gay press of the day.

15 January 1982 (Friday):

I skimmed through Gay News *– there's too much of all this rather crude, coarse, obscenely-worded stuff, that's as boring and tedious as 'tis vulgar. The magazine must of necessity be eclectic, but if this is the impression it makes on me, how much more will it influence the disgusted indignant anger of our enemies?*

In essence – and this might seem odd to say – Mr Lucas was something of a prude. He preferred sex to be sly, underhand and in private. Sunlight shone on the sexual act – or the male nude figure – on stage or television, ruined the illicit thrill of the unknown, the sexual tension of undressing a young man. If you know what you're going to get, he seems to say, there's no point having it. And, given the age we're talking about – the liberal sixties – his is a constant battle against the loosening sexual mores of the day.

17 September 1968 (Tuesday):

This nasty American play Hair *(the very name is offensive) opens at the Shaftesbury Theatre on the 27th of September, the day that theatre censorship is abolished. With indecent exposure taking place on the stage we can, I suppose, expect before long to have copulation, simulated or real, performed in public... and surfeited with open sex, our enjoyment of sex will wane and flag. Reticence, puritanical restraint and public decorum are essential if private nakedness, private lechery, are to retain their former power to thrill and inflame. These apostles of emancipation, these psychologically corrupt producers and playwrights, are, I suspect, themselves frigid, and seek to choke people's appetites by surfeiting them.*

Mr Lucas was rather coy about detailing the sex he had, describing the local Romford cottages as the 'pissotières' and – here in a snippet from May 1948 – describing his sex in French: *'J'ai fait un péché, à mon grand remords'* ('I have committed a sin, to my great remorse'), presumably as he knew his mother – who regularly read his diary – wouldn't be able to understand. What's undeniable is that Mr Lucas lived for the pleasure of intercourse, even if it was simply someone talking dirty to him.

3 September 1968 (Tuesday):

I'm feeling dispirited and rather devitalized these days. No doubt half-an-hour's sex with someone both enjoyable and reliable would set me up again.

Many times, however, Mr Lucas backed out at the last minute, either leaving the young man waiting by a Tube station or paying them off. Last-minute nerves set in.

21 August 1968 (Wednesday):

Tired on leaving the office, and quite disinclined for sex with Michael Wylie or anyone else. I went straight to dinner and was near finishing when who should come into the Trafalgar but Wylie himself, having spied me from the street. It was but five minutes past the time of our meeting and I made out I had been delayed at the office and had been about to come on to keep the appointment. We walked about, through the Embankment Gardens, to the Square (where Tony Brown was walking also) and at last I made my excuses, gave him £2 [£43.23] (had hoped to save the £3 put by for sex, but could not decently part with less) and so home.

The guilt he felt earlier due to his Catholic religion has dissipated by the late sixties – indeed he is able to counsel others as to their own feelings after gay sex. He writes earlier in

August 1968 of first meeting the 'dark-haired' Irishman Kevin Farrell on Trafalgar Square.

2 August 1968 (Friday):

With an agreeable Irish voice, he discussed his feelings of guilt and depression after homosexual intercourse, feelings that he did not have after sex with a woman, and that he thought attributable 'to the Catholic religion'. I commented appropriately, mentioning my own Catholicism and my own familiarity with these guilty feelings (and I do indeed remember how I felt when I was twenty-three and looked upon my sexual enjoyment in the light that convention and orthodoxy persuaded me was appropriate). This Farrell seemed somewhat astonished at my conversation and manner, remarking, 'You're not a bit like what I thought you would be; you're not a pansy at all, and you talk very well. You've got a posh accent like Edward Heath.'

Let's not pull any punches here, Mr Lucas is also fully aware of the 'semi-sadism of [his] penis in a guardsman's straight mouth', as he writes in May 1958. For him, the rent boy's character comes down to one essential factor: honesty. Can he trust the person whom he takes home not to rob or attack him? Mr Lucas constantly bemoans the fickle, facile nature of the gay scene, yet is there most nights.

6 June 1964 (Saturday):

It is ten years now since I came to the gay world of the West End. At first I thought that the homosexual society would resemble the world of office and suburb where the ordinary decencies and courtesies of life are observed; where colleagues and neighbours are uninteresting, or reliable; where people come to tea but one need not count the spoons afterwards; where a smile or a handshake are what they appear to be – an indication of goodwill. Before long, I found that the world of the 'Fitzroy' and the 'Standard' now gone, the 'White Bear' and the Coffee-House and the gay clubs is not like this at all. Even so, hope continues. Hope that honesty and truthfulness and good nature are still to be found more frequently than snow in August.

Yet not once does he ask whether he himself is an 'honest' person. Indeed, quite the opposite: it is presumed that he is the benchmark of probity. Here Mr Lucas is reflecting on how a year has now passed since his mother died – and the legacy she left him both financially and spiritually.

25 January 1973 (Thursday):

I have more to thank [my mother] *for than £1,700* [£27,000] *and a flat. From her, I learned those elements of religious belief on which reading and reflection and the bent of my mind have built an orthodox or near-orthodox personal creed; from her, I learned those middle-class values so scorned today, respect for truthfulness, for honesty, a fierce scorn and loathing for the dishonest and the deceitful; and from her, I gained by unconscious imitation a speech and accent [...] and untainted by the vowels and intonations of suburban London. All these are a rich and lasting inheritance.*

Perhaps they are, but there are numerous examples in the diaries of those who have been initially helped by Mr Lucas, partly out of simple friendship but usually determined by an ulterior motive to get them into bed, finding themselves swiftly out of favour if they do not conform to his ideals, like the 'plasterer living in Bromley', John Joyce, who lasted a month living with Mr Lucas before he was asked to leave.

This, for me, shows the limitations of Mr Lucas's goodwill: he is willing to help, but only ever on his own terms. It is a streak of selfishness that also informs his relationship with the various rent boys and Irish labourers: he might convince himself that he is doing them a good turn, but in fact he's only ever satisfying his own desires.

Does that make him a predator per se? Probably yes by today's standards, but not one with evil intentions, hopefully only misguided ones. His lack of success in finding mutual love has exposed a misanthropic tendency that, unfortunately, runs very deep. This diary entry from 1961 shows him struggling to reconcile the two – benevolence and bitterness – after bringing home a young man who makes a comment about his lack of hair, a touchy subject for Mr Lucas at the best of times:

7 November 1961 (Tuesday):

Furiously angry, frightened, dismayed and outwardly polite, I did have sex with him – the worst kind, in a hostile spirit, wishing to humiliate. He sucked me off as I knelt over him and came in his mouth. Then, giving him 30/- [£41.12], I got rid of him. I regret that I used sex as a means of satisfying resentment, that is 'unnatural vice' in the strict sense; and I ought to confess it. In future, I really must control these periods of general benevolence – indiscreet confidences, indiscreet kindnesses – as West End rent boys usually have inconvenient and dangerous sequels.

Does this damn him in our modern eyes? Yes and no. For me, it is simply the mark of a complicated man living in complex times. Yet his misanthropic nature – not just in terms of his attitudes towards his sexual partners, but life in general – would probably still be in place even if he hadn't lived through the end of the Second World War and the illegality of gay sex. His hateful, homophobic parents have indeed 'fucked him up', to paraphrase Philip Larkin, leaving him unloved and – at times – unlovable.

11

The Death of Mr Lucas

THE END, WHEN it came late in the evening of 28 December 2014, was squalid. It was sordid. And it was alone. The last man standing, Craig Hoy, who had met Mr Lucas in the eighties and remained one of his few genuine friends rather than the parade of paid part-timers, was in jail for punching a policeman (of which more later).

I had no idea Mr Lucas was so near the end. I had seen him earlier that year when I'd received a croaky indistinct growl over the phone and rushed round to see what was wrong. As far as I could tell, it wasn't terminal, but at that point Mr Lucas had suffered a stroke and was pretty much incapacitated. That fine mind was still there but trapped in an unresponsive body that required regular visits from a troupe of NHS care workers. Craig had been doing his best: running errands; keeping the bills paid; and, more importantly, fending off thieving rent boys who could smell money in the offing from their now even more vulnerable former punter.

THE DEATH OF MR LUCAS

Mr Lucas's official death certificate states he died of 'aspiration pneumonia' and 'acute kidney injury', which suggests he'd eaten something that had gone down the wrong way and then fallen heavily out of his chair onto the floor. He'd been unwell for a number of years. In 2001, he'd been hit by a van while out shopping in his Clapham neighbourhood, which severely affected his mobility and pretty much confined him to the upstairs maisonette at 24a Mandalay Road, with only Craig as his regular companion and friend. At that point, I was still living in Georgia, unable to visit as much as I had previously. And when I did finally make it back and went round, I found a man much diminished. Eight decades now hung heavy on him; the black suit still buttoned and covered in dust and dirt, but hanging loose on his smaller, weaker frame.

We fell back into our usual pattern of coffee before midday or brandy if it was later; at that stage, as Mr Lucas very rarely drank at home, brandy only for me. If he was feeling well enough, we'd meet occasionally at the Green Man & French Horn. By rights, of course, we should have been at the Golden Lion, but Mr Lucas had alighted on this pub a few years earlier, drawn by, as he described it, 'the peace and quiet and decent soup'. I'd pass on the soup and accept a pint of lager. Occasionally, an older friend would join us. And, as with every moment of every day for the past sixty years, our meetings would be faithfully recorded in the diaries I hold now.

Before he'd been hit by the van, Mr Lucas was still relatively active, both physically and sexually. His need for sex – or for physical contact – was still strong. A quote from Hanya Yanagihara's book, *To Paradise*, neatly sums up his desires – and how the need to be touched, held, fucked, does not dissipate with age:

> *You forget, sometimes, how much you need to be touched. It's not food or water or light or heat – you can go years without it. The body doesn't remember the sensation; it does you the kindness of allowing you to forget.*[1]

Craig had first met Mr Lucas when he was hired to do some building work and repairs around the flat – something I still find surprising given the state of 24a Mandalay Road when I first visited in the mid-nineties. 'What you have to remember is that flat was basically a fifties flat in terms of how it was built,' Craig tells me. 'The other problem which we had to get sorted out is everything was still based around the old round three-pin sockets. So if people came round and tried to plug something in, nothing worked.'

I asked him whether Mr Lucas, when they first met, was still having sex – and yes, yes, yes was the answer... 'All the time,' Craig laughed. 'I mean, I used to meet people over there all the time, and he used to do his Polaroid photos.'

I still have many of those semi-pornographic Polaroids. Men, usually semi-naked, rather than fully unclothed; but some patently for pornographic purposes: erect and staring directly at the camera, they raise more uncomfortable questions about exploitation. No one is smiling; no one looks particularly happy. 'Oh god, when we cleared the flat, the amount of photos I took out!' laughs Craig now. 'Later on, he used to just put photos in on normal film into the chemists. I was doing some shopping for him and, I thought, "I'll pick these up", so I went to the chemist and they didn't give me a funny look or anything like that. But obviously I got in the car and thought I'd have a look and when I saw them, I was like, "Oh my god..."'

Craig and I have known each other for almost as long as I've known Mr Lucas. We've met for drinks, laughed about our mutual friend's foibles and failures and enjoyed swapping some of the tales we've heard. Mr Lucas, beyond the diaries, knew how to hold a table.

'There was a young girl who used to deliver his paper. At Christmas, he went down and said to her, "Give me a knock tomorrow, and I'll give you a Christmas box [present]." So she knocked on the door and he gave her a grand! That was before his stroke when he was going a bit doolally sometime in the early noughties. He caused so much fucking trouble by doing that! She walked home thinking, like, "What have I got?" Her parents were worried about whether she'd nicked it. And when they found out she hadn't, they were, of course, worried about what else had happened. I had to say, "No, don't worry; you've got nothing to worry about there..."'

Her parents insisted on giving the money back to a much-bemused Mr Lucas, who managed to get them to at least accept £50 on behalf of their daughter. Doolally or not, his actions echo those decades before on the streets of Soho and around Piccadilly Circus. Up until the end, Mr Lucas was still handing out money to those he liked and thought deserved it. Does this give us, perhaps, a back door into his motives back in the fifties and sixties? Did he exploit the vulnerable? Did he, to use a current term, use his privilege in order to get what he wanted?

I still favour the idea that Mr Lucas was a force, if not entirely for good, then certainly for some form of patrician benevolence.

Craig and I talked further. I told him I had never realized, in the twenty or so years that I had been visiting the flat, that it actually had a balcony, just off the kitchen to the back of the property.

'That was one of the jobs he got me to do,' Craig said. '"I want you to sort the patio out." And I said, "Patio? I didn't know you had a patio." He told me it was just off the kitchen, but when I tried to open the back door, I couldn't; it was impossible because there was something behind it. Basically, the whole patio was infested with roots, and I spent two days just with hacksaws and secateurs cutting them away.'

I was keen to hear Craig's impressions, particularly as a professional relationship drifted into what was probably our diarist's longest-lasting friendship. Did he actually like Mr Lucas? I know that might be a strange question to ask, but Mr Lucas could be awkward and obdurate – never allowing me to choose even the time of our meetings (or the place) or allowing me to pay for anything (not that I complained about that).

'He was really smart and always used to make me laugh,' Craig says. 'He would come home, take off his coat and put on a smoking jacket, which was falling to pieces by the way. Everything he had was monogrammed with his initials. He was just weird, eccentric.' But Mr Lucas aged and became ornery, and the friendship flexed and warped, though never quite to breaking point.

'To be honest, I did like him even after he had [lost his voice] and all the rest of it. But, I mean, he used to make my life so difficult. There were so many meetings with social services to try and get him the help he needed,' Craig said with an audible sigh. 'We had bleeding carers in twice a day – for £1,500 a month. They would phone me and say he wasn't washing. So I'd say to the carer, look just put him in the shower; I've already asked him to wash properly. But there was only so much I could do without being accused of elder abuse by doing things against George's wishes.'

The contradictions within Mr Lucas's character also became more pointed, particularly when it came to money.

'He was very generous,' says Craig. 'But then he would fixate on something. For example, he always used to use monogrammed paper, but then it got too expensive, so he stopped using it – but he was never happy about it.'

And then eventually, his health deteriorated even further, with a stroke destroying his ability to talk properly. 'For the last two years, he couldn't really speak to me,' Craig sighed. 'I mean, he would ring me up and all I get is like this silence. And I'd say, "George, I cannot understand what you're saying." And of course, he'd get annoyed with me as I couldn't understand him at all.'

Nearer the end, events caught up with Mr Lucas – and Craig. 'I had a court case coming up and I ended up in prison for eleven weeks. When he died I was in there.' Ah yes, the prison sentence. Did you punch a policeman, Craig? 'I got done for assaulting a policeman, yes. I was in prison for all of Christmas and I think I got out on the 31st of December.' Craig, freshly out of jail, phoned social services to find out Mr Lucas had already gone.

George Leo John Lucas died alone on the night of 28 December 2014. It had been a long life, living to the age of eighty-eight and five months. Not bad, considering he had foretold his death much earlier. And, very poignantly, frequently wished it had occurred much earlier. Even in the earliest diary I have from 1948, at age twenty-one, we find him musing on death.

13 February 1948 (Friday):

I fell to reflecting on my melancholy situation, forever cursed to love those that can never love me, tormented by love in a hell of loneliness, reduced to loving, silently, lance-corporals and drivers met by chance on inspections.

'The end is death or madness: there's the torment with the poisonous anodyne of physical satisfaction…

'My Love is of a birth as rare,
'As 'tis for object strange and high:
'It was begotten by Despair
'Upon Impossibility.'

And then later, as the sixties trip into 1970, he is once more moved to consider his mortality.

17 February 1970 (Tuesday):

Thinking on the prostatitis this warns me of and going on to savour the comfortable thought of death – never far from my imagination, a sweet I suck often.

His father had died in 1958 and his mother in 1972. Even when he was suffering from a chest tumour in 1963, Mr Lucas was relatively blasé about the idea of dying. I say relatively, as the thought of death appealed, but it's also obvious there's an undercurrent of terror as to why he delayed seeking medical attention for so long.

27 August 1963 (Tuesday):

It occurs to me that if indeed this whole set of events was designed to get me under medical care before my tumour had progressed too far – if the quarrel with my mother and the dirty man at Magdalen Green [public lavatory in Clacton-on-Sea] *were intended to bring this about – then it's also intended I should survive the operation, and need no longer dally and amuse myself with imaginations of death. The whole scheme would be pointless else. (Unless, of course, it was a practical joke of an involuted subtlety – but this would not be in character. God is a jester, a joker, with a fine ironical humour, but He's kindly too, and His benevolence infinite.) This has reassured me considerably. I don't think I need be looking my 'last on all things lovely' this autumn.*

While Mr Lucas certainly hankers for death over the years, fortunately for us, the end does not come quickly. But Mr Lucas's longing for death is long-standing and ever-present in the diaries throughout the sixties.

3 March 1968 (Sunday):

So home, reflecting gloomily that tomorrow it all starts again, a mountain of work to be shifted, Chilton back to press down on me, another dismal weekend at the end of five days, and so… how long before I crack under steady, inexorable pressure? Too late, or not at all, I fear. Madness would be an agreeable escape, though death is better; but I shall be granted neither.

It is a theme he returns to time and time again in the diaries.

26 January 1973 (Friday):

So home, sleepy and very despondent at the bombardment of lewdness that assails me on every side. A film, a comedy, so-called, is soon to leer and simper from the cinema screens; and one cannot avoid sight of the placards archly heralding it coming. There's no remedy now in the law... yesterday, a jury acquitted the publishers of obscene comics intended for juveniles and inculcating copulation, drugging and sadistic cruelty; and after the verdict was delivered, one of the jurymen, a long-haired fellow, embraces the main defendant in open court, judge King-Hamilton looking on. This would be a very good year to die in.

Time has passed quickly and, with it, the familiar faces of Soho and the 'Dilly. The problem with reading someone's diary is that there is no structured narrative; characters appear and then disappear; what might seem earth-shattering – the death of JFK, the moon landing – flickers briefly and then goes out. Some of the people whom Mr Lucas writes about are destined to always remain side notes of history – remembered only by friends and relatives – and memorialized only here in the diaries themselves. But for Mr Lucas, ever with an eye for the memento mori, each individual death adds up to the greater feeling that his is a life bound by fate, time ultimately crushing any individual concerns or meaning.

2 January 1964 (Thursday):

Death seems to be in the air. Going today to my barbers in Old Compton Street, I missed the little spry bald-headed manager and Italian with thin moustache who has cut my hair and chatted intelligently enough since Michael

McLachlan in the 'Palace Tavern' recommended the place to me four years ago. The assistant doing my hair told me the little man had fallen ill with a heart attack in the evening of Christmas Day and died in his sleep the next morning. I reflected that he who cut my hair and chatted to me only last month is gone. The 'Palace Tavern' is gone. Flesh and blood, bricks and mortar. Their faces and hearts must all be ground away to find dust in the rolling mill of time. This is comforting. There is:

'delight

'In life's discovered transitoriness.'

Sometimes death is brutal and nasty, brought on by love and passion gone awry. There is a particularly poignant account towards the end of the sixties of what seems to be a *crime passionnel*: the murder of Mr Lucas's acquaintance David Jackson by his boyfriend, Michael Luke. Mr Lucas first hears of David's death while flicking through his *Evening Standard* on the way home.

8 November 1969 (Saturday):

So David Jackson is dead, killed by Michael Luke, so a brief notice in the evening paper says. It was a crime passionnel, of course, and not surprising. When two self-centred homosexuals of the lower classes live together, each of them with a hysterical personality, without taste or insight, and coming from a situation of society where violence is not unusual, it's pretty certain something like this will happen.

A rather harsh reaction from Mr Lucas, tempered slightly by feelings of remorse for Jackson's parents – and also for those of Luke. 'I'm... even more sorry for Luke's poor old mother, a decent Catholic widow, I think, and not to be blamed for her son. But Jackson is no loss – a vicious rent boy six years ago, later one of a Clapham Common rolling gang and in recent years dabbling in whatever small dishonesty came to his hands. There's bad blood in that family and it's to be hoped his brother Stewart, Dave the Roller, doesn't pass it on.'

One factor that does come into play is Mr Lucas's continuing fixation with Irish Peter. 'As always,' he writes in November 1969, 'when I hear of the death of someone in the homosexual underworld, I wish "if only it had been Peter!"' If only indeed. But the ending to the Jackson murder is even more tragic.

12 December 1969 (Friday):

That odd youth, very plain and gawky, who used always to be asking where David Jackson was, came hurrying up to tell Lynch of the murder, produced Jackson's lighter, now his... and declared that Michael Luke had committed suicide in Brixton early this week. I don't know whether to believe this... but if it's true, it may not be any matter for regrets. I didn't dislike Luke, and indeed found him a pleasant fellow; but I doubt he'd have been either happy or honest had he lived.

London in the twenty-first century was shocked by the crimes of Stephen Port, a serial killer and rapist sentenced in 2016 to a whole life order, meaning he will never be released, for murdering four young men and raping countless others between 2014 and 2015. The case exposed many faults, particularly in terms of how London's Metropolitan Police handled the case, even when confronted with evidence that a serial killer was loose in the city. A report by Her Majesty's Inspectorate of Constabulary and Fire & Rescue Services into the Met's handling of the case published in 2023 was damning in its judgement of London's police force.

Between June 2014 and September 2015, Stephen Port drugged, sexually assaulted and murdered four young men in East London. Despite the obvious similarities between the deaths, the Metropolitan Police Service (MPS) failed to recognize that they might be connected. They even failed to recognize, until after the last death, that Port's four young victims – Anthony Walgate, Gabriel Kovari, Daniel Whitworth and Jack Taylor – had been murdered. Had the police conducted a professional and thorough investigation after Anthony Walgate's death, it is entirely possible that the other three men would still be alive. But the MPS's initial response to each of the deaths was reprehensible. As the coroner who held inquests into the four deaths said, there were a 'large number of very serious and very basic investigative failings'.[2]

The Metropolitan Police did not respond to a request for further comment.

The report's findings notwithstanding, the Stephen Port murders stand as a reminder that the dangers of the past are still very much with us in the present.

22 June 1968 (Saturday):

There's another homosexual murder reported. A quiet middle-aged Scotsman called Stephens was stabbed to death in his bathroom at a little before 2 o'clock this morning – fifty deep stab wounds in him, and his trousers off. He had brought a young man back earlier, and it's pretty clear what happened; the sort of thing that can happen to any of us.

Mr Lucas's own experience of violence had started much earlier. Growing up was a horror for him. In 1974, Mr Lucas witnessed the closure of his old school, Clark's in Ilford, which acted as a trigger to ponder his own future – and look back with hopelessly rose-tinted glasses at the past. And I say rose-tinted as we've already heard how he was bullied mercilessly at school. 'I must go to Ilford this weekend and find out what's to be done about the school furniture, etc.,' he writes in April that year. 'I want to be in at the death of the old school I left thirty years ago this July. I should like to revisit those rooms where I spent five pleasant years, the pleasantest, I think, of all my years.'

Reading that sentence feels almost as if Mr Lucas is employing very rare irony, but no, I don't think he is being ironic. Despite the bullying, despite the name-calling – despite everything – on occasion he seems to believe his life now is worse than it was then. He is, in essence, a miserabilist.

Part of his reoccurring fears are to do with drifting into penury and dying destitute, despite being a constant saver and always finickity over his finances. His diaries are full of how much he spends on cake – Battenberg ('stale') for 5s [£5.40] – as well as rent boys (usually £3–£4 [£65–£86]). We hear about his bank balance, which at the end of 1968 stood at £497-2s-8d [a touch under £10,750], 'thanks to my mother's gift and the other windfalls during the year'; his pension fund and building society savings and money held in a unit trust – £248 [about £5,400]; and funds held in his savings bank and premium bonds – £21-8s-6d [a little over £460]. Mr Lucas is not poor by any means, but worry he still does.

19 February 1968 (Monday):

Lying in bed last night I thought of my saving for retirement, of the £10,000 [£220,000] I hope to have, in eighteen years' time, to purchase an annuity so that I shall have an undiminished income from sixty-five onwards. But I don't want to live another twenty-three years, or even eighteen. The times are bad enough now for one of my temperament and, once my mother is no longer here to be grieved at my going, I too would be gone, before the world of the eighties is come. And even if I do live on to sixty and sixty-five, I can have no certainty that inflation will not have made £10,000 inadequate for my purpose; or perhaps, twenty years hence, a socialist administration will have put an end to such devices as annuities, and to private savings too, very like. And, of course, there's a very real chance that, sometime in the next decade or two, the flaccid shallow democracy that is Britain will fall to the strong clear-sighted enemy in the East. There will be no cushioned old age for me then.

Yet despite his regular hand-outs, his retirement was distinctly well cushioned. Estimates varied as to how much his estate was worth, but 24a Mandalay Road sold in May 2018 for £650,000. It shows just how many repairs were needed as it resold just under a year later for £905,000 – a cool £255,000 profit in just eleven months.

There was money apportioned in the will for his funeral, but that was a painfully soulless affair held at a crematorium in north London with only three of us present: myself, Craig and the long-suffering downstairs neighbour. Mr Lucas had initially asked that his body be left to medical science, which in itself would have been the perfect way to end not just this book, but indeed his entire life: what made Mr Lucas tick – literally? I have the will in front of me as I write this. 'I direct that after my death any organs or parts of my body, which are required for therapeutic or research purposes, shall be removed without delay and made available for the said purposes and my body then made available for dissection.'

But it was not to be. His body had lain too long unfound at 24a Mandalay Road for it to be of much use to medical science. Fortunately, his will had also made provision for this. 'And I further direct that if my body shall not be accepted for dissection, my Trustees shall cause it to be cremated and my ashes to be disposed of in accordance with my wishes, which I communicated to them. No unnecessary expenses other than the expense of a convivial party after cremation to be incurred and no religious service to be held.'

'Unfortunately, he died shortly after Christmas,' Craig told me. 'And he'd kind of been lying around indoors. So I mentioned the medical science bit to some people, and they basically said, "Thank you, but no thank you." So I went off to the undertaker's and just arranged the basic funeral.' There was also to be no convivial party other than me and Craig in the pub with a couple of pints. Not quite the death Mr Lucas wanted, but then even his best-laid plans went awry at the very last part of his life. He'd asked for his ashes to be scattered in his old garden at Bath Road, where he'd lived with his parents – something Craig attempted to do but didn't quite succeed. 'I couldn't just dump them in someone's garden,' he said. 'What would have happened if someone had turned up while I was doing it? So I did the best compromise I could think of, and I scattered the ashes in a park opposite.'

I'd like to say that was it. But, of course, it wasn't. Craig and I had been named as co-executors of his will, but in the chaos of Mr Lucas's death, the rush to clear the flat and the general melee that occurs when someone dies, the original will was lost. The most organized and pernickety person in the world, this would have horrified Mr Lucas. Every time – every single time – I went round to see him, he would bring it out and check my address and phone number were still the same. In his latter years, he even went as far as to have the will laminated… I'm almost surprised it didn't end up alongside his rent boys on a commemorative plate. But lost it was, kick-starting an incredibly torturous eight-year process that would only come to an end for Craig on 31 January 2023. 'I finally got paid today,' he wrote in an email to me, going on to detail how he had received about a sixth of what he had initially thought he would get.

Because Craig and I could only locate a copy of the will, we were not able to gain probate easily – or quickly. Our lawyer battled valiantly and steadfastly but probate was not awarded until several years after Mr Lucas's death. In the meantime, professional heir hunters had got a whiff of the potential value of the estate and went in search of potential benefactors as, technically, Mr Lucas had died intestate. Several months later, more than twenty third cousins twice-removed were located and a Battle Royale began. I bowed out in 2016, heartily sick of the whole process and just in despair at what Mr Lucas would have made of it all – and how he would have hated to let Craig down.

The will I'm looking at now is the same as I saw often between 1994 and 2014, both in paper and laminated form. It's full of wonderfully antiquated curios – as you'd expect Mr Lucas's last will and testament to be.

To Mrs June Field of 15 Crestfield Mews Hazlewood Glanmire in the County of Cork Ireland, my silver vase and silver crumb scoop, formerly the property of my late mother.

To the Cats Protection League of 17 Kings Road Horsham West Sussex RH13-5PN, a registered charity no.203644, the sum of Three Thousand Pounds (£3,000).

To the Pink Triangle Trust of 34 Spring Lane, Kenilworth, Warwickshire, a registered charity no. 1015629, the sum of Three Thousand Pounds (£3,000).

And, for the sake of transparency, to me as well:

To Hugo Greenhalgh aforesaid, the sum of Ten Thousand Pounds (£10,000).

Mrs Field died several years ago and her appreciation – or otherwise – of the silver crumb spoon is, like many of the characters who flit in and out of the diaries, lost to the mists of time.

To fast forward slightly, Craig finally came to an agreement with the heir hunters that saw his inheritance split 60:40 between

THE DEATH OF MR LUCAS

them and him. Again, Mr Lucas, who very rarely mentions his distant relatives in his diaries, would be utterly dismayed that the one person left at the end did not receive his rightful due.

'I mean, he was a funny old bugger right at the end,' Craig told me. 'But there were some funny things that happened over the years that make me laugh to look back at him. There was the time when he got his foot run over. He was down the West End and stepped off the kerb and a taxi ran over his foot. And then I got this mad phone call from St Thomas's [Hospital] to come and collect him. At the end, it was so funny, he was going around trying to tip the staff.' Like he was Princess Margaret, I interjected. 'Yeah, exactly that – but that's who he was right until the very end.'

Postscript

So he's gone, leaving behind fifty-six diaries and millions upon millions of words. Other than the mess of the will, he left pretty much nothing else; his books, long collected and cared for, dumped in a skip at the front of the Clapham flat before I could rescue them. Yet the diaries stand as the summation of a long life, eighty-eight years partly spent in the shadows, both accidentally and deliberately. A life complaining about penile discomfort while celebrating his conquests, the diaries are both banal and brilliant.

12 March 1968 (Tuesday):

A letter from my mother, in her accustomed style, complaining 'I am not well. I wish I had never come here' and tartly adding 'You have pain after food. Surely you can get tablets for that.' No pain or discomfort tonight. If I can move my normal time of defecation to morning or midday, I may be free of penile numbness by evening.

14 January 1973 (Sunday):

A clear bright day, not cold. Intermittent defecations this morning, with much use of lavatory paper, resulted in partial choking of the W.C. outfall, I was dismayed to see the water rise almost to seat level when I flushed it, and it took several flushings to disperse this paper bolus.

Why should we care? Why is Mr Lucas remarkable despite his classically unremarkable life? Put yourself in his well-worn, but always polished, shoes. Almost fifty years as a civil servant; many, if not all, spent alone. Passions left from decades ago; obsessions masquerading as love. Was it a life he enjoyed? Was it a life well led? For Mr Lucas, always aware of how history might remember him – and for us, the readers of his diaries – the answer would probably be no.

4 June 1969 (Wednesday):

I wish I could withdraw altogether from the West End. Better the stodge-pudding of office, flat and cinema than the gay painted apples of Piccadilly and Soho with their so-bitter core.

Yet there is something that does make him remarkable. Not just his diaries, not just how he lived his life, but the man himself. Throughout this book, I've tried to tell the story of Mr Lucas from his own words, but also, somehow, to separate him from them. That constant question of whether we can trust his diaries to really tell us who he was still stands. At the risk of asking too many questions, have I, as his friend, the executor of his will and the custodian of his diaries, actually managed to answer that question of who Mr Lucas was?

To be frank – and perhaps counterintuitive – I hope not entirely.

Every life is messy; every life cannot be tucked neatly into a book, even with his extensive diaries to help us. We can parlay his life into a metaphor for the times: Mr Lucas as a guide to a lost queer London. It's happily not that simple. Mr Lucas is no long-lost hero. His views, right-wing and not even right of centre, are spectacularly out of favour in today's more liberal age. Predator or prey, either way, some of his actions damn him through the lens of modern eyes. What we do see, though, is the passing of time, passing Mr Lucas by to a very large extent, but also allowing the reader to trace the history of London as its weaves and wends its way through the middle of the twentieth century.

1 January 1968 (Monday):

I look back eighteen years to 1950. When I was twenty-four, the London scene was not changed much; places, buildings, familiar to the homosexual world of 1950 had been familiar for a long time. And how many there were – the public rendezvous at Marble Arch and Piccadilly Circus and Trafalgar Square; the numerous gay bars: the

'Standard' in Piccadilly Circus, the celebrated 'Fitzroy' in Rathbone Place, the 'Bunch of Grapes' on the south side of the Strand, with its stone canopy carved in the form of a cornucopia over the door; 'Rainbow Corner' by the Monico in Shaftesbury Avenue... and, of course, the lavatories of the 'Grand Tour'; starting with Falconberg Court and ending at York Place.

The descriptions of the time are acute, even down to Mr Lucas's distaste for modern life – and life in general. And, mercifully, amid the gloom, they are also funny.

13 July 1961 (Thursday):

To see La Dolce Vita *this afternoon – an incoherent and episodic film of the 'decadent' society of Rome – which appeared to be as 'decadent' as Nuneaton or Bournemouth!*

26 September 1968 (Thursday):

I woke to the splashing of rain, but this ceased during the morning, and the rest of the day was dull, cloudy and dry. The chattering banality of the radio in the morning is so unbearable that to escape these disc-jockeys, I tuned to Radio 2, as they call it, that by day is disturbed by crackling and interference. But these noises are preferable to the bright silliness of Mr Tony Blackburn.

There are no lessons we can take from Mr Lucas's rackety life; no moral message relevant today that his diaries offer us an easy in to. Consider the man beyond the diaries: difficult, but important to do. His life was wracked with pain, seeped in the associated misery of living in an age that simply meant being gay, having sex, was illegal. But he kept on going. So did hundreds, thousands, hundreds of thousands of gay and bisexual men, so this does not make him remarkable. What does? For me, it was his resilience, his tenacity and – to be frank – his ability to turn a neat sentence.

9 June 1965 (Wednesday):

In these rather cool overcast days, I have been visiting in thought that brilliant summer of twenty-five years ago. Memory is the frail bridge leading back across the misty years to those days of May and early June. I see the sunlight dazzling the trees in Valentine's Park, and behind the school yard shining in on the black scarred desks of form six or the newer lightly varnished worn ones in form three. The German armies were driving across the low countries and northern France in those days, but more important to us was whether last night's homework would pass muster. Where are they now, my fellows who shared that golden term of long drowsy afternoons?

Yet why do we read diaries? Here's Anaïs Nin writing in one of her earliest diaries:

> *By beginning a diary, I was already conceding that life would be more bearable if I looked at it as an adventure and a tale. I was telling myself the story of a life, and this transmutes into an adventure the things which can shatter you.*[1]

'An adventure and a tale.' This remove, this level of distance, is reminiscent of another approach: that of Christopher Isherwood as outlined in his 1939 novel, *Goodbye to Berlin*, detailing the dying days of Weimar Berlin:

> *I am a camera with its shutter open, quite passive, recording, not thinking. Recording the man shaving at the window opposite and the woman in the kimono washing her hair. Some day, all this will have to be developed, carefully printed, fixed.*[2]

The pain of his life, the horror of his personal experiences, the sheer exhaustion of just being, rings loud and true throughout Mr Lucas's writing. His views on the age, on the scene, are not unique, but his diaries are. And that is what makes him remarkable. Every night scratching away at his diary; not one day missed.

Do we – did I – revel in his misery? More questions fall as I write this, but what is the appeal of reading the diaries of strangers other than living life vicariously? Mr Lucas was rarely happy, hardly ever even content. He had few actual friends; he never spent a night out with friends at dinner.

By modern standards, he was unhappy, and from a very early age.

24 December 1949 (Christmas Eve – Saturday):

I was too miserable to go to mass and went home after to cry quietly to myself at 2.30 a.m. on Christmas morning, and then to creep miserably to bed.

A friend of mine for twenty years, I both looked forward to seeing him and also dreaded it. Dreaded, as I'd be an audience. Frankly, at times I was bored. His stories were fascinating; the level of detail remembered and recounted was incredible. But I was there to sit, to soak in his life and never to engage.

In 1994, the age-of-consent campaign had just come to a messy end when the M.P.s voted for eighteen. My relationship with Will was falling apart; my career, such as it was, had yet to really start. If I'd wanted someone to listen to my problems, my issues, Mr Lucas was never that person. Yet round I went. Cynically at first with an eye to eventually getting my hands on the diaries, but as we passed year ten, year twelve, my motivation changed. I owed it to him – much as, indeed, I had promised him I would try to publish his diaries in some form after his death. So yes, I liked him. He was in his late seventies to my mid-twenties, so we obviously had few things in common beyond our sexuality. Yet his stories were spectacular – and, on occasion, very funny.

1 February 1966 (Tuesday):

I sent David Potter into fits of laughing as to his inquiry, 'Had I done anything enjoyable this weekend?' I replied, 'Yes, I did rather raise my spirits by starting negotiations to buy a grave.'

18 January 1973 (Thursday):

A clear bright coldish day. This morning, reaching out to pick false teeth from the cup where I placed them overnight, I was exceedingly astonished to find it empty; and peering and searching in the kitchen and bedroom no trace of my teeth could I find. So at last out, wearing my new ones, that fit ill, marvelling what can have become of these false teeth. I cannot have forgot to take them out, and then swallowed them sleeping, nor can they have dissolved to nothing... but where, then, are they? Home, and after some further casting about discovered my teeth in the King Edward VIII beaker I stand the toothbrush in. I suppose [the man who stayed the previous night] *so disordered my customary routine that I misplaced these teeth inadvertently.*

Queer history might try to claim Mr Lucas as one of its heroes, but I am fairly certain he would be uncomfortable with this. He wanted his diaries published in some form, but as per his pulling out of the initial documentary back in 1994, saying his words should be read by an actor, after a lifetime avoiding the spotlight, he did not want it in death either.

For historians, however, the diaries are critical, opening up important parallels with his life and the battle for LGBTQ+ rights over the decades and still today. For most gay and bisexual men and women, legal oppression is a thing of the past. Yet for many trans people, the battle for equality is still very live in the UK at present.

'The way trans people are being talked about now is very resonant with the way in which gay men in the fifties were talked about as a danger to children, as predatory, as treacherous, as damaging to the national fabric,' Matt Cook, Britain's first ever tenured professor of LGBTQ+ history, told me. 'And now we're seeing the same mentality all over again.'

Looking back so as to be able to look forward is crucial, Cook added. 'The debate in the UK about trans rights is particularly febrile... There's been some intense fearmongering,' he said. '[But] if you look historically, you can see that people across the centuries, have gender crossed and lived as a gender different from that assigned at birth. History can help us understand some of the particular fractures of our present.'

Trans people appear occasionally in the sixties diaries, usually as a result of trouble with the law. Mr Lucas even writes about early attempts at so-called conversion therapy. He is quick to note that it has little effect. Indeed, in the example below, quite the opposite.

2 January 1964 (Thursday):

Over a cup of tea in the Pronto, [a friend] *told me something he had heard from a psychiatric social worker in his social welfare group of a man several times in trouble for importuning in female dress and some time ago subjected to aversion therapy – the current nostrum* [now known as conversion therapy]. *This was employed enthusiastically and perseveringly with the result, it seems, that the poor man now wears women's clothes all day, and no longer experiences any aversion even under the treatment. This particular instance is not likely to be published as psychiatrists are as unscrupulous as swindling financiers in cooking their accounts, and probably do a good deal more harm. 'Suppression of material facts' in a company prospectus may cheat people out of their money; in a psychiatric case history, it may rob them of all peace of mind.*

Looking more broadly, how do the diaries compare with those of, say, Anne Lister and John Addington Symonds in the nineteenth century, Edward Carpenter a few decades later and, running in the twentieth, with those of actor Kenneth Williams, playwright Joe Orton and politician and social gadfly Chips Channon? For British actor, writer and director, Mark Gatiss, the diaries are 'like this amazing cross between Joe Orton and Mr Pooter; this sort of extraordinary, raffish sex life of this civil servant combined with his really quite ordinary observations on the state of the world. I find them absolutely fascinating.'[3]

Mr Lucas stands out from his diarist peers by his very ordinariness. Of those mentioned above, even Lister was a wealthy landowner and businesswoman, so remarkable within her own community, if not the wider world. Mr Lucas was, unlike Williams, Orton or Channon, not a public figure by any close margin.

Perhaps the best comparison, as Gatiss mentioned, is with the quite gloriously dull *The Diary of a Nobody*, a fictional account of the deeply tedious Charles Pooter, a middle-ranking office clerk in nineteenth-century London. Add a century or so and the main character is starting to sound somewhat familiar. Written in 1892 by brothers George and Weedon Grossmith, the book is riven with class concerns – still familiar to us today.

5 June 1951 (Tuesday):

The [conference] *speakers were all lower middle-class men with a twang to their voices and no very high intellectual standards.*

18 January 1969 (Saturday):

Piccadilly Circus underground at 11.30 on a Saturday night is a scene requiring the brush of Hieronymus Bosch to depict it – the small working-class lads, noisy, many with football scarves, their close-cut hair emphasizing their bony vicious faces, the rollers [robbers] *and rent boys, the shabby sinister men, the boozy home-going oiks and yobs, beatniks departing to their nocturnal lairs, and various sorts of homosexual, some demure and discreet, with rapid step and swift sidelong look, some vulgar, brash with loud voice and appraising stare.*

For me, Mr Lucas is far closer in temperament and attitude to Mr Pooter than Joe Orton, who, for all his escapades, both in terms of his West End success and eventual murder, is never mentioned by our diarist. But, that said, Orton died gruesomely in August 1967 – beaten to death with one of his awards by his lover Kenneth Halliwell – and Mr Lucas's diary from that year is lost to us. It is fair to say, Mr Lucas would have loathed Orton as a person and as a type of homosexual. Everything about him – his success, swagger and showiness – would have been anathema to our shadow seeker – although the sordid nature of Orton's death would surely have been catnip to him as a diarist. Indeed, celebrity does interest Mr Lucas, not only in terms of pointing out the sexuality of those in the news and understood by those in the know.

9 September 1961 (Saturday):

The film Victim, *that had its premiere last week, deals with the blackmail of homosexuals vulnerable under the present law. It is the first film explicitly dealing with homosexuality to be screened in England, with the romantic Dirk Bogarde as leading actor (or leading lady as everyone in the know would say).*

The American author and social gadfly Gore Vidal had much to say on anything and everything. But on writing, he is worth citing. '"Write what you know" will always be excellent advice for those who ought not to write at all. Write what you think, what you imagine, what you suspect!'[4] Not what you know, but what you think and imagine: this might be at odds with diary keeping, but the advice does chime with much of Mr Lucas's frantic scribblings: it's not just what he sees and experiences; we have a far greater sense of the age through how he feels and what he thinks. Admittedly, Vidal also once exhorted people to 'write something, even if it's just a suicide note'[5], which would have also been dear to Mr Lucas's heart, given his utterly bleak outlook on life at times. Not for him living 'on honeycomb' as per Oscar Wilde, but he does indeed write what he thinks, imagines, suspects.[6]

But is Mr Lucas frank and open in his depiction of homosexuality? I'd argue he is, certainly far more than the, for me, somewhat fey and ponderous diaries kept by British socialist poet and philosopher Edward Carpenter, who lived from 1844 to 1929. The echoes, the same themes, travel through time. In comments often ascribed to the nineteenth century writer, Carpenter talked of how it was time that the queer world was provided with a literature that would reflect itself and its own nature.

Mr Lucas's diaries stand as testament to a man trying to understand his own nature and, I'd add, how that can be defined by love – or the lack of it. Ultimately, the diaries stand as testament to one man's search for love: Flannan O'Hehir, briefly John Joyce and, most destructively, his almost decade-long acquaintance of Irish Peter, Miss Peter of the 'Dilly. And, kept diligently, they are continued until Mr Lucas can physically write no more, his body incapacitated by several strokes. Yet try he does – the final entries are from his very last diaries written in 2009. They are no more than almost illegible scrawls; the effort that has gone into the attempt to write is obvious as his hand skirted across the paper. Mr Lucas would live, his sharp mind trapped in a weakened body, for five more long years. But, for once, after more than sixty years, we hear no more.

18 November 2009 (Wednesday):

I attempted to move the fire and had to wait for young McMahon to find my glasses. Young McMahon brought a much larger pie for my dinner and will bring my fire on Thursday when I have the price, which the father is quiet about.

19 November 2009 (Thursday):

A day as usual.

20 November 2009 (Friday):

Young McMahon failed to bring back my laundry and this evening spilled the whole of my large pie on the floor.

21 November 2009 (Saturday):

McMahon senior brought my missing laundry and spoke harshly of his son.

22 November 2009 (Sunday):

Gary did what I asked him, getting eggs and toothpaste.

23 November 2009 (Monday):

So uncomfortable did I feel that I rose at 5 o'clock and gradually felt better.

25 November 2009 (Wednesday):

Daniel McMahon back and all back to normal.

26 November 2009 (Thursday):

A rare disaster when my knee gave way and I lay in the hall until Mrs Bowler came home and sent the ambulance people to rescue me.

27 November 2009 (Friday):

Kernaghan's brother asked for a £460 cheque for his Christmas trip to Belfast – but I gave him this on 9 October.

Notes

Preface

1. Clark, A. (2010). *Alan Clark: A Life in His Own Words, The Edited Diaries 1972–1999* (edited by Ion Trewin). W&N.

1. George Leo John Lucas

1. Crisp, Q. (1968). *The Naked Civil Servant*. Cape: chapter 15.

2. The Early Years

1. Powell, W. R., ed. (1978). 'Romford: Local government', in *A History of the County of Essex: Volume 7*. Victoria County History: 76–82. *British History Online*. Retrieved from http://www.british-history.ac.uk/vch/essex/vol7/pp76-82.
2. Hansard (3 Dec. 1953). Sexual offences. Retrieved from https://hansard.parliament.uk/commons/1953-12-03/debates/6bb0d43c-41b6-4bd6-8855-183f35292116/SexualOffences.

3. A Fateful Night in Germany

1. Bourne, S. (25 Jul. 2017). Fighting Proud: The untold story of the gay men who served in two world wars [blog]. London School of Economics and Political Science. Retrieved from https://blogs.lse.ac.uk/politicsandpolicy/fighting-proud/#:~:text=What%20

surprised%20me%20was%20the,homophobic%20attitudes%20 and%20make%20friends.
2. Higgins, P. (1996). *Heterosexual Dictatorship: Male Homosexuality in Postwar Britain*. Fourth Estate.
3. The National Archives (n.d.). Sexual Offences Act 1956. Retrieved from https://www.legislation.gov.uk/ukpga/Eliz2/4-5/69/section/13/enacted/data.xht?view=snippet&wrap=true.
4. National Army Museum (n.d.). The Army and the occupation of Germany. Retrieved from https://www.nam.ac.uk/explore/occupation-and-reconstruction-germany-1945-48.
5. Rose, S. O. (2003). *Which People's War?: National Identity and Citizenship in Wartime Britain 1939–1945*. Oxford University Press.
6. Gscene (3 Jan. 2020). Peter Tatchell calls on government to compensate all LGBT+ military personnel it unfairly dismissed. Retrieved from https://www.gscene.com/news/peter-tatchell-calls-on-government-to-compensate-all-lgbt-military-personnel-it-unfairly-dismissed/.
7. Banks, C. (10 Jan. 2020). Defence Minister apologises to LGB community for 'unacceptable' military ban. Forces Network. Retrieved from https://www.forces.net/news/minister-apologises-lgb-community-unacceptable-military-ban; Gov.uk (19 Jul. 2023). Government apologises to veterans for egregious historic LGBT policy in the Armed Forces. Retrieved from https://www.gov.uk/government/news/government-apologises-to-veterans-for-egregious-historic-lgbt-policy-in-the-armed-forces.
8. The Army Act, 1950. Retrieved from https://www.mod.gov.in/sites/default/files/TheArmyAct1950.pdf.
9. Crowther, B. (19 Sep. 1949). 'Abbott and Costello Meet the Killer, Boris Karloff' Opens at the Globe – New film at the Mayfair. *New York Times*. Retrieved from https://www.nytimes.com/1949/09/19/archives/abbott-and-costello-meet-the-killer-boris-karloff-opens-at-the.html.

10. Rose, S. O. (2003). *Which People's War?: National Identity and Citizenship in Wartime Britain 1939–1945*. Oxford University Press.

4. The Tragic Tale of Flannan O'Hehir

1. Kynaston, D. (2015). *Modernity Britain: 1957–1962*. Bloomsbury.

5. Irish Peter

1. Hadleigh, B. (1996). *Hollywood Gays*. Barricade Books Inc.
2. Teale, D. (2022). *Surviving the Krays*. Ebury Publishing.

6. England on Trial

1. Wolfenden60 (n.d.). About the Wolfenden Report. Retrieved from https://www.thewolfendenreport.com/about/the-wolfenden-report#:~:text=The%20report%20recommended%2C%20%E2%80%9Cthat%20homosexual,of%20stricter%20penalties%20for%20soliciting.
2. Traini, Robert (23 Nov. 1962). Union chief is found beaten to death. *Daily Herald*.
3. *Daily Mirror* (23 Nov. 1962).
4. *The Scotsman* (11 Dec. 1962).
5. Dunton, M. (17 Dec. 2012). The scandalous case of John Vassall: Sexuality, spying and the Civil Service. The National Archives. Retrieved from https://media.nationalarchives.gov.uk/index.php/scandalous-case-john-vassall/https://media.nationalarchives.gov.uk/index.php/scandalous-case-john-vassall/.
6. Leitch, D. (9 Dec. 1996). Obituary: John Vassall. *Independent*. Retrieved from https://www.independent.co.uk/news/obituaries/obituary-john-vassall-1313796.html.
7. *Birmingham Daily Post* (14 Mar. 1963).

8. *Guardian* (12 Oct. 1963): https://www.newspapers.com/article/the-guardian-laurence-bell-clifford-lu/14498524/.
9. Frampton, W. (9 Dec. 2013). Sexual abuse case against ex-BBC reporter Clifford Luton is put on hold indefinitely. *Daily Echo*. Retrieved from https://www.bournemouthecho.co.uk/news/10863392.sexual-abuse-case-against-ex-bbc-reporter-clifford-luton-is-put-on-hold-indefinitely/.
10. Walter, N. (10 Jul. 1997). Obituary: Lord Horder. *Independent*. Retrieved from https://www.independent.co.uk/news/people/obituary-lord-horder-1249901.html.
11. Davenport-Hines, R. (2013). *An English Affair: Sex, Class and Power in the Age of Profumo*. HarperPress.

7. A Brush with the Krays

1. Popham, P. (10 May 1994). 24 hours in Piccadilly: Peter Popham spends an all-human-life day at the circus (Eros is not what he was). *Independent*. Retrieved from https://www.independent.co.uk/life-style/24-hours-in-piccadilly-peter-popham-spends-an-allhumanlife-day-at-the-circus-eros-is-not-what-he-was-1434777.html.
2. Lucas, N. (12 Jul. 1964). Peer and a gangster: Yard inquiry. *Sunday Mirror*.
3. *Sunday Mirror* (28 Apr. 1963). How to spot a possible homo.
4. BBC News (23 Oct. 2015). Ronnie Kray and Tory peer Lord Boothby 'attended homosexual parties'. Retrieved from https://www.bbc.co.uk/news/uk-34612729.
5. Staveley-Wadham, R. (27 Sep. 2021). 'Persons of the worst possible character' – The story of the Kray twins as told by our newspapers [blog]. The British Newspaper Archive. Retrieved from https://blog.britishnewspaperarchive.co.uk/2021/09/27/the-story-of-the-kray-twins/#:~:text=We%20now%20wish%20to%20apologise,our%20reports%20caused%20to%20him.

6. Baker, R. (26 Oct. 2018). Gangsters, nude models and pill-popping teens – the hidden history of Gerrard Street. *Daily Telegraph*. Retrieved from https://www.telegraph.co.uk/travel/destinations/europe/united-kingdom/england/london/articles/london-chinatown-history/.

8. Out on the Scene

1. Campkin, B., Marshall, L., Raze Collective and Queer Spaces Network (Jul. 2017). LGBTQ+ nightlife spaces in London. UCL Urban Laboratory. Retrieved from https://www.ucl.ac.uk/urban-lab/research/research-projects/lgbtq-nightlife-spaces-london.
2. Vaines, C. (17 May 2015). Soho stories: Celebrating six decades of sex, drugs and rock 'n' roll. *Guardian*. Retrieved from https://www.theguardian.com/culture/2015/may/17/london-soho-stories-sex-drugs-rock-and-roll.
3. Waddell, B. (1993). *The Black Museum: New Scotland Yard*. Little, Brown.
4. Huggett, R. (1989). *Binkie Beaumont: Eminence Grise of the West End Theatre, 1933–1973*. Hodder & Stoughton.
5. McKinley, B. (2 Jun. 2017). London 40 years on: In search of my musical youth. *Irish Times*. Retrieved from https://www.irishtimes.com/culture/books/london-40-years-on-in-search-of-my-musical-youth-1.3105615.
6. Ferry, K. (2011). *The 1950s Kitchen*. Shire Library.
7. *East Kent Times and Mail* (13 Mar. 1970). Peter Dolphin of Dolphin Square gets a ducking – in the dolphinarium.

9. The Slow Train to Ireland

1. Ruhs, M. and Quinn, E. (1 Sep. 2009). Ireland: From rapid immigration to recession. Migration Policy Institute. Retrieved

from https://www.migrationpolicy.org/article/ireland-rapid-immigration-recession#:~:text=With%20the%20exception%20of%20the,a%20country%20of%20net%20immigration.
2. O'Connell, P. J. (Feb. 1997). The Irish labour market: Working paper no. 81. Economic and Social Research Institute. Retrieved from https://www.esri.ie/system/files?file=media/file-uploads/2015-07/WP081.pdf ; Central Statistics Office (27 Jun. 2006). Measuring Ireland's progress, 2005. Retrieved from https://www.cso.ie/en/csolatestnews/pressreleases/2006pressreleases/measuringirelandsprogress2005/.
3. Gallagher, C. (30 Nov. 2016). Gay community recalls dark days before decriminalisation. *Irish Times*. Retrieved from https://www.irishtimes.com/news/social-affairs/gay-community-recalls-dark-days-before-decriminalisation-1.2886652.
4. Varadkar, L. (19 Jun. 2018). In the three years before I was born... [tweet]. X. Retrieved from https://twitter.com/LeoVaradkar/status/1009127511295393792.
5. *Irish Times* (24 Sep. 2016). Barry Dunne: All were welcome in his family's pub, Bartley Dunne's. Retrieved from https://www.irishtimes.com/life-and-style/people/barry-dunne-all-were-welcome-in-his-family-s-pub-bartley-dunne-s-1.2803432.
6. Ibid.
7. Hansard (19 Jun. 1967). Overseas travel allowance. Retrieved from https://api.parliament.uk/historic-hansard/commons/1967/jun/19/overseas-travel-allowance.

10. Sex, Money and Death

1. *Scotsman* (21 Jul. 2004). Man convicted of killing paedophile teacher he befriended in jail. Retrieved from https://www.scotsman.com/news/man-convicted-of-killing-paedophile-teacher-he-befriended-in-jail-2509381; Collins, R. (29 Nov. 2016). Grub's in good nick. *Scottish Sun*. Retrieved from

https://www.thescottishsun.co.uk/news/236137/wheelie-bin-killer-ian-sutherland-who-chopped-up-teacher-into-five-pieces-boasts-about-festive-prison-food-in-magazine/#:~:text=The%20court%20heard%20how%20Sutherland,it%20in%20a%20back%20garden.
2. Khan, S. (15 Feb. 2004). Horror tale stranger than fiction. *Guardian*. Retrieved from https://www.theguardian.com/uk/2004/feb/15/ukcrime.stephenkhan.

11. The Death of Mr Lucas

1. Yanagihara, H. (2022). *To Paradise*. Picador: 639.
2. HMICFRS (27 Apr. 2023). An inspection of the Metropolitan Police Service's response to lessons from the Stephen Port murders. Retrieved from https://hmicfrs.justiceinspectorates.gov.uk/publications/inspection-of-the-metropolitan-police-services-response-to-lessons-from-the-stephen-port-murders/.

Postscript

1. Nin, A. (1969). *The Diary of Anaïs Nin, Vol. 1: 1931–1934* (edited by Gunther Stuhlmann). Mariner Books.
2. Isherwood, C. (1939). *Goodbye to Berlin*. Hogarth Press.
3. Comments made by Mark Gatiss during a reading of the Mr Lucas diaries for a Queer Britain fundraiser on 6 Feb. 2020 at London's Bishopsgate Institute.
4. *The Essential Gore Vidal*, edited by Fred Kaplan (Abacus, 2000)
5. Ibid.
6. Wilde, O. *De Profundis, The Ballad of Reading Gaol & Other Writings* (Wordsworth Classics, 1999)

Acknowledgements

The book has been a labour of love, but one underpinned by the incredible professionalism of the team who brought it to fruition – and there are many people I'd like to thank.

Huge thanks must first go to my wonderful agent Eli Keren (Agent E), who has been with me all the way from the very beginning when the idea was no more than a jumbled collection of scrappy notes.

Also, my editor James Pulford has shown both editing acumen and judicious patience – particularly in the face of working with a journalist used to filing at the very last minute. That goes for all the team at Atlantic Books, who have been fabulous to work with.

I definitely need to thank Julia Kellaway for polishing my ragged sentences into the pellucid prose you've hopefully just read.

My former colleagues at the *Financial Times*, Rohit Jaggi and Stephen Foley, very much deserve a mention for suggesting that I pluck a year at random and start a blog on Facebook that is still unfolding today, many years later (https://www.facebook.com/mrlucas1927).

Huge thanks also to Dr Clifford Hampshire Williams and Tim Burford, both seasoned writers themselves, for their steer and help (and not least their eagle-eyed subbing skills). Craig Hoy, one of Mr Lucas's friends, provided me with invaluable details of a life led away from the diaries. I owe a huge amount to my former team at the Thomson Reuters Foundation, not least Lucy Middleton, Hayley Watson, Sadiya Ansari and Enrique Anarte – and my much-missed fellow TRF traveller, Rachel Savage – for allowing me to bang on and on (and on) about Mr Lucas. I should also mention my former editor, Belinda Goldsmith, for her support, as well as my very dear friend – and now landlord – Robert Jarman, without whom a vast amount of silly fun – both in the UK and Georgia – would not have happened. Much-needed thanks to Stef Dickers at the Bishopsgate Institute and historian and writer Dominic Janes. David Cook and Mark Gatiss, please take a well-deserved bow for a really rather incredible documentary on Radio 4 (https://www.bbc.co.uk/programmes/m00138hx) about Mr L; and, additionally, Mark, Joe Galliano and Queer Britain for the 2020 reading of the diaries (https://queerbritain.org.uk/history-2020-mr-lucas-diaries). I must also credit Bryan Karetnyk and Matt Pagett for being the most perfect sounding boards. Almost there, but just to add, sorry Jack, you're not the most famous Greenhalgh yet…

And last, but certainly not least, to the many readers of

ACKNOWLEDGEMENTS

the weekly Facebook blog for your charm, humour and – on many, many occasions – assistance. I look forward to spending many more weekends with you.

Index

age of consent, 242–3, 284
Army Act (UK, 1950), 53
Attlee, Clement, 29

Bacon, Francis, 195
Bad Oeynhausen, Germany, 49, 52
bars, 33, 68, 111, 141–2, 160, 166, 176, 192–218, 280–81
Bartley Dunne's, Dublin, 228–30, 233, 235
Beatles, The, 217
Bell, Laurence, 137, 138, 151–7
Bennitt, M. W., 157
Binkie Beaumont (Huggett), 199
Black Museum, The (Waddell), 195–6
Blackburn, Antony 'Tony', 281
Blair, Anthony 'Tony', 53
Board of Trade, 2, 35, 71, 80, 85, 113, 141, 148, 164, 183, 187, 204

Boothby, Robert, Baron, 169–72, 174
Bourne, Stephen, 48
Bow Street, London, 73–4, 114
Brinham, George, 137, 141–6, 157, 161
British Army of the Rhine, 49–67
Brixton, London, 104, 113, 164, *164*
Buggery Act (England, 1533), 40
Bunch of Grapes, Strand, 201, 281
Burgess, Guy, 137, 138, 147
Burgh Quay, Dublin, 225–7
Byrne, Dermot, 239–40

Cambridge Spy Ring, 137, 147
Campaign for Homosexual Equality, 73
Campaign for Homosexual Law Reform, 227

Caravan club, London, 33
Carpenter, Edward, 287, 290
Casement, Roger, 32
Catholicism, 3, 18–19, 31, 75, 82–5, 87, 197, 253–4
Channon, Henry 'Chips', 287, 288
Churchill, Winston, 164
Clacton-on-Sea, Essex, 31, 36, 78, 113, 265
Clark, Alan, 5
Clark's school, Ilford, 271
class, 5, 51, 76, 157
Coe, Godfrey, 200
Coffee-House, London, 102, 142, 158–60, 255
Communism, 19
Connellan, Noel, 231
Connolly, Pat, 34, 35–8, 43, 67
Conservative Group for Homosexual Equality, 73
conversion therapy, 286–7
Conway, Russ, 200
cooking, 205–6
Cornwall, England, 221
cottaging, 20, 31, 33, 46, 51, 52–67, 68, 72, 107, 196, 252, 281
  decline of, 215–16, 217
  in Dublin, 225, 226
  policing of, 52–67, 136, 199, 209
Criminal Law Act (ROI, 1993), 227

Criminal Law Amendment Act (UK, 1885), 40
Crisp, Quentin, 2, 14
cruising, 20, 31, 33, 38, 46–67, 68, 72–5, 107, 252
  decline of, 215–16, 217
  policing of, 46–67, 72–5, 136, 199, 209

dating apps, 192
Davenport-Hines, Richard, 160
Davidson, Colonel, 182–4, 189
Davidson, Harold, 115–16
Davy Byrne's, Dublin, 228–9, 230
Diary of a Nobody, The (Grossmith), 288, 289
Dolphin, Peter, 211–12
drugs, 112–13, 125–6
Dublin, Ireland, 221–38
  assault in, 235–8
Dunne, Bartholomew, 229–30
Düsseldorf, Germany, 46, 50–67

Edinburgh, Scotland, 13, 52, 239–46
English Affair, An (Davenport-Hines), 160
Euston Tap, London, 219–20

Farrell, Kevin, 248, 249, 254
Ferry, Kathryn, 205

films, 57, 60, 66, 129, 281
Fitzroy, Rathbone Place, 36, 255, 281
Fletcher-Cooke, Charles, 137, 138, 148–51, 152, 156, 157, 161
Fyers, Fitzroy Hubert, 42

Gardler, Ray, 48
Gatiss, Mark, 2, 287, 288
Gay News, 251
'gay panic' defence, 144
Georgia, 222, 246, 259
Germany, 46, 49–67
Gielgud, John, 75, 139–40, 199, 215, 216
glory holes, 52
Golden Lion, Soho, 33, 142, 160, 194, 210–14
Goodbye to Berlin (Isherwood), 283
Granger, Stewart, 117
gross indecency, 40–45, 48–9, 52–67, 73–4, 80, 137, 151
guardsman's defence, 144

Hadleigh, Boze, 117
Hair (musical), 252
Harvey, Ian, 73–4
Hazell, Martin, 198
Heterosexual Dictatorship (Higgins), 48
Hideaway Club, London, 172–91

Higgins, Patrick, 48
Hollywood Gays (Hadleigh), 117
homophobia, 31–2, 33, 99, 138, 170
homosexuality, 3, 31, 40, 99
 age of consent, 242–3, 284
 armed forces and, 53, 58
 Buggery Act (1533), 40
 conversion therapy, 286–7
 cruising, *see* cruising
 Labouchere amendment (1885), 40, 48
 Lady Austin case (1932), 32
 marriage rights, 227
 Offences Against the Person Act (1861), 40
 Sexual Offences Act (1956), 48–9
 Sexual Offences Act (1967), 6, 31, 53, 98, 99, 204, 218
 World War II and, 1, 6, 48, 53, 107
Horder, Mervyn, 2nd Baron, 158
Household Cavalry, 218
Hows, Julian, 197
Hoy, Craig, 258–64, 273–5
Hudson, Rock, 200
Huggett, Richard, 199

Ireland, 221–38
 Celtic Tiger economy (c. 1995–2008), 226

Criminal Law Act (1993), 227
emigration, 225–6
Irish Peter, 9–10, 21, 25, 97, 98–135, 269, 291
    fencing work, 100, 122
    Flynn, relationship with, 105
    Krays, connections to, 110, 125, 162–3, 172–91
    murder, contemplation of, 98, 131–3
    physical appearance, 103–4
    probation officer blackmail (1961), 111
    robbery of Lucas (1965), 129
    robbery of Lucas (1968), 25, 133
    torture (1968), 125, 134–5
Isherwood, Christopher, 283
Istanbul, Turkey, 222, 247

Jackson, David, 268–9
John XXIII, Pope, 151
Joyce, John, 165–9, 256, 291

Keane, Richie, 231
Keeler, Christine, 72, 137, 152
Kelly, Anthony, 180–81
Kennedy, John Fitzgerald, 207–8, 267
Kildoran Road, Brixton, 104, 113, 164, *164*
Kit-Cat Club, London, 33

Kray twins, 1, 9–10, 110, 122, 125, 162–3, 169–91, *180*
    Boothby affair (1964), 169–72, 174
    Irish Peter and, 110, 125, 162–3, 172
    trial (1965), 125, 172–91
Kynaston, David, 74

Labouchere, Henry, 40, 48
Labour Party, 142, 143–4, 145
Lady Austin case (1932), 32
Larkin, Philip, 257
Lister, Anne, 287, 288
Loftus-Tottenham, Frederick Joseph, 62
Lucas, George Leo John, *17*, *32*, *108*, *277*
    car accident (2001), 259
    Catholicism, 3, 18–19, 31, 75, 82–5, 87, 253–4
    chest tumour (1963), 265
    childhood, 18, 271–2
    class, views on, 5
    court-martial case (1950), 52–67, 187
    death (2014), 4, 7, 257–64, 273–7
    death, views on, 265–70
    Dublin assault (1966), 235–8
    finances, 272
    first sexual experience (1942), 20, 31
    hair loss, 18, 108–9, 257

Irish Peter, relationship with, *see* Irish Peter
National Service, 8, 30–31
O'Hehir, relationship with, 70–71, 75–83, 87–97, 103, 109, 118, 291
parents, relationship with, 3, 18–20, 33, 68, 78, 84, 92, 113, 252, 255–6, 257, 265
penile discomfort, 204–5, 278
penises, views on, 214–15
photo collection, 12, 16, 46, 260–61
pornologophilia, 249
prudishness, 251–2
robbery (1968), 21–8, 133
'street philanthropy', 77, 114–16, 248, 256, 261–2
voice, 16–17
will, 273–7
Luke, Michael, 268–9

MacLeod, Ian, 109
Macmillan, Harold, 137, 160
Mandalay Road, Clapham, 14–17, 97, 258–64, 273, 274
Marble Arch, London, 33, 40, 69, 81–2, 84, 107, 198, 217, 280
Margaret, Countess of Snowdon, 162
Marlborough Street, 70, 72, 81, 88
marriage rights, 227
Maxwell Fyfe, David, 41–2
McAleese, Mary, 227
McCowan, Hew, 172–89
McKellen, Ian, 195, 242
McKinley, Barry, 202
McVitie, Jack, 191
Melly, George, 173
Mercer, Johnny, 53
Missionary, The (1982 film), 116
Modernity Britain (Kynaston), 74
Montagu, Edward Douglas-Scott-Montagu, 3rd Baron, 75, 139
Moran's Hotel, Dublin, 225, 237
Morris, Chris, 243

National Service, 8, 30–31
Niece, Charles, 9, 194, 201–2, 205, 210–14
Nilsen, Dennis, 196
Nin, Anaïs, 283
Norris, David, 227, 229
Northern Ireland, 227

O'Hehir, Flannan, 70–71, 75–83, 87–97, *93*, 103, 109, 118, 291
Offences Against the Person Act (UK, 1861), 40
Old Compton Street, Soho, 192, 267

Orton, Joe, 287, 288, 289
Osborne, George, 103

Parker, David, 203
Parnes, Larry, 200
Parry, Will, 13, 242
Payne, Les, 125
penises, 215
Piccadilly Circus, London, 27–8, 68, 82, 102, 110, 139, 280, 288–9
  Irish Peter at, 98, 99, 101, 105, 122, 124, 177
  'Meat Rack', 114, 126
  police crackdown (1961), 111
  Ward's Irish House, 166, 176
Pitt-Rivers, Michael, 139
pornologophilia, 249
Port, Stephen, 270–71
Pratt, James, 40
Profumo Affair (1961–3), 1, 72, 136–7, 149, 152, 153–4, 160
Pronto Café, Piccadilly Circus, 207–9, 224
prostitution, 7, 12–15, 69, 105–7, 109, 110, 239–57
  car trade, 114
  exploitation, 239–57, 260–61
  at Golden Lion, 196, 197–8, 201
  at Piccadilly Circus, 111, 114, 126
  'street philanthropy', 77, 114–16, 248, 256, 262
  at Ward's, 203

Quant, Mary, 217

Radio Two, 281
Rainbow Corner, Shaftesbury Avenue, 201, 281
Raphael Park, Romford, 33, 38–45, 196
Redgrave, Michael, 116–17
Reid, George, 68
Rice's bar, Dublin, 228–9, 231
robbery (1965), 129
robbery (1968), 21–8
Robinson, Mary, 227
Rohm, Ernst, 50
Rose, Sonya, 53, 58

Sexual Offences Act (UK, 1956), 48
Sexual Offences Act (UK, 1967), 6, 31, 53, 98, 99, 204, 218
Shepherd, William, 41
Smith, John, 40
Snowdon, Antony Armstrong-Jones, 1st Earl, 122–3
Soho, London, 192, 195
Soviet Union, 137, 146–8
Standard, Piccadilly Circus, 106, 201, 255, 281
Stonewall, 242, 243
Surviving the Krays (Teale), 125

Sutherland, Euan, 243
Symonds, John Addington, 287

Tatchell, Peter, 53
Teale, David, 125
Teddy Boys, 1–2
Thorndike, Sybil, 199
To Paradise (Yanagihara), 260
Tokyo Rose, 9, 28
Ton of Malice, A (McKinley), 202
Trafalgar Square, London, 102, 140, 188, 217, 226, 254, 280
transgender people, 180–81, 286
travel, 232
Turkey, 222, 247

University of Edinburgh, 13, 52, 239–46

Varadkar, Leo, 227
Vassall, John, 137, 138, 146–8
Vaughan, Frankie, 200
Victim (1961 film), 289–90
Vidal, Gore, 290

Waddell, Bill, 195–6
Ward's, Piccadilly Circus, 111, 166, 176, 186, 202, 203, 204, 208, 216
Welsh Harp, Covent Garden, 33, 115, 141, 151, 160, 209–10
Which People's War? (Rose), 53
White Bear, Kennington, 33, 111, 141, 148, 156, 160, 197, 202, 208, 255
Wilde, Oscar, 32, 40, 65–6, 72, 290
Wilde, Ralph, 243
Wildeblood, Peter, 139
Williams, H. D., 9
Williams, Kenneth, 287, 288
Wilson, Alan, 241–6
Wilson, James Harold, 217
Wolfenden Report (1957), 140, 149
World War II (1939–45), 1, 6, 48, 53, 107, 282

Yanagihara, Hanya, 260